THE CON5OLE
50 Years of Home Video Gaming

MIKE DIVER

WHITE OWL
AN IMPRINT OF PEN & SWORD BOOKS LTD.
YORKSHIRE - PHILADELPHIA

First published in Great Britain in 2023 by
Pen and Sword WHITE OWL
An imprint of
Pen & Sword Books Ltd
Yorkshire - Philadelphia

Copyright © Mike Diver, 2023

ISBN 978 1 39904 046 4

The right of Mike Diver to be identified as Author of this work has been asserted by **him** in accordance with the Copyright, Designs and Patents Act 1988.

Some images courtesy of mobygames.com

A CIP catalogue record for this book is available from the British Library.

All rights reserved. No part of this book may be reproduced or transmitted in any form or by any means, electronic or mechanical including photocopying, recording or by any information storage and retrieval system, without permission from the Publisher in writing.

Typeset in 11.5/14.5 pts Avenir by SJmagic DESIGN SERVICES, India.

Printed and bound in China by 1010 Printing International Limited

Pen & Sword Books Ltd incorporates the imprints of Pen & Sword Books Archaeology, Atlas, Aviation, Battleground, Discovery, Family History, History, Maritime, Military, Naval, Politics, Railways, Select, Transport, True Crime, Fiction, Frontline Books, Leo Cooper, Praetorian Press, Seaforth Publishing, Wharncliffe and White Owl.

For a complete list of Pen & Sword titles please contact

PEN & SWORD BOOKS LIMITED
George House, Units 12 & 13, Beevor Street, Off Pontefract Road,
Barnsley, South Yorkshire, S71 1HN, England
E-mail: enquiries@pen-and-sword.co.uk
Website: www.pen-and-sword.co.uk

or

PEN AND SWORD BOOKS
1950 Lawrence Rd, Havertown, PA 19083, USA
E-mail: Uspen-and-sword@casematepublishers.com
Website: www.penandswordbooks.com

CONTENTS

Credits	4
Introduction	6
Foreword by Julian 'Jaz' Rignall	7
The 1970s – From One Man's Inspiration to a Global Sensation	9
The 1980s – Japan Rises to Rule the Gaming World	24
The 1990s – A Sleeping Giant Becomes a Gaming Superpower	68
The 2000s – One Console to Rule them All	130
The 2010s – The Collapse and Comeback of an Icon	163
The 2020s – Brand New, You're Retro	184

CREDITS

Select photos courtesy of **Evan Amos**, whose free-to-use shots of gaming hardware are an unmatched resource for anyone documenting this history. Amos' book *The Game Console 2.0: A Photographic History* is out now.

Select photos courtesy of **The Museum of Obsolete Media**. A unique collection of over 800 media formats covering data, audio, film and video, the UK-based museum was started in 2006 by Jason Curtis and its website was launched in 2013. The museum is not open to the public but does occasionally arrange exhibitions, and more information can be found online at obsoletemedia.org.

Select photos courtesy of **The Centre for Computing History** (CCH). CCH is a pioneering educational charity that opened at its current site in Cambridge, UK, in August 2013. CCH was established as an educational charity to tell the story of the Information Age through exploring the historical, social and cultural impact of developments in personal computing. CCH has an internationally significant collection of vintage computers, memorabilia, artefacts, documents and hands-on displays – in total about 24,000 items. For more information visit computinghistory.org.uk.

Select screens and box art courtesy of **mobygames.com**, the world's oldest and largest video game database covering over 300 different platforms. The site collects art, screens, credits and more, and is both for gamers and built by gamers. At the time of writing over 303,000 games are featured on the database, running to almost a million screenshots.

All Collector Spot photographs are provided courtesy of the collectors in question.

Adam Mills via Unsplash (page 59); Alex Handy (page 44); Alex Hansen (page 159); Amazon Official Product Photography (page 183); Artem Podrez via Pexels (page 171); Audrey & Max (page 83); Atari Official Product Photography (page 188); Baptiste Herrmann via Unsplash (page 62); Billy Freeman via Unsplash (page 184); Blake Patterson (page 147); Blaze Entertainment (pages 189, 190); Celso Mejía via Pexels (page 170); Charles Sims via Unsplash (page 186); Corentin Detry via Pexels (page 175); Creative commons (pages 92, 101, 104, 114, 121, 124, 131, 143, 159, 161, 165); Cristiano Pinto via Unsplash (page 182); Dell Inc Official Product Photography (page 177); Denise Jans via Unsplash (page 135); Duncan Aird (pages 110, 111, 112); Dynamic-Gaming-Twinz (page 87); Erik Mclean via Pexels (page 178); Famicom Tsushin Magazine (page 76); Faith Johnson (pages 127, 128, 129); Frazer Rhodes (pages 72, 73); Greg Dunlap (page 13);

Henry Walkley (pages 41, 42); Hello I'm Nik via Unsplash (page 47); Lara Ferroni (page 151); Lewis Clark (pages 19, 20); Liane Enkelis (page 10); Liftarn (page 15); Louis-Philippe Poitras via Unsplash (page 175); Lucas Santos via Unsplash (page 178); Mariah N via Pexels (page 116); Mats Lindh (page 80); Max Mustermann (page 28); Michael Adeleye via Pexels (page 179); Microsoft (pages 144, 145, 185); Mike Rouse (pages 64, 65, 66); Mikey Dowling (page 119); Museum of Play Estate of Jerry Lawson (page 14); necretro.org (page 55); Nikita Kachanovsky via Unsplash (page 170); Nikita Kostrykin via Unsplash (pages 103, 130, 153, 157); Nintendo Official Product Photography (page 180); OnLive Official Product Photography (page 163); Possessed Photography via Unsplash (page 32); Public domain (pages 94, 135, 150); Retro-Computing Society of Rhode Island (page 113); Schnurrikowski (page 56); SEGA Official Product Photography (page 189); SEGA wiki (page 61); segaretro.org (pages 48, 49, 51, 100); Sony Interactive Entertainment Official Product Photography (page 187); Taito Corporation Official Product Photography (page 189); Taylor R via Unsplash (page 120); Tiia Monto (page 30); Tomasz Filipek via Pexels (page 37); unknown (pages 57, 75, 76, 77, 84, 93, 95, 97, 132, 148, 155); Courtesy of the Smithsonian National Museum of American History (pages 10, 11); Wikipeda user Greenpro (page 153); Wikipedia user Artikbot (page 77); Wikipedia user Baz1521 (page 138); Wikipedia user Beeblebrox (page 69); Wikipedia user Bilby (page 31); Wikipedia user Ilhuday (page 79); Wikipedia user JCD1981NL (page 79); Wikipedia user LucasVB (page 48); Wikipedia user Muband (pages 42, 78); Wikipedia user Newoikkin2113 (page 48); Wikipedia user Nomancam (page 35); Wikipedia user Paquitogio (page 80); Wikipedia user Takimata (page 166); Wikipedia user Talkkaris (page 148); Wikipedia user ze bear (page 167); Xavier Caré (page 147).

INTRODUCTION

My relationship with games consoles started with a SEGA Master System in the early 1990s, but I was obsessed by these machines long before having one of my own. I'd visit friends' houses to use their SEGA or Nintendo consoles, spending hours gawping at *Super Mario Bros.* and *Hang-On*, while one pal had a rarely sighted Commodore 64 Games System and another an old Atari VCS. I didn't really acknowledge the generational differences or the 'bits' at play – I just loved the speed of the experiences, the plugging in of a cartridge and the game being right there, ready for you. To my young mind this was like putting a coin into an arcade machine: instant gratification, and a long way from the tape-loaded ZX Spectrum games I'd known before.

    I graduated from the Master System to the Mega Drive – and became one of those people who slapped a Mega-CD and a 32X onto their 16-bit machine (no regrets). Nowadays my (too small) house is filled with (too many) home consoles, from largely forgotten hardware like the Amstrad GX4000 and Wii U (ha) to Sony's iconic series of PlayStations. I'm smitten with the mini-consoles from Nintendo and SEGA (and the PC Engine CoreGrafx Mini's a joy, too), and love to spend an evening in the company of Xbox's backwards compatibility – a wonder of modern technology that's kept my 360 games on the shelf long after the console itself was stored away.

    But for all my love for older-school experiences, my favourite console ever is probably the Switch. I don't think any gaming hardware has fitted into my life so brilliantly, providing invaluable escape from depressing commutes and handheld excitement when my partner's watching the TV, as well as countless big-screen thrills. Its categorisation as a home console first and a handheld second is debatable – many players hardly ever dock theirs – but since that's what Nintendo officially positions it as, it's included in this book.

    Speaking of which: home consoles alone are the focus of this 50-year history because portables have their own story, and it's one that's worth telling separately from TV-necessitating systems. A tale for another time, perhaps. Regarding these pages, there are some systems and console variations I've had to omit for space, likewise high-end modern retro hardware like the machines produced by Analogue, but I've got to draw a line somewhere (and not every Famiclone can get a mention).

    I need to thank Louise, because without her help you wouldn't be holding this; and I'd also like to extend my gratitude to the contributors within these pages for sharing their passions with me. This book was written in Brighton, UK and Bourguébus, France (when I was supposed to be having a holiday, whoops), and I sincerely hope you enjoy it.

Mike Diver, August 2022

FOREWORD
BY JULIAN 'JAZ' RIGNALL

I've always been a huge console fan. Probably because, despite my first video gaming system being a second-hand Atari 400 home micro, the collection of games that came with it included an excellent range of cartridges. Since this was the early 1980s and most of the machines that I'd previously experienced (BBC, Commodore PET, ZX Spectrum) required you to load their games from cassette, being able to plug in a cartridge and instantly start playing was hugely appealing to me. Especially considering that some games took up to 20 minutes to load – and would oftentimes crap out during the process and you wouldn't know what had happened until the cassette finally reached its end.

My love for video game consoles was reinforced in late 1983 when, after winning *CVG*'s UK National Arcade Championships, I was invited down to London to attend the launch of the ColecoVision. What an immensely exciting day that was! Not only was it the first of what would become many system launch events that I would go on to attend, I also got to play on a brand-new console and experience some seriously great games. Sure, the ColecoVision failed to make any kind of impression in the UK, but I always thought its range of games were terrific for the time. Indeed, due to the ripple effects of the Great US Video Game Crash of 1983 that we felt in the UK, I was able to buy one of these machines and a bunch of games for absolutely peanuts a year or so later.

While the mid-'80s gaming scene in the UK was dominated by home micros, that changed toward the end of the decade as consoles began to appear in shops around the country. The first wave of these didn't exactly fly off the shelves, though. SEGA's Master System and Nintendo's Entertainment System didn't really capture British players' imaginations because their games weren't a whole lot better – and were indeed considerably more expensive – than those available for the home micros of the era. However, when NEC's PC Engine and SEGA's Mega Drive arrived at the end of the decade, and the Super Nintendo was launched a couple of years later, gamers' attitudes rapidly began to shift. The former two machines' extremely accurate arcade conversions clearly showcased their considerable capabilities, and the SNES's launch titles were simply astonishing. The subsequent, seemingly endless parade of high-quality shooters, platformers, brawlers, beat 'em ups, RPGs, and sports games swiftly ensured that any gamer worth his or her salt had at least one of these machines on their Christmas list during the early 1990s.

That pretty much sounded the death knell for home computers, and while the PC would go on to become a great gaming platform in its own right, consoles ultimately became the most common and popular way to play video games.

I don't lament that at all. As someone who has always been far more interested in playing games than fiddling about with machine languages or practical software, video game consoles made sense to me. They were laser focused on what I wanted to do – play games – and they didn't have to compromise like home computers did by featuring additional hardware and features that had nothing to do with gaming.

Nope. Consoles were hardcore gaming systems, and as a hardcore gamer, they were absolutely the thing I wanted. Always did. Always will.

Long live the console!

Julian 'Jaz' Rignall, legendary games journalist as seen at Personal Computer Games, Zzap!64, Computer and Video Games, Mean Machines, Sega Magazine, IGN, GamePro and USgamer.

THE 1970s
FROM ONE MAN'S INSPIRATION TO A GLOBAL SENSATION

The 1970s witnessed a rapid evolution and escalation of video gaming, a medium that had blinked into existence in 1962 with the creation at Harvard of the two-player game *Spacewar!* and the spread of electro-mechanical arcade games like SEGA's *Periscope* of 1966 and Chicago Coin's *Speedway* of 1969. The decade began with the rise in popularity of purely electronic arcade games, dedicated coin-operated cabinets playing a single title. In 1971, *Computer Space* took the gameplay of *Spacewar!* into arcades, and its designers – Ted Dabney and Nolan Bushnell – subsequently co-founded Atari, whose *Pong* became a global phenomenon in 1972. However, the tennis-like gameplay of *Pong* had a precedent in the form of the world's first home video games console, whose makers would soon act against Atari for stealing their idea.

MAGNAVOX ODYSSEY

Manufacturer: Magnavox

Released: September 1972 (North America); 1974 (Europe)

Given the most elementary meaning of the word 'odyssey' – a long and exciting journey of challenges and triumphs – it feels right that the first-ever home video game console bore that name. Yet it could have been so different. The Magnavox Odyssey was briefly called the Skill-O-Vision by its manufacturers, which isn't quite so foresightful as the moniker it released under. But nomenclature never-weres aside, the Odyssey was a passion project turned commercial endeavour that could have, at any moment of its lengthy gestation, ceased to progress as it struggled to make it into the homes of consumers.

Ralph Baer was born Rudolf Heinrich Baer in Pirmasens, Germany, in March 1922. His Jewish family fled their home in 1938, as atrocious anti-Jewish policies turned to persecution and murder under the Nazi Party. They moved to New York City, and soon after Baer (pictured below) enrolled in Washington, DC's National Radio Institute, graduating as a radio service technician in 1940. After serving in the United States Army during World War II, working in military intelligence, he achieved a Bachelor of Science degree in Television Engineering, and gravitated towards defence contractors for his career. It was at one of these companies, the Bronx-based Loral Corporation, where Baer first conceived of something radical: using a television set to play electronic games.

That was 1951. His boss at Loral advised him to forget about it. Speaking to Declan Burrowes for arstechnica.com in July 2013, Baer called this moment, despite its cool reception, his 'epiphany'. Loral were not convinced – 'management said no', is how Baer bluntly recalled the moment – but the notion of playing electronic games on a TV refused to budge from his brain. In 1966, Baer was on a business trip in New York for his then-employer Sanders Associates, a defence contractor headquartered in New Hampshire, when he had his self-described 'eureka' moment, and properly noted down how these games – how *video games* – would work on an everyday TV set, which were now commonplace in homes.

Upon returning to Sanders, he turned his notes into a pitch document outlining a 'game box', to use his words, which could run action and sports games, card games, artistic software and educational exercises. It would, he wrote in his own book *Videogames: In the Beginning*, 'do neat things' – and how right he'd be. In September 1966 he worked with a technician to create something physical to showcase the theoretical to the Sanders R&D department. This ramshackle device, which could move a line on a TV screen but little more, was named the TV Game Unit #1 (pictured below) – and it impressed his bosses sufficiently for them to give Baer and technical engineer Bill Harrison a $2,500 budget to proceed with prototyping.

A handful of TV Game Units and several fresh injections of funding later, Baer and colleagues arrived at TVG #7, which featured two controllers, a light gun, a joystick and seven playable games activated using bespoke circuit boards, aka the Unit's game cards. Covered in woodgrain-patterned vinyl, this unit came to be named the Brown Box. It was early 1968, and Baer and his team had cracked it: TVG #7, the Brown Box, was the first finished, totally functional, ready-to-sell home video game console. But it'd be over four more years before the public would be able to buy what would become the Magnavox Odyssey.

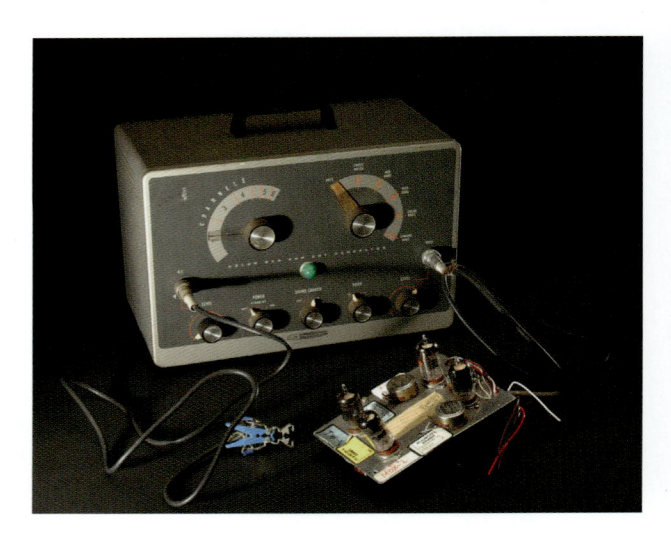

Sanders' patent attorney, Lou Etlinger, invited prominent TV manufacturers to look at Baer's Brown Box, hoping they'd want to take the device to market. But despite meeting the likes of Zenith, Motorola, Sylvania, Magnavox and General Electric, licensing negotiations wouldn't stick. One company, Warwick, put Sanders in touch with the department store Sears, but that came to nothing as the retailer had visions of parents leaving their kids with the games while they shopped elsewhere. RCA, the first potential partner to see the Brown Box (pictured below), was keen but the two parties couldn't agree terms. However, when RCA's Bill Enders left to join Magnavox – at the time known for its TVs, record players and radios – he wanted a second bite at Baer's creation and encouraged his new bosses to see it for themselves.

Having been persuaded by Enders' enthusiasm, Magnavox's VP of Console Products Planning, Gerry Martin, was equally enamoured with the Brown Box, and sought approval from his superiors to negotiate a deal. It was now July 1969, a year and a half on from TVG #7's completion – but Martin didn't receive the OK from management until March 1970, and it took until January 1971 before Magnavox and Sanders agreed licensing terms.

Magnavox's own engineers, under the leadership of Bob Fritsche, revised the Brown Box, changing the controller and radically altering the appearance of the console. The name Skill-O-Vision came and went before, in May 1972, the Magnavox Odyssey was officially unveiled at a corporate event in Las Vegas. Press demonstrations followed across the United States, and in September 1972 customers were finally able to buy the console for an RRP of $99.99 – double Baer's expectations, and over $680 in 2022 money. To add insult to financial injury, the console's AC adapter had to be purchased separately, likewise its light gun.

As revolutionary as the Odyssey was for the time, all it could really do was draw and move white dots and lines against a black screen, with no sound effects. Games were made different by using screen overlays, which attached to TV sets through static alone. One of its launch games, *Tennis*, required players to use the controllers' aftertouch function – oddly called 'English' on the peripherals themselves – to spin the 'ball' beyond the reach of their opponent. It was the direct inspiration for Atari's *Pong*, and this bat-and-ball gameplay also underpinned many other Odyssey titles, overlays and physical extras like cards and dice bringing variety and colour to the on-screen experiences. While the Odyssey, like the Brown Box, did use swappable 'cartridges' – its total of 28 games spread across 11 of them – these weren't ROM carts like those of later years. Rather, they were complete circuit boards, altering how the console's logic responded to the player's inputs.

The Odyssey released in Europe in 1974 and sold between 330,000 and 350,000 units worldwide before its discontinuation in 1975. Between 1975 and 1977, the manufacturer put out eight dedicated consoles with games built in and no cartridge functionality, before an all-new console proper, the Odyssey 2, was released in December 1978. Named the Philips Odyssey 2 (stylised as Odyssey[2]) and the Philips Videopac G7000 in certain territories, due to the Dutch electronics company now owning Magnavox, it used a more conventional joystick controller instead of the Brown Box's three knobs approach; and with 12 on-screen colours and mono audio output, it supported games that appeared far more advanced than the original Odyssey's offerings. A model with a built-in black-and-white screen, the Videopac G7200, was also released in very limited quantities across Europe.

The Odyssey 2 was a relative success, selling two million units globally and launching in Japan and South America. It couldn't match the sales of the 1977-launched Atari VCS or Mattel's Intellivision console of 1979, but it enjoyed a steady stream of software support, including arcade conversions of games like *Frogger* and *Q*Bert*, until 1983's video game market recession, primarily impacting North America but felt worldwide, took Magnavox and several of its competitors out of the gaming business completely. The Odyssey was over, but its place in gaming history was secured. No Ralph Baer, no Brown Box, no Odyssey … and the gaming world turns out very differently.

HOME PONG

Manufacturer: Atari
Released: Late 1975

In November 1972 Atari released *Pong*, the world's first true arcade hit. It transformed the fledgling company into a gaming giant, and its quarter-munching success bred a wealth of clones. But *Pong* was something of a clone itself, its bat-and-ball gameplay inspired by Atari co-founder Nolan Bushnell's experience of seeing the Magnavox Odyssey's *Tennis* at a showcase event in mid-1972. Magnavox sued Atari for patent infringement in April 1974, the parties ultimately settling out of court two years later to the tune of $1.5m – by which point Atari had taken *Pong* from the coin-op world and into the home.

Home Pong is exactly what you think it is: a small device that plays *Pong* on your TV. What you might not realise is that despite *Pong*'s huge arcade revenues, retailers were reluctant to stock the home version. While initially benefitting from *Pong*'s mainstream breakthrough due to the similarity of its games, Magnavox's Odyssey was struggling by 1975, making stores unsure about taking on new video games products. However, an exclusive deal was agreed with Sears for Christmas 1975, and the store's own 'Tele-Games'-branded *Pong* rolled out for customers.

Atari revised *Home Pong* several times – there was *Ultra Pong*, *Super Pong*, *Ultra Pong Doubles*, *Super Pong Pro-Am Ten* and more. It faced competition from toymaker Coleco's Telstar series, which dressed *Pong* up as tennis and hockey across several iterations before culminating in 1977 with the triangular Telstar Arcade, featuring a light gun and steering wheel. Also participating in the domestic clone wars was Magnavox, which discontinued its Odyssey console to focus on the Odyssey series, the 2000 model of which gave consumers the first single-player home version of *Pong*; Concept 2000 with its Spectrum 6 and TV +4 consoles; and the Monteverdi TV Sports 825 console of 1976 combined a few *Pong*-likes with built-in light gun games.

Outside the US, further manufacturers launched their own takes on the bat-and-ball hit. In Japan, Epoch's TV Tennis

Electrotennis was co-developed with Magnavox and launched in September 1975, slightly ahead of the Sears *Home Pong*. In the UK, Binatone's TV Master Mark IV came out in 1976, offering players four games – tennis, football, squash and squash practice – which were all basically *Pong* (a later model, the Mark 6, added two more games); while in Germany, the SHG Black Point Multicolor FS 1001 was a clone released in 1977. Many more *Pong* clones were released for the home market in the 1970s and '80s, from makers including Intel, Commodore and Philips, but there's one manufacturer in particular that warrants a spotlight of its own.

COLOR TV-GAME SERIES

Manufacturer: Nintendo
Released: June 1977

Nintendo, based in Kyoto, Japan, was a company with a long history by the 1970s. It was founded as a manufacturer of hanafuda playing cards in 1889, and in 1959 acquired a Disney licence to produce cards featuring the world-famous animation studio's characters. It went public in 1963, produced the wildly successful Ultra Hand toy in the mid-1960s (an extendable grabber designed by Gunpei Yokoi, who'd later invent the D-pad and lead development on the Game Boy), and in 1970 produced its first electronic toy, the Beam Gun. This light gun device worked with targets that would split apart when 'shot', and the technology caught the eye of Magnavox, who worked with Nintendo to create the Odyssey's own light gun peripheral. In return, Nintendo gained the right to import the Odyssey for the Japanese market in April 1975.

This small taste of the video game world must have appealed to Nintendo, as it moved to further its operations in the market despite having little prior experience in the electronics field. With *Pong* now a worldwide phenomenon, Nintendo – with assistance from Mitsubishi, a company that did understand electronics – released its own clone of Atari's game in June 1977 as the Color TV-Game 6, a system that was made possible due to its relationship with Magnavox, who licensed the use of its tennis-like game. The 6 in the name references the six modes of play, but Nintendo's first video games console doesn't offer anything other than TV tennis with a few extra bells and whistles (or more accurately, walls and added paddles).

A mere week after the release of the Color TV-Game 6, Nintendo followed it up with the Color TV-Game 15, featuring 15 variations of *Pong*. Further models followed, and in 1979 the Color TV Block Kuzushi (pictured left) came out, which switched its focus from *Pong* to copying another Atari arcade hit of the era, 1976's block-busting *Breakout*. This console is notable not only for its commercial success – Nintendo sold over 400,000 units, a huge result at the time – but also because it's one of the first video game projects that Shigeru Miyamoto worked on. Miyamoto had joined

Nintendo in 1977 and designed the Kuzushi unit's layout, which proudly displayed the Nintendo brand name on its casing for the first time. Afterwards, in 1981, he would design *Donkey Kong*, following it up with *Super Mario Bros.* in 1985, *The Legend of Zelda* in 1986, and *Star Fox* in 1993. Every legend starts somewhere.

The final Color TV-Game console, named the Computer TV Game, released in 1980 and featured Nintendo's 1978 arcade release *Computer Othello*, making it the world's first arcade-perfect home version. *Computer Othello* was the debut game from Nintendo's R&D1 team, which would later produce *Metroid* and *Kid Icarus*, and the first title to be both developed and published by Nintendo, making it quite the landmark. By 1983, such dedicated consoles were forgotten at Nintendo in favour of something far more fascinating, not to mention lucrative: the Family Computer.

FAIRCHILD VES/ CHANNEL F

Manufacturer: Fairchild Semiconductor International

Released: November 1976 (North America), October 1977 (Japan); the console was rebranded for other territories

Whereas the insides of the Magnavox Odyssey were comprised of so many diodes, capacitors and transistors, the Fairchild Channel F used microprocessor technology. Intel spearheaded the commercial use of these CPUs with its 4-bit Intel 4004 in 1971, used in calculators and pinball machines. In 1972 the 4004 was succeeded by the 8-bit 8008, and Fairchild Semiconductor International, not to be outdone by a competitor in this cutting-edge space, developed its own 8-bit processor, the F8. It quickly became a big seller in the microcontroller market, and in 1975 a computer engineer called Jerry Lawson used the F8 in his home-made arcade game, *Demolition Derby*, creating one of the first-ever video games to use the technology.

At the time, Lawson was a Fairchild employee. Born in Brooklyn, New York, in December 1940, he'd joined the San Francisco-based company in 1970. Come the middle of the decade, he'd moved up the ranks from an engineering consultant to Fairchild's chief hardware engineer, and it's in this position where Lawson encountered the product that'd define his career.

When Magnavox launched the Odyssey in 1972, the computing world inevitably took notice. Two employees at Alpex Computer Corporation in Connecticut, Lawrence Haskel and Wallace Kirschner, set about working on their own system in 1974, but this time using ROM chips that could be swapped in and out of a console to change the game. Alpex's founder, Norman Alpert, was keen to break into the gaming market, so with Haskel leading software development and Kirschner the hardware side of the operation, he was hopeful of not only rivalling the Odyssey, but bettering it.

However, just as Sanders Associates had struggled to secure a partner to manufacture the Brown Box for commercial purposes, Alpex found negotiations with TV makers, including RCA and Motorola, just as tough. The company contacted Fairchild buyer Shawn Fogarty, who they already had a business relationship with – perhaps a semiconductor company would take on the Alpex prototype, at the time called RAVEN: Remote Access Video Entertainment. Luckily, Fairchild was interested, and Gene Landrum – a consultant in the company's consumer products division – turned to Lawson, asking him to evaluate the RAVEN. Lawson liked what he saw and recommended that Fairchild license the technology from Alpex.

Landrum filed a report to senior management in November 1975, claiming that 5.5 million consoles could be sold by 1978. A deal was signed in January 1976: Fairchild would use the technology of the RAVEN system to develop its own video games console. The RAVEN used an Intel microprocessor, but Lawson replaced that with an F8. His colleagues, Ron Smith and Nick Talesfore, developed a unique controller that could be pulled and pushed, used like a joystick and even rotated like the Odyssey's knobs. The team also worked on refining the ROM cards that Alpex was using, transforming them into the world's first ROM cartridges. Development sped along, and Fairchild's console was released in November 1976 – first as the Video Entertainment System, the VES, but later rebranded to the Channel F (the F stands for 'fun') to avoid confusion with 1977's Atari VCS (itself later rebranded as the 2600).

As chief hardware engineer, it was Lawson who oversaw Fairchild's evolution of the Alpex prototype to the commercial release of the Channel F. Today, he's acknowledged as a pioneer for introducing players to both the world's first games console to use a microprocessor, but more importantly the first system to use swappable cartridges as we've come to know them. A total of 26 'Videocarts' were released for the Channel F, all made with bright yellow plastic and some of which contained more than one game. The console itself featured two games built in, *Hockey* and *Tennis*, both of which were essentially *Pong* clones.

Of the Channel F's games, a couple are notable for very different reasons. Videocart-17 is called *Pinball* but isn't pinball at all, instead a clone of *Breakout*. Rather less confusing and far more influential is Videocart-12, *Baseball*. As with all pre-1980 Channel F games, it was developed in-house, and its makers really used it as a showcase for the console's controller. The player can vary their pitch greatly by twisting and tilting the stick, and alter the speed of their delivery, and this unprecedented level of detail made Videocart-12 the cornerstone of the Channel F library, and it would inspire all future baseball games.

While the Channel F was the first games console to use now-traditional cartridges to support a varied array of software, its sales were poor. It couldn't compete with Atari's VCS and its popular arcade conversions, and despite licensing deals overseas – the Channel F was marketed as the Adman Grandstand in the UK, the Luxor Video Entertainment Computer in Sweden and the SABA Videoplay in Germany, and appeared under other names with slightly modified designs in further territories – it had only sold between 250,000 and 350,000 units by 1979, when Fairchild cut its losses and sold its gaming tech and inventory to Zircon International. Clearly, the prediction of 5.5 million sales was somewhat detached from reality. Zircon remodelled the console and relaunched it as the Channel F System II, but later discontinued the line in 1983 as the US video games market crashed through hardware oversaturation and an abundance of sub-par software.

Lawson left Fairchild in 1980 and set up a game development studio called Videosoft. It produced titles for the Atari VCS, the very system that'd killed off the console he'd help bring to life. In March 2011, the International Game Developers Association honoured Lawson for his contributions to the gaming medium. He died the next month, aged 70. It's sad that it's only after his passing that Lawson's career has really been highlighted for being so important. A collection of his contributions to gaming is on permanent display at New York's Strong National Museum of Play; he received a posthumous award at the 2019 Independent Games Festival for his Channel F work; and Netflix's gaming history documentary series *High Score* detailed his achievements in 2020.

Fairchild Channel F: Play One Game

Desert Fox (1976)
One of two games featured on the Channel F's *Videocart-2* alongside *Shooting Gallery*, *Desert Fox* is a game of tank-based combat where the player, controlling a blue tank, must navigate a field of mines to destroy their opponent – also a tank, but in green. It's a simple game but one that even incredibly primitive visuals and sound don't compromise the enjoyment of, as you duck behind barriers and carefully pick your shots. Your tank can aim in directions other than the one you're moving it in, giving *Desert Fox* the feel of a twin-stick shooter, and while the on-screen mines are able to deflect shots and keep you safe if you're behind one, driving over them will scrap your tank and give your opponent a point. While briefly entertaining played solo, *Desert Fox* is far better with a second player controlling the green tank.

ATARI VCS/2600

Manufacturer: Atari, Inc

Released: September 1977 (North America), 1978 (Europe), 1983 (Japan, sold as the Atari 2800)

Fairchild's ROM cartridge breakthrough might have made its products the market leaders in a different timeline – but Atari, enjoying ongoing arcade popularity in the wake of *Pong* with titles like *Space Race*, *Pursuit*, *Breakout* and *Tank*, would wholly steal its home gaming thunder with the release of its Video Computer System, or VCS, in September 1977. Going on to sell between 25 and 30 million units across a lifespan of 15 years, official discontinuation only coming in early 1992, this is home gaming's first heavyweight and it made Atari a byword for video games.

The success of the VCS – later rebranded as the Atari 2600 – wasn't solely built on Atari's arcade experience. The company knew that the home market was a different beast entirely. In 1973 Atari purchased a company called Cyan Engineering, which was tasked with developing a home console that'd translate arcade thrills to lounges and bedrooms the world over, using ROM cartridges for its games. MOS Technology's 1975-made 6507 8-bit microprocessor was chosen to power the console, and a prototype called Stella was built the same year, showing that such a product was viable.

Atari looked to Fairchild for further expertise. Gene Landrum was consulted to determine the look of the VCS and can be credited for recommending its woodgrain finish; and Douglas Hardy, who'd helped to design the Channel F's cartridges, worked on Atari's carts, ensuring they weren't so close to Fairchild's as to lead to legal complications. But there remained a problem: money. The *Pong* revenues were slowing down, and Atari needed extra investment to get the VCS manufactured and marketed to a level where it could really stake a claim as the number one console on the market. So in 1976 Atari co-founder Nolan Bushnell sold the company to Warner Communications for $28 million, while staying on as president. This injection of funding got the VCS over the line and into stores – and from there, into the homes and hearts of millions.

But the VCS started slowly. Its release was slightly delayed, allowing the dust to fully settle on Magnavox's legal action over *Pong* (see page 12). Its nine launch games included the console-bundled *Combat*, which was inspired by the successful *Tank* arcade game, *Star Ship* and *Video Olympics*, and its CX10 model joysticks (later updated to CX40 models) were brilliant representations of what players were used to in arcades. The VCS's CX6000 launch model would become known as the 'heavy sixer' for its six on-console switches and extra weight when compared to a lighter 1978 revision called, expectedly enough, the 'light sixer'. But consumers were wary, still unsure of the swappable cartridge gimmick and reluctant to shell out the $199 asking price – double the cost of the Magnavox Odyssey in 1972 and 30 dollars above the RRP for the Channel F. Shipping delays ate into sales too, and by the end of 1977 Atari had only sold a high estimate of 400,000 units. The next year saw 550,000 units shifted, necessitating further Warner funding to keep Atari's home console going. With fresh competition arriving from the Odyssey 2, and Mattel's Intellivision on the horizon, the VCS needed something to increase its appeal. And it got it from Japan.

A licensing agreement was struck with Taito to release its global arcade hit *Space Invaders* exclusively on the VCS. This was the first deal of its kind, and the Atari version of *Space Invaders* landed in March 1980, its impact immediate and incredible. The cartridge sold two million copies in its first year, shooting (freshly redesigned, four-switch CX2600-A model) VCS sales upwards, and the game would ultimately reach 6.25 million lifetime sales for the platform. But another legendary Japanese game would fare even better on Atari's console. A similar deal was agreed with Namco to bring its 1980 worldwide smash *Pac-Man* to the VCS, and while the game that eventually emerged in March 1982 was more *Pac-Man* in name only rather than an accurate conversion of the arcade experience, a whopping eight million copies were sold. By the end of 1982, Atari's machine – now called the 2600 as its successor, the 5200 SuperSystem, was also available – had achieved global sales of 15 million.

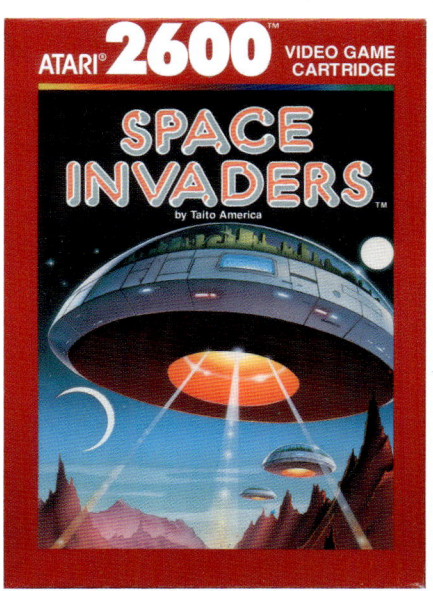

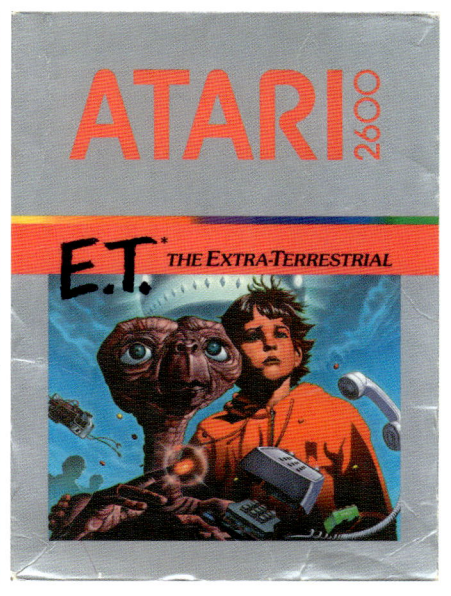

While *Pac-Man* and *Space Invaders* played a huge part in Atari's home market success, they were far from the only hit titles on the VCS/2600. In 1982 Nintendo's *Donkey Kong* was released for the console, albeit via Coleco's port; Activision's *Pitfall!*, developed by ex-Atari staffers; and Parker Brothers' conversion of Konami's *Frogger*. Titles familiar to arcade-goers arrived thick and fast: *Defender*, *Asteroids*, *Centipede*. And then there was movie tie-in *E.T. the Extra-Terrestrial*, fast-tracked through its development to release for Christmas 1982.

E.T. was *not* a good game (although it's far from the worst game on the VCS), but it sold exceptionally well, with 1.5 million copies shifted on release. However, Atari – which had paid $25 million for the licence – had massively over-estimated the demand for the game and manufactured as many as five million *E.T.* cartridges. Unsold stock collected dust, returns from disappointed players grew through 1983, and *E.T.* became gaming's first great commercial failure. In 2014, several *E.T.* carts were found at a New Mexico landfill site alongside other 2600 releases and hardware – unable to sell these things, and with manufacturing switching from the US to China, Atari had simply buried them.

The North American games market, where Atari ruled, was hit by a major recession in 1983, brought about by too many carts on sale at once, a flood of utterly wretched software, and too many manufacturers pushing similar hardware. Revenues dropped by 97% between 1983 and 1985, and in the middle of these testing times Warner sold Atari's home division to former Commodore CEO Jack Tramiel.

Tramiel had scored a huge hit with 1982's Commodore 64 home computer.

It was a machine 'for the masses, not the classes', as his mantra went, and he took this philosophy into the new age of Atari. His Atari Corporation released both the backwards-compatible Atari 7800 (launch price, $79.99) and a wallet-friendly 2600 revision in 1986 (pictured below), affectionately called the 2600 Jr (launch price, $49.99) – two new ways to enjoy the huge 2600/VCS catalogue without breaking the bank. It would later produce the XEGS and Jaguar consoles, the portable Atari Lynx, and several Atari-branded home computers. Atari didn't begin and end with the VCS, then, but its legacy in the home console market is absolutely tied to this system of flick switches and woodgrain.

Atari VCS/2600: Five Must Plays

Space Invaders (1980)
The first officially licensed arcade port, the VCS version of Taito's *Space Invaders*, plays just like the coin-op cab, only with rather drabber visuals and sputtery sound effects. Destroy each wave of aliens, move onto the next level, repeat: it's a formula that struck an immediate chord with players in the late 1970s and its appeal hadn't waned whatsoever by the time it came to Atari, with this cartridge selling two million copies in its first year and over six million by 1990. *Space Invaders* was such a huge acquisition for Atari that its release saw VCS sales quadruple, leading some to see this as gaming's first-ever 'killer app'.

Adventure (1980)
This pioneering action-adventure game laid the foundations for the likes of the Legend of Zelda series to follow, the player's exceptionally simple square avatar exploring

a semi-open world to find progress-enabling items while avoiding deadly enemies. You'll need a rich imagination to play this one today, painting in your mind's eye what your adventurer might be seeing before them, but *Adventure*'s innovations – its use of a screen-obscuring 'fog of war', randomised item placement, and free-roaming enemies that move around the game world independently of the player's actions – make it a game that anyone who loves role-playing titles today should check out just the once.

Pitfall! (1982)

Thirty-two treasures, 20 minutes, *go*. That's essentially *Pitfall!*'s sole instructions to the player as they steer its protagonist, Harry, through 255 screens of hazards and shortcut tunnels. The end game is either you lose all three lives, the timer runs down, or you find all the treasures within the time limit and win. Sounds simple enough, but exploration and experimentation are key cornerstones of the experience, with every crocodile, scorpion and rolling log deadly to the touch and the passages beneath the ground full of annoyingly placed brick walls. It's unlikely you'll beat *Pitfall!* on a first attempt, but the game – designed by David Crane and which really announced Activision as a publisher of note – has terrific longevity as you learn its secrets.

Pole Position (1982)

Atari licensed Namco's arcade racer for US distribution and wasted little time in also bringing the game to the 2600, where it immediately became the go-to game for speed-seekers among the console's audience. Its visuals are simplistic yet bright, with high contrast between racers and track ensuring that you always see a rival coming up ahead of you, but it's really the amazing sense of speed that *Pole Position* delivers that made it such a highlight of the 2600 library. It's lacking in features and game modes, but if you're after a 2600 game that lets you feel the wind in your hair while staring at the screen this is the one.

Mario Bros. (1983)

Before its own consoles made waves around the world, Nintendo regularly licensed their games for play on other platforms – and *Mario Bros.* on the 2600 is a fairly faithful version of the arcade game that'd come out just a few months before this port. A single-screen platformer, *Mario Bros.* sees Mario and Luigi defeat enemies appearing out of pipes, but unlike later 'Super' games, they can't just jump on their heads to do so. Instead, critters need to be flipped onto their backs by hitting the platform below them, and then kicked into oblivion. It's quite the change in gameplay for anyone used to *Super Mario Bros.*, but stick with it and this is a lot of score-chasing fun, especially with two players.

Atari VCS/2600 Collector Spot

VCS/2600 collector Lewis Clark from London, who also collects Atari 7800 games, shares some of his thoughts on the console, and his favourite titles. When not acquiring Atari titles, Lewis is focused on SEGA games and runs the SEGADriven website and YouTube channel.

'I was enamoured with the VCS the moment I got it. I had been specifically after a Light Sixer and was biding my time until one came up at the right price. Interestingly, my future girlfriend would be the one to reserve the Light Sixer I ended up owning! I think it's one of the most beautiful gaming consoles ever made, and the way the cartridges jut out of the machine and display them in all their monolithic glory is an iconic image.

'The VCS game that really made the biggest impression on me, at the start of my collecting, was *H.E.R.O.* – it holds up incredibly well, with a level structure that beckons you to keep trying. It really feels like an early take on the modern action game formula that would be better established later, on the NES.

'I'm a big racing game fan, and *Enduro* and *Sprint Master* are two excellent examples of the genre, with *Enduro* doing a fantastic job of being a third-person, *OutRun*-style driving game and *Sprint Master* being a great top-down, *Super Sprint*-style racer. *Solaris* is a technical showpiece for the system, with some outstanding effects and some great variety as you explore the galaxy; and *Cosmic Ark* has a fantastic gameplay loop that sees you defending your mothership from asteroids before you send out a smaller UFO, which must be used to beam up the different lifeforms on each planet. It's a simple set-up that becomes extremely compelling. I think *Pitfall II: Lost Caverns* is the game I cherish the most as it's the one I spent the longest time trying to get at a decent price. It's a fantastic follow-up to the David Crane classic that features a huge map to explore alongside an actual soundtrack, which is a rarity among VCS games.

'I think the VCS is a great system for retro collectors to get into nowadays because the system's modus operandi is bringing the arcade home, and despite the notorious *Pac-Man* port there's actually a lot of great arcade games available. *Ms. Pac-Man* and *Jr. Pac-Man* are considerably better ports and well worth a try! Most of the VCS's library is made up of arcade ports and it's very rare you need an instructional manual to figure out how to play them. The games boot straight away and you're playing within seconds, which has always been a big appeal for me as I'm particularly fed up with having to sit through minutes of publisher logos at the start of modern games!'

INTELLIVISION

Manufacturer: Mattel Electronics
Released: 1979 (North America), 1981 (UK), 1982 (mainland Europe, Japan), 1983 (South America)

A major toy manufacturer in the United States, and the name behind such brands as Barbie and Hot Wheels, Mattel had started to dabble in electronics in the mid-1970s, releasing its pioneering all-digital *Auto Race* handheld game in 1976, which was swiftly followed by *Missile Attack* the same year. But these portable playthings weren't in the same ballpark as what Fairchild and Atari were producing, so the company began development of its own home console in 1977. Two years later, at the Las Vegas-held consumer electronics trade show CES, Mattel unveiled the fruit of its labours: the 'Intelligent Television' console, or Intellivision.

Mattel's aim from the beginning of the Intellivision's development was to offer something better than what was already on the market. And that came at a price. Its 16-bit GI CP1610 processor (this is technically the world's first 16-bit games console) could produce sounds and visuals beyond anything the Atari VCS or Fairchild Channel F could muster, and it had over 1,400 bytes of RAM to play with against Atari's 128 and Fairchild's 64 – but at launch the Intellivision's RRP was as high as $299.

The Intellivision wasn't just a games console, though – again, its makers were thinking bigger. The main unit was called the Master Component, and Mattel released expansions – a keyboard module could be attached to create the Intelliputer, although only around 4,000 of these components were ever made; and the Intellivoice module could generate speech, but just five of the Intellivision's 125 games supported it. Despite its high price and low-appeal add-ons, Mattel's machine genuinely, albeit briefly, threatened Atari for the position of home console market leader. After a full rollout across North America in 1980, including the specially manufactured Tele-Games Super Video Arcade for Sears (identical on the inside to the standard Intellivision), and international launches in the following years, some two million units had been sold by 1982.

The Intellivision's games weren't half-bad, either. *Lock 'N' Chase* was a great conversion of Data East's *Pac-Man*-like arcade game; *Night Stalker* a tense game of cat and mouse as a human protagonist is hunted by deadly robots; and *Shark! Shark!* a compelling eat 'em up where you start as a small fish and consume even smaller fish to grow, while avoiding the shark that swims around on screen. Several popular arcade games made the leap to the Intellivision, with the console receiving excellent versions of *Bump 'n' Jump*, *Burger Time* and *Q*bert*.

One thing that might well have held the Intellivision back was its controller – its 16-direction 'control disc', side buttons and numeric keys layout just wasn't as intuitive or as fun to use as the VCS's joystick, and reviewers of the era compared it unfavourably to its rivals. The console underwent a few revisions, including 1983's Intellivision II (which could play Atari 2600 cartridges with an adapter, the aptly named System Changer) and 1985's INTV System III, and moved from being a Mattel product line to being owned by INTV Corporation because of the 1983 market crash. With over three million units total sold the Intellivision was no flop, but it staggered through its final years. It simply couldn't compete with the new champions of home gaming, SEGA and Nintendo, and was officially discontinued in 1990.

The Intellivision name carried through into the 21st century. A dedicated mini-console, the Intellivision Flashback, released in 2014 and featured 60 built-in games. More significantly, an all-new console proper called the Intellivision Amico, referencing the original system's design but with a curved finish and Bluetooth controllers with touchscreen functionality, was announced in 2018. But as of June 2023, the Amico not only remains unreleased, but certain stockists have pulled pre-orders completely. A fourth round of fundraising for the console in early 2022 flopped, and there have been significant layoffs at Intellivision, suggesting that the Amico may never see the light of day.

Intellivision: Play One Game

Lock 'N' Chase (1982)

The best Pac-Man game of the early 1980s that wasn't actually a Pac-Man game, Data East's *Lock 'N' Chase* turns the ghosts into patrolling policemen and the dot-munching pizza monster into a robber that looks like a tomato in a top hat. Rather than gobble down Power Pellets to gain an advantage over its pursuers, the player can instead close doors on the map to block the officers' paths. The maze of each stage is a vault, the dots are coins, and you don't immediately win when you collect them all – instead, exits open. But otherwise, this plays like you already know *Pac-Man* does, albeit much better than the popular but flawed Atari VCS port of Namco's arcade classic.

The Also-Rans and Never-Weres

The late-1970s saw a glut of other companies rush to get on board the home gaming gravy train – and most of them swiftly fell by the wayside. The first to try its luck was the RCA Studio II, released exclusively in North America in January 1977 – after the Fairchild Channel F but before the Atari VCS. Developed from an original concept for a home computer, the Studio II only produced black and white visuals, its audio was restricted to primitive bleeps, and much of its software was educational, cartridges including such titles as *Word Spelling Drill* and *Logical Deduction Test*. Thrilling stuff.

Despite stealing a march on Atari, the Studio II suffered from extremely low sales, with high estimates only placing it around 25,000 units shifted, and it received a measly 11 game cartridges. The tech inside the Studio II would be licensed for products including the Japan-only Toshiba Visicom Com-100 and the Conic M-1200 Colour in Europe, but RCA left the gaming market after only a year, discontinuing its console in 1978. In the April of that same year, the amusement company Bally – well known for its pinball machines – played its home console hand with the full release of its Professional Arcade system. It too struggled to find a foothold, with its high launch RRP of $299 and poor advertising leaving it floundering.

What the Professional Arcade offered that no other console of the time could, though, was the ability to use its built-in programming language, Bally BASIC, to make games. This appealed to hobbyist programmers, and the console was essentially host to the world's first proper homebrew scene. It also shipped with *Gun Fight* built in, the first game to show human against human duelling and depict the death of the loser. But this wasn't enough to drive sales, which flatlined in comparison to its main competitors, and Bally bailed on video gaming in 1980, selling the console rights to Astrovision, who marketed it as the Astrocade until its mid-1980s cancellation. The console sold between 40,000 and 60,000 units in total, and its games library only reached 28 releases.

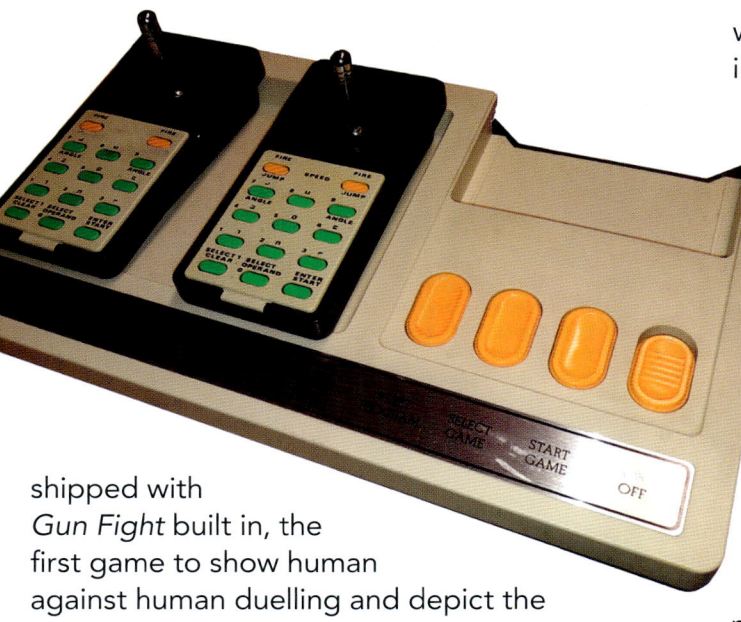

In Europe, German hearing aid manufacturer Interton put out its own home console using ROM cartridges, the VC 4000, the successor to a series of *Pong*-clone systems. As well as launching the VC 4000 domestically in 1978 for 500 Deutsche Marks, Interton sold the console in other European markets including the UK, France and the Netherlands, and also in Australia. The insides of the VC 4000 were widely 'cloned', and other contemporary consoles that were stylistically different but internally identical included the Voltmace Database (pictured left), Audiosonic's 1292 Advanced Programmable Video System, and the Acetronic MPU-1000. Uniquely, the 35-plus VC 4000 cartridges loaded their programmes into the console's internal RAM, and they played just fine on other compatible systems. Sales figures for the VC 4000 are unknown, but it was discontinued in 1983 and Interton never produced another console.

Another that came and went was APF Electronics' MP1000 console of 1978. The New York company had previously manufactured *Pong* clones (the TV Fun range) and its one and only proper gaming machine was compatible with a keyboard expansion called the Imagination Machine, which also expanded its RAM and basically turned the console into a home computer. However, only 12 games were released for the MP1000 before APF declared bankruptcy in 1983. Perhaps the rarest games console of the era, Unisonic's Champion 2711 system came out in 1978 and only sold between 500 and 1,000 units. Unisonic, also based in New York, had produced its own *Pong* clones but was better known for calculators, and its dalliance with home consoles was brief indeed. The Champion 2711 focused on card games – *Poker Games* was one of its four released cartridges – and was marketed in Japan as the Casino TV Games system. Don't expect to find one down your local car-boot sale anytime soon.

THE 1980s
JAPAN RISES TO RULE THE GAMING WORLD

While the 1970s had seen Japanese developers focus largely on arcade releases, the following decade brought with it a sea change. SEGA and Nintendo took their experience of producing coin-op classics into the home console market, with both the Mega Drive and Nintendo Entertainment System becoming iconic machines. But while the Western 'console war' was waged between these two titans, Atari having become a bystander, NEC's unassuming PC Engine made it a three-way race in Japan, briefly knocking even the mighty Mario makers into second position. The 1980s was also when 'bits' started to matter to home console players, as 8 gave way to 16, and a crash in the major North American market saw a few big names taken out of the game completely.

COLECOVISION

Manufacturer: Coleco Industries, Inc

Released: August 1982 (North America), July 1983 (Europe)

Initially founded as a leather supplier in the 1930s, the Connecticut-based Coleco's greatest claim to fame in the world of toys and games is probably the Cabbage Patch Kids, which it introduced in 1982. But in the 1970s, while also producing playhouses and paddling pools, it entered the video gaming market with the Telstar series of dedicated *Pong*-clone consoles.

These systems grew in complexity from the first model in 1976 to 1977's bizarre-looking Coleco Telstar Arcade, a triangular contraption with a different interface on each side: *Pong* controls, a steering wheel, and a light gun. With an amazing 14 variations produced in just two years the Telstar range inevitably burned itself out, but Coleco wasn't done with video games. Company president Arnold Greenberg wanted to follow Atari's lead and take arcade games into the home, and it was left to lead designer Eric Bromley to make the magic happen.

The magic stalled. Despite Bromley having a clear idea for Coleco's home console as early as the late 1970s, the cost of its component parts, particularly the 16kb of RAM that it would demand, was too much for Greenburg. This changed in 1981, when Bromley spied an article in The Wall Street Journal on the declining price of RAM. He rushed to his boss, telling Retro Gamer magazine several years later: 'I burst into his office [and] before he could react I showed him the new figures. Ten minutes later we were working on a new project with the working name "ColecoVision".'

The working name stuck, and the ColecoVision was ready for release in August 1982. It promised – and delivered – visuals that were leagues ahead of the Atari VCS, and its price point of $179 was 20 dollars less than the market leader had launched for in 1977. But what mattered most of all to Bromley was the pack-in game. It had to be special, and as a big arcade-goer himself, he knew who to approach. Atari might have secured the rights to *Space Invaders* and *Pac-Man*, but in 1981 another Japanese arcade game sent shockwaves around the world, and Coleco was determined to make it theirs.

Nintendo's Shigeru Miyamoto and Gunpei Yokoi had worked together to create *Donkey Kong* – the first game in what would become a franchise for the titular ape *and* the first appearance of Mario, who'd go on to be the company's mascot. It was North America's highest-grossing arcade cabinet in 1981 (and 1982), and Bromley travelled to Nintendo's headquarters in Kyoto to secure the exclusive rights to produce a ColecoVision conversion. The negotiations proved expensive for Bromley, who convinced Greenburg to agree to a $200,000 advance and for Nintendo to receive $2 from every unit sold. The deal was done – but upon returning home, Bromley realised that he had no legally binding paperwork. Further months of negotiations followed before Nintendo president Hiroshi Yamauchi finally put pen to paper on something that mattered – but even then it was only the intervention of Yamauchi's daughter, Yoko, that saw Nintendo sell the *Donkey Kong* rights to Coleco and not Atari. 'She believed me that this was not just a product, but also my dream,' Bromley recounted to *Retro Gamer*, adding that he'd told Yoko, '*Donkey Kong* would look like crap on the VCS.'

Donkey Kong became the pack-in game for the ColecoVision, included in every purchase, and this was a huge shot in the arm for the console – it sold half a million units in five months. Atari's new 5200, released in November 1982, couldn't keep pace, while the 2600 now looked incredibly dated. And it's not like newcomers to home gaming needed to make a choice between the ColecoVision or Atari either – the higher-spec system featured an expansion module interface, and its Expansion Module #1 allowed 2600 carts to be played using Atari's own joysticks. Atari was incensed and filed a $350 million lawsuit. It was settled out of court with Coleco – who'd made their module using off-the-shelf parts and nothing specifically from the

The 1980s

25

2600 – agreeing to license Atari's patents. The module remained on sale and Coleco even produced a standalone console, 1983's Gemini, which played 2600 carts as standard.

Further expansion modules added a steering wheel and pedal – essential for the ColecoVision's port of SEGA's 1981 arcade hit *Turbo* – and the ADAM computer add-on, complete with keyboard and cassette drive. With a drawn-out development period and a high RRP of over $700, ADAM was a costly misstep for Coleco and ultimately put them in a precarious financial situation right before the North American games market crash of 1983. Through 1983 and into 1984, Coleco lost almost $50 million – and as good as the ColecoVision was as a games machine, it couldn't sell enough units to turn its makers' fortunes around, and the console was officially discontinued in October 1985.

Like the Intellivision, however, the ColecoVision name reappeared in the 21st century as a dedicated plug-in-and-play mini-console, the ColecoVision Flashback, went on sale in 2014 with 60 built-in games. It includes some of the system's finest releases, like its arcade ports of Stern Electronics' intense title *Frenzy*, SEGA's isometric shooter *Zaxxon*, and Taito's Tarzan-like *Jungle Hunt*. And while its estimated two million sales don't make the ColecoVision one of gaming's biggest-ever machines, it sure left an impression on Nintendo. Having seen *Donkey Kong* running on the American-made console, it knew its Family Computer (or Famicom) would need to raise its game to not only outshine Atari but also this superior system. It also learned from the collapse of the American gaming market that sent Coleco back to the comfort of kids' toys, and when the time came to sell the Famicom in the US, Nintendo would be *very* careful about the language it used.

ColecoVision: Five Must Plays

Donkey Kong (1982)
A superb version of Nintendo's arcade game, *Donkey Kong*'s inclusion as the ColecoVision's pack-in title guaranteed it plenty of attention from players, but even those coming to the console later on would put this port near the top of their second-hand shopping list. Bright and crisp visuals and great sound and music really did highlight how powerful the ColecoVision was compared to the Atari 2600, and for many reviewers at the time this was just about as faithful as any arcade conversion could be.

Zaxxon (1982)
SEGA's isometric shooter looks and plays brilliantly on the ColecoVision, its clear visuals making oncoming obstacles easy to read and avoid, although enemy ships are far trickier since they have a habit of firing back at you. *Zaxxon* was incredibly striking as a coin-op when it debuted in Japan in 1981, and this is probably its best home port outside of more modern versions that truly replicate the arcade look and feel.

Frenzy (1984)
This high-adrenaline game has you controlling a guy with a gun through several screens full of deadly robots, also with guns. The aim is to escape each of these screens, navigating your way through breakable access points and using blaster-proof walls to bounce your shots off of. The enemies can be destroyed by their own friendly fire as they go after you – but linger too long on a single screen and a bouncing smiley face named Evil Otto will appear, which can pass through any solid barrier and will eliminate you on contact. There's no end to *Frenzy* except the loss of the player's three lives, the sole goal being a high score, but played in feverish short-session bursts it's a thrill even so many years since its debut.

Burger Time (1984)
Another amazing ColecoVision arcade port, *Burger Time* shows how great this console was at bringing the coin-op experience home. Data East's fast-food-forming puzzle-platformer has large and colourful sprites,

its catchy music carries over intact, and the whole thing's fun enough to keep you hooked for several rounds per session. Just don't be surprised when you're feeling hungry once the controller's finally put down.

River Raid (1984)

River Raid began as an Atari 2600 title but is another game that shines brighter on the ColecoVision, leaving the Atari version's stiffer, slower action in its shadow. A vertical shooter that adds the additional challenge of keeping your fighter filled with fuel – just fly over the indicated sections of the water below – *River Raid* looks a lot more simplistic than *Zaxxon*, but it's a speedy, twitchy game that demands fast reactions as you take out enemies and avoid slamming into the riverbanks and bridges.

VECTREX

Manufacturer: General Consumer Electronics/Milton Bradley Company

Released: November 1982 (North America), 1983 (Europe, Japan)

The Vectrex was truly unlike any console to come before it – and it didn't inspire many imitators either. It could have been something *very* different, however, as its development at Smith Engineering, under the guidance of John Ross, started in 1980 with the intent to release a handheld system with a tiny one-inch display. Ross and his team were calling this the Mini Arcade; but once the project was licensed to General Consumer Electronics it shifted in size and focus, becoming a larger, tabletop device.

The most striking feature of the Vectrex is its built-in screen. This design was somewhat echoed by Entex's elusive Adventure Vision, a hard-to-find and self-contained portable device also released in 1982, although that console's display used red LEDs reflected onto an oscillating mirror (Nintendo would adapt this technique for its ill-fated Virtual Boy in the 1990s). In contrast, the Vectrex's monitor was a fairly standard monochrome CRT, made by Samsung and measuring nine inches wide by 11 tall. It was more the visuals that played out across it that made this console special.

Rather than use the sprites typical of other home systems for its games, Vectrex titles were displayed using vector graphics. These were generated by following the player's movements on the X and Y axis, with bright white lines drawn and objects moved against a stark black background. Colour was added to the console's games via Magnavox Odyssey-recalling screen overlays, or by using the 3-D Imager peripheral with its blue, red and green filters. Vector graphics weren't unprecedented in video gaming – arcade titles like 1977's *Space Wars* by Cinematronics and 1979's *Asteroids* by Atari showcased the approach – but General Consumer Electronics took a chance with its product.

The very *Asteroids*-like *Mine Storm* came built into the Vectrex, appealing to arcade fans, and the console attracted early plaudits and sold steadily. Indeed, it sold well enough that board game makers Milton Bradley opted to acquire General Consumer Electronics and distribute the

Vectrex in Europe; while in Japan, Bandai won the licence to sell the system. But this good fortune wouldn't last – with the North American gaming market in freefall in 1983, Milton Bradley lost over $31 million in a year, and halved the console's initial RRP of $199 to offload stock. A colour model was scrapped, and official discontinuation dawned in February 1984, with total consoles sold reaching around 100,000.

The Vectrex received 27 game cartridges, several of which were ports of Cinematronics titles – including *Space Wars*, the military themed *Armor Attack*, and *Starhawk*, which shamelessly ripped off the Death Star trench scene from *Star Wars: A New Hope*. One of the Vectrex's most historically notable games was *Cosmic Chasm*, the first title to be developed for a home console before subsequently being released as an arcade cabinet.

Several years after Milton Bradley's involvement, the rights to the Vectrex name reverted back to Smith Engineering, who permitted enthusiasts to make new games for the console free of any charge. This led to the creation of brand-new Vectrex games in the 21st century, such as 2003's *Defender*-like *Protector* and the 2004 shooter *I, Cyborg*. It's an odd one, then, but the Vectrex definitely has its fans – then and now.

Vectrex: Play One Game

Space Wars (1982)

Intense sci-fi shooter action for one or two players, *Space Wars* is dogfighting made simple with the added fun of being able to warp to random parts of the screen. The player must not only contend with the actions of their rival ship, but also asteroids passing by and the presence of a sun in the middle of the screen that, if thrusted into, means immediate destruction. Defeat your rival and it's a point to you; become space debris, and it's a point to them. First to ten wins the contest. *Space Wars* is an incredibly intuitive game that'll keep a pair of competing players content for many an afternoon.

ATARI 5200

Manufacturer: Atari, Inc

Released: November 1982 (North America only)

As the 1980s arrived, Atari needed to freshen up its console line to compete with the Intellivision and ColecoVision. The Atari VCS had sold well but its games now looked tired. The company's answer was the 5200 SuperSystem, an upgrade from the VCS – now called the 2600 to align with the new branding – and internally based on the company's popular range of 8-bit home computers. But lightning did not strike twice, and the 5200 was a comparative failure with around million units sold, exclusively in North America.

It's not that the 5200 was a bad system, but it was let down by incredibly poor peripherals – its box-in controller featured an analogue stick that would break if you so much as looked at it and a keypad that was used with a bare minimum of titles. Also diminishing the 5200's appeal was its lacklustre updates of well-known games, and no backwards compatibility with the massive VCS/2600 library. Atari did produce an adapter for the 5200 that would allow it to play the carts of its older machine, but much like the new console itself it never caught on.

Further playing against the 5200 was Atari's choice of pack-in game. Whereas the ColecoVision came with the huge arcade hit *Donkey Kong*, Atari's new console included *Super Breakout*, a barely upgraded version of a game that'd released for the 2600 only a year earlier. The 5200 was powerful enough to compete with the ColecoVision graphically, but so little of its software made the most of the custom processor under its substantially sized hood. With the ColecoVision's games looking more impressive than Atari's 5200 line-up, and the rival console having its own 2600 adapter, many consumers switched brands and left Atari behind.

A revised version of the 5200 went on sale in 1983, changing the storage for its controllers – which went from a compartment in the top to a space at the rear – and switching from the original's four controller ports to just a pair. (The decision to include four at the start was based on a four-player version of *Asteroids* being the pack-in game, before it was switched to *Super Breakout*.) This reduced-price remodel might have stood a chance of success if not for 1983's collapse in gaming revenues in North America, which saw it discontinued in 1984 with only 69 games released as ownership of Atari switched from Warner Communications to former Commodore CEO Jack Tramiel. Atari would be back with more hardware, *better* hardware, but not before a nascent gaming superpower in Japan took its domestic console global and planted its flag in the US like no overseas company before it.

Atari 5200: Play One Game

Qix (1983)

Drawing lines on a screen might not sound like a thrilling way to spend time in the company of a games console, but in the puzzling *Qix* progression is all about claiming territory by connecting together a series of 'land grabs' while avoiding the erratic titular presence that moves around the play area. Connect your cursor to an existing line, creating a closed-off rectangle, and you'll claim more of the territory, with between 50% and 90% needed to progress depending on your difficulty level. Get intercepted by the Qix, or by the Sparx that chase your diamond-shaped cursor along unfinished lines, and it's a life lost. This is an initially unremarkable-looking game that quickly becomes hard to put down.

Early 1980s Console Contenders

History largely only remembers its winners, and in the 1980s it was Nintendo and SEGA that ruled the home console market. But at the beginning of the decade a few other systems took their shots. They all missed.

In 1982, Hong Kong-based VTech released its CreatiVision console, marketing it mainly in Asia, Australia, and parts of Europe. However, those territories had started to take a shine to computers over consoles, and although the CreatiVision *could* be used like a computer – its controller keypads, when docked, form a semi-traditional keyboard – its hybrid model failed to find a large audience. A high estimate of 70,000 units were sold, and only 20 games released – but VTech stayed active in the space for several years more, putting out a series of home computers and, in 1988, the education-focused Socrates console. Another console-computer hybrid, Commodore's low-spec MAX Machine, was briefly available in Japan in 1982, but its poor reception saw an international rollout cancelled. Its makers would nevertheless see great success in the 1980s with the Commodore 64 and Amiga home computers, before unwisely re-entering the console market in the 1990s.

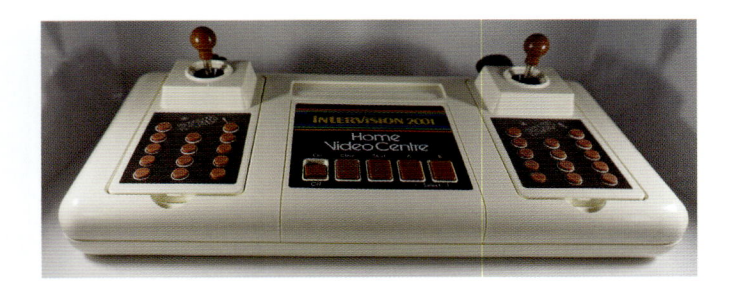

Other not-so-notable consoles of the early 1980s included the Emerson Radio Arcadia 2001, released in North America in May 1982 and much-cloned by overseas manufacturers. In the UK it morphed into the Rowtron 2000, in Finland it was the Intervision 2001, in the Netherlands it became the Ormatu Video Spelcomputer 2001, while Bandai gained an official licence to sell the system under the name Arcadia in Japan. In Germany in 1982, SHG released its Black Point FS-1003 and FS-2000 consoles, both of which ran the same range of cartridges, only a small handful of which were released. And Philips issued the Videopac+ G7400 as a European exclusive system in 1983. It ran the same cartridges as its Odyssey 2/Videopac G7000 console as well as enhanced games specifically made for it – but that only three of these higher-resolution releases came out tells you everything you need to know about the G7400's success, or lack thereof.

SG-1000

Manufacturer: SEGA

Released: July 1983 (Japan), 1983 (Australia and New Zealand), 1986 (China, SG-1000 II)

Just as Nintendo didn't blink into life with electronic gaming products, SEGA's history also predates the arrival of battery-powered handhelds, home consoles and coin-op arcade cabs. Or rather, it predates arcade cabs as they became in the 1970s and early 1980s with the rise of Atari, Taito, Nintendo and Namco (and, indeed, SEGA itself). Because SEGA has always been a name connected to gaming – just not quite how we think of it today.

In 1940, three Americans formed a company called Standard Games in Hawaii. It distributed slot machines to US military bases, and over time changed both its business and its name: Standard Games became Service Games, and in the 1950s it started selling coin-operated amusement machines – mechanical, not electronic – in Japan and other Asian locations, as Service Games of Japan. Service Games was abbreviated to SEGA on its products, the first dating back to 1954; but the early 1960s saw a shift in fortunes and Service Games of Japan was dissolved.

In June 1960, two Japanese companies took over Service Games of Japan's business; and after an acquisition or two and a few CEO handovers, what was SEGA Inc. became SEGA Enterprises, Ltd and focused itself on amusement machines, pinball tables and jukeboxes. One of its first electro-mechanical arcade machines, *Periscope*, was released in 1966 and distributed internationally, its 1968 US release effectively standardising the one-quarter-per-play payment model. It was a huge success for SEGA, and the company would go on to be a major player in the arcade world.

At the start of the 1980s, though, the purely electronic thrills of the arcades were becoming increasingly popular in homes, too. Atari was selling stacks of VCS consoles, and Mattel's Intellivision was popular too. SEGA was not about to be left behind, and on July 15 1983 its first home console was released: the SG-1000 (the S and G standing for SEGA Game). Development for a home system had begun with the aim of incorporating a keyboard, and SEGA went ahead with this model alongside the SG-1000: the SG-3000, aka the SEGA Personal Computer, was compatible with peripherals including a data recorder, disc drive and printer. But SEGA wouldn't stick to this approach to hardware, as focus switched to a range that could rival Nintendo's Famicom, released on the very same day in Japan as the SG-1000.

The SG-1000 got off to a decent start, selling 160,000 units by the end of 1983. Playing its games today, it's clear the system could sing in the right hands: *Sonic the Hedgehog* programmer Yuji Naka's *Girl's Garden* is a cheery collect 'em up; *Flicky* and *Zaxxon* are aesthetically compromised but very playable ports of SEGA's own arcade games; and *Gulkave* is a fast and tough horizontal shooter. But Nintendo caught up after being plagued by failing consoles in 1983, and the Famicom overtook SEGA's sales in 1984 thanks to first-party arcade ports and savvy licensing deals.

A revised SG-1000, the Mark II, was released in July 1984 and swapped the original's hardwired joystick for detachable pads much closer in look and feel to the Famicom's controller – but it too stumbled while Nintendo's machine soared. SEGA, however, realised that its home turf wasn't the only territory up for grabs, and while the SG-1000 and its update never received official releases outside of Asia and Australasia (although a clone from China's Bit Corporation, the Dina, was released in the US as the Telegames Personal Arcade, and also played ColecoVision carts), the next revision, the SG-1000 Mark III, would transform into a masterful system of worldwide ambition.

FAMILY COMPUTER

Manufacturer: Nintendo
Released: July 1983 (Japan)

The Home Cassette-type Video Game: Family Computer – to give Nintendo's first home console to use swappable game cartridges its full name, but from here we'll go with its widely used abbreviation of Famicom – was released on 15 July 1983, the same day as SEGA's SG-1000. Developed from the arcade hardware of Nintendo's own *Radar Scope* of 1980, inspired by the ColecoVision's capability for smooth and clear graphics, and originally envisioned as being compatible with a wealth of come computer add-ons, the Famicom really is the foundation upon which its maker's entire modern reputation is built upon. The console sold almost 20 million units in Japan alone and was home to breakthroughs like *Super Mario Bros.*, *Metroid* and *The Legend of Zelda*, albeit via an add-on with the last two. And yet, the Famicom could have been one of gaming's greatest failures.

At least it wasn't *actually* a joke, though – which is what designer Masayuki Uemura originally thought upon receiving a phone call in 1981. He spoke to Matt Alt for kotaku.com in 2020, a year before he died, aged 78: 'President (Hiroshi) Yamauchi told me to make a video game system, one that could play games on cartridges. He always liked to call me after he'd had a few drinks, so I didn't think much of it. I just said, "Sure thing, boss," and hung up. It wasn't until the next morning when he came up to me, sober, and said, "That thing we talked about, you're on it?" that it hit me: he was serious.' Uemura subsequently bought every games console he could and pulled them apart, studying their components, but nothing really inspired him. 'They simply didn't have expressive enough graphics,' he said. 'They were old fashioned, and I couldn't use anything from them.' While impressed by the ColecoVision, Uemura didn't want to match it – he wanted to surpass it.

The Famicom, powered by a Rioch 2A03 processor evolved from Nintendo's own arcade tech, released with three launch titles of huge arcade appeal: *Donkey Kong*, *Donkey Kong Jr.*, and *Popeye*. Bearing a toy-like design, it came with two hardwired controllers that took cues from Nintendo's Game & Watch series of handheld titles (that's where the cross-shaped D-pad originated), and its price of ¥14,800 was marginally cheaper than SEGA's simultaneously released system. With exceptional visuals for the time and arcade ports that pretty much replicated the coin-op originals, Nintendo's console should have enjoyed a flying start. But it was marred by chipset failures with many consoles returned as faulty, leading to Nintendo issuing a complete recall of stock at the end of 1983, costing the company millions of dollars.

Embarrassed but unprepared to concede defeat – not just to SEGA but also the likes of Japanese competitors Epoch and Casio and the American imports of Atari and Intellivision – Nintendo fitted the Famicom with a new motherboard and went back to retail. This time the console's failure rate was insignificant, and by the end of 1984 the Famicom had become the dominant video games console in Japan with sales of over 2.5 million units. The console didn't yet have *Super Mario Bros.* as an enticement, but its 19 releases in '84 were of a consistently high quality: the likes of the Zapper light gun game *Duck Hunt*, the motocross racer *Excitebike*, Namco's arcade hits *Pac-Man* and *Galaxian*, *Donkey Kong 3* and *Devil World* all played their part in making the Famicom a success. Any console is only as good as the games you can play on it, and some of these were exceptional.

The Famicom's controller set a clear precedent for games consoles, with its A and B buttons, Select and Start, and the D-pad for directional movement. The D-pad, ubiquitous ever since the Famicom's breakthrough, was born through necessity as the 1982 Game & Watch version of *Donkey Kong* required four-way movement – up and down, left and right – and designer Gunpei Yokoi felt that four individual buttons just didn't feel right, while a joystick was too fragile and impractical for the portable device. Using a single button, albeit one that connected to four separate inputs, was more fluid, more responsive, and didn't necessitate the player to look down at what they were doing. Yokoi originally called this the 'plus controller', but D-pad became the conventional name after SEGA used the term 'D button' in its manuals. Nowadays, almost every console controller features a D-pad, the one notable exception being Nintendo's own Switch, which due to its Joy-Con play pattern uses four individual buttons for movement.

Super Mario Bros. was released for the Famicom in September 1985 and would go on to be the best-selling game for the console – including sales on the Nintendo Entertainment System (NES), the revised Famicom for the international market, its total sits at over 40 million copies on original hardware (with several million more sold on subsequent platforms). Directed, produced and co-designed by Shigeru Miyamoto, who'd previously designed *Donkey Kong* for arcades and *Devil World* for the home console, *Super Mario Bros.* became the benchmark for side-scrolling platformers, its smooth gameplay, tight controls and hidden secrets nowadays the stuff of legend. The game's popularity saw it become a bundled title with new purchases of a NES, often packaged alongside *Duck Hunt*, and it was ported from the Famicom/NES to other platforms: to arcades via Nintendo's VS. System (basically a coin-op NES, using the same CPU), home computers with Hudson Soft's *Super Mario Bros. Special* for the NEC PC-8801 and Sharp X1, and to the Famicom Disk System.

The Famicom Disk System, released exclusively in Japan in February 1986, was a peripheral that enabled owners to buy games on floppy discs instead of the usual cartridges. These 'Disk Cards' were sold for less than Famicom cartridges and could even have their games replaced by others using special kiosks in stores – so you could buy a copy of *Super Mario Bros.*, finish it, and overwrite the disk with something else entirely (a headache for collectors today due to labels not matching software). Nintendo really pushed the Disk System, claiming that all of its new first-party games would release on it and not as cartridges. That didn't quite prove to be the case as the cost of cartridge production fell in the late 1980s, but *The Legend of Zelda*, *Metroid* and *Castlevania* all debuted on the Disk System, taking advantage of the format's increased storage capacity of 128k and enhanced audio.

While it only sold 4.4 million units – representing less than a quarter of the Famicom's 19.3 million sales in Japan – Nintendo's technical support for the Disk System lasted until 2007. The Famicom itself wasn't officially discontinued in Japan until 2003, giving both the console and its add-on 30-year lifespans, far longer than the NES enjoyed in the rest of the world.

Alongside Nintendo's Famicom models, Sharp was active in the Japanese market, releasing its own versions of the hardware. In 1983, the company released its C1 NES TV, a television set with an integrated Famicom available in both 14-inch and 19-inch screen sizes; and July 1986 saw the debut of its Twin Famicom, a two-in-one console combining the Famicom and Disk System, which sold for ¥32,000 – around ¥2,000 more than the buying the original system and its add-on separately. A second model of the Twin Famicom followed in 1987, with a reshaped shell and turbo functions on its controllers. Sharp also produced a high-end Famicom variant capable of RGB and S-Video output, the Famicom Titler (or Editor), which came out in 1989 for a massive ¥43,000 and was aimed at users wanting to record their gameplay.

The Famicom was widely cloned, with perhaps its most famous knock-off being the Dendy Junior, released for the Russian market in 1992 and selling several million units. Dendy redesigned its console a few times, while elsewhere in the world other clones included the Chinese-made Micro Genius IQ-201 and its numerous successors including the IQ-1000; Brazil's Dynavision range, some of which played both Japanese and American games; and the officially licensed (and incredibly hard to find today) models of Samurai's Electronic TV Game, sold in India from 1987, and the Korean market's Hyundai Comboy, both of which were NES consoles sold under alternative names to get around local trading regulations.

Not-So-Big in Japan
While Nintendo and SEGA were just getting started at being rivals, a handful of other Japan-based manufacturers were taking their own steps into the video game

console world. The biggest of these was Epoch, whose Cassette Vision console released in July 1981 and would sell around 400,000 units, making it the market leader until the Famicom and SG-1000 series arrived on the scene.

Despite its tapes-referencing name, the Cassette Vision used ROM cartridges like most other consoles of the time. Unlike many competitors, the Cassette Vision did not have its controllers running on leads to the main system, instead placing all the necessary inputs on the console itself – two knobs and two buttons were on each side of the cartridge slot, rather like the *Pong* clones of the mid-1970s. Eleven games were released for the Cassette Vision, which was also revised into a smaller and cheaper Cassette Vision Junior model in 1983, before Epoch, losing ground to Nintendo and SEGA, responded with a more powerful system: the Super Cassette Vision.

Also released in 1983, in October, was Casio's debut games console, the PV-1000. It failed to gain any market traction and was swiftly discontinued with only 13 games released – among them ports of Namco's *Dig Dug* and Konami's *Super Cobra*. Despite this failure, Casio would put out another console, the 32-bit Loopy, in the mid-1990s.

In 1983 there was also the release of Nichibutsu's My Vision console, which focused on electronic versions of traditional board and card games like mahjong and *Mastermind*; and Gakken's Compact Vision TV Boy, a strange-looking system with a large built-in T-shaped joystick and handle, for which only six cartridges were ever released (again including *Super Cobra*, and another Konami arcade hit, *Frogger*). The Compact Vision TV Boy looks more like a retro-futuristic telephone than a games console, and its unusual design makes it a favourite with collectors today.

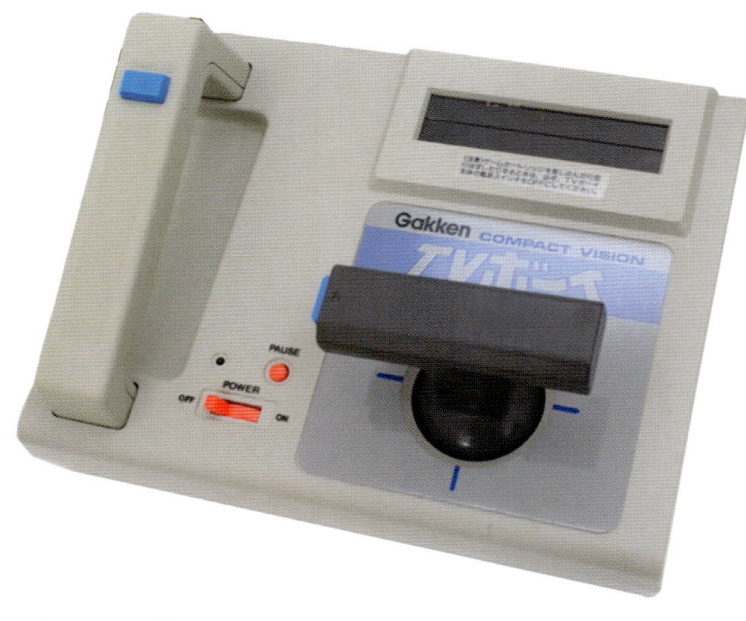

SUPER CASSETTE VISION

Manufacturer: Epoch
Released: July 1984 (Japan), late 1984 (France)

With the Cassette Vision looking exceptionally primitive compared to the SG-1000 and Famicom, both in terms of its under-the-hood hardware and on-screen visuals and action, Epoch needed to get an upgrade into stores. And it did just that with the aptly named Super Cassette Vision, which used an 8-bit processor just like SEGA and Nintendo to produce bright, bold colours and gameplay that could match that of its rivals. The Super Cassette Vision also moved its controls off the console, coming with a pair of hardwired joysticks with side-mounted buttons that store away in the front of the casing. By all accounts, the Super Cassette Vision was a great console that simply had the misfortune to be up against a pair of rising industry titans, with total sales before its discontinuation (and Epoch's withdrawal from the console market) in 1987 coming in at a high estimate of 300,000.

Thirty games were released for the Super Cassette Vision, including licensed titles based on manga series Doraemon, Dragon Ball and Lupin III, and ports of Namco arcade games like *Mappy*, *Sky Kid* and *Pole Position II*. Around half of these games made it to Europe as the Super Cassette Vision was released in France courtesy of the company YENO, which slapped its name on the system but otherwise left it largely untouched aesthetically, maintaining its Japanese colour scheme. Epoch itself also produced a version of the Super Cassette Vision in bright pink, ostensibly aimed at the Japanese female market, which they named the Lady edition. It was sold in a larger case that offered game cartridge storage, and was bundled with *Milky Princess* (pictured above), a sort of interactive horoscope game full of fairies with magic wands.

While the Super Cassette Vision was Epoch's final home video games console, the company – which had a strong background in toys and electronics and had manufactured the first games console ever released in Japan, 1975's TV Tennis Electrotennis – would reappear in 1991 with a very odd gaming system: Barcode Battler. Not *exactly* a games console, it scanned barcodes to generate player characters, power-ups and more, for one-on-one fights played out on a stats-filled LCD screen. It was also compatible with a limited number of Epoch-made and published Famicom and Super Famicom games. A redesigned Barcode Battler received a worldwide release in 1992 and '93, with an English-language interface replacing the Japanese original.

Epoch scored a world first in 1984 with the Game Pocket Computer, a handheld that was the first portable console to use swappable ROM carts, played on a 75-by-64-pixel display. It didn't catch on though, with only five games coming out for it. Perhaps it was simply too ahead of its time, as Nintendo's handheld console proper, the Game Boy, would fare much better five years later.

NINTENDO ENTERTAINMENT SYSTEM

Manufacturer: Nintendo

Released: October 1985 (North America), September 1986 (Europe), 1987 (Australia), 1993 (Brazil)

As Nintendo's Famicom console dominated the Japanese market, its makers began looking overseas. North America was the best next step for the hardware, and Nintendo already had an established presence there, Nintendo of America, founded in 1980 to oversee the company's arcade business in the territory. However, the region was rocking from a recession in the gaming space: total revenues of over three billion dollars in 1983 fell to around $100m by 1985 as Atari and its domestic competitors bore the brunt of excessive releases of poor quality control and consumers burned out on substandard products.

Negotiations with Atari were held in 1983, the idea being that the US company would distribute the Famicom in North America – but they collapsed when Atari discovered Nintendo had sold the home rights to *Donkey Kong* to Coleco, leaving Nintendo to go it alone. In 1984, Nintendo of America showcased the Famicom – now called the Advanced Video System, redesigned with modular components including a wireless joystick and control pads, a data cassette recorder, and featuring a full keyboard – at the CES trade show in Las Vegas, and its reception was exceptionally negative. Attending toy distributors, having seen so many game carts and consoles flood bargain bins over the previous 12 months, passed on the opportunity to take on Nintendo's machine, despite the impressive performance of *Donkey Kong*, *Mario Bros.* and more in stateside arcades. But Nintendo's president, Hiroshi Yamauchi, refused to take no for an answer, and the next year the Famicom was back at CES having undergone a transformation.

Nintendo of America understood the domestic resistance to new video gaming hardware in the early 1980s, so completely redesigned the Famicom, scrapping the Advanced Video System concept for something simpler. The result was the Nintendo Entertainment System, or the NES. Its cartridges slid inside the machine like cassettes into a VCR, using a front-loading opening and gentle lock-in mechanism; its grey and black colour scheme helped it blend into homes beside televisions, video recorders and hi-fi separates; and the language used for the range – the console was the Control Deck, the cartridges Game Paks – generally eschewed then-conventional nomenclature for such products. The designer of the NES, Nintendo of America's Lance Barr, spoke to nintendojo.com about the design process in 2005, saying that he wanted it to 'look more like a sleek stereo system rather than an electronic toy', and how the console's zero-force cartridge connector dictated the proportions of the end product: 'The [console's outer] case had to be designed around the movement of the game [cartridge], and required the size of the NES to grow.'

Side by side, the NES dwarfs the Famicom, and its Game Paks are around twice the size of the carts that came out in Japan. But in this instance size mattered, and retailers took notice. To further persuade curious parties to take a punt, Nintendo of America sweetened the deal: store owners in the test market of New York could have Nintendo come to their locations and set up displays for them, plus the consoles – the 'Deluxe Set' version of which was bundled with the largely useless R.O.B. the Robot peripheral and the Zapper light gun, essential for playing the included *Duck Hunt* – were provided on a sale-or-return basis, lessening the financial risk for everyone but Nintendo itself. The gamble paid off: next to no consoles were returned, and the New York test encouraged retailers across the country, with a little extra persuading from Teddy Ruxpin and Lazer Tag makers Worlds of Wonder (more on page 50), to give the NES a chance.

With the ColecoVision console discontinued, the Intellivision on life support and Atari's 5200 having faded into the sunset – its successor, the far-superior Atari 7800, would arrive too late to mount a notable commercial challenge, and the same can be said of SEGA's Master System – the NES had a largely competition-free run at the North American market. Nintendo sold 1.1 million units in the US alone in 1986, at an RRP of around $180, and a wave of high-quality first- and third-party games kept the NES out in front throughout the rest of the 1980s. Shigeru Miyamoto's seminal side-scrolling platformer *Super Mario Bros.* was made a pack-in game with new NES purchases in 1988, on a dual-game cartridge alongside *Duck Hunt*; ground-breaking Famicom Disk System titles *Castlevania*, *Metroid* and *The Legend of Zelda* were released for the NES on cartridge, as the add-on never officially made it out of Japan; and developers like Konami, Capcom and Hudson Soft released a steady stream of hits for the console. There were strict licensing agreements to follow when bringing a game to the NES (they would ease by the time of the Super Nintendo), but that didn't stop the likes of *Mega Man 2*, *Duck Tales* and *Teenage Mutant Ninja Turtles* from becoming cornerstones of many collections.

In 1990 *Super Mario Bros. 3* was released in North America, which arrived in a flurry of press hype having been revealed to US audiences in 1989's film *The Wizard*, essentially a feature-length showcase of NES games with a basic road movie plot plonked on top. The game was a phenomenal hit for Nintendo, selling 11 million copies worldwide by the end of 1990 – it had come out in Japan in 1988 – and earning near-perfect review scores. Even as Nintendo's great rivals SEGA began to see modest success in the American market with the 16-bit Genesis console – the localised version of the Mega Drive was released in the States in August 1989, replacing the Master System – *Super Mario Bros. 3* helped to keep NES sales high, and by the end of 1990 *Computer Gaming World* reported that an amazing 30% of American households owned one. With the Famicom enjoying an even better market share in Japan – it was in 37% of homes by the end of 1989, according to the *New York Times* – Nintendo had two of the world's largest gaming markets all sewn up. But elsewhere, things didn't go so smoothly.

The NES trickled its way into Europe via a handful of regional distributors, initially arriving in Scandinavia and Germany in September 1986. Bandai picked up the rights to sell the NES in the Netherlands, and a company called Spaco handled distribution in Spain. In the European autumn of 1987, players in France and the UK could finally pop to their local electronics or toy store and pick up a NES, with Mattel overseeing sales in Britain. Mattel was the name behind toy lines like Masters of the Universe, Barbie and Hot Wheels, but it wasn't able to lift the NES to the sort of success it'd seen in Japan and North America, with SEGA's Master System console outselling Nintendo's machine in the UK throughout the late 1980s (a situation only aided by Nintendo's relatively lacklustre promotion of its products in Europe). *Super Mario Bros. 3* gave the NES a boost when it arrived in Europe in 1991, but for much of the 8- and 16-bit generations, the region belonged to SEGA.

With the American landscape very different, though, Nintendo remodelled the NES after the release of the 16-bit Super Nintendo, to give consumers the chance to explore its 8-bit catalogue of games for a budget asking price. The New-Style NES, or NES-101, came out in the US in October 1993 for just $49.99 (significantly less than the SNES's £199) and Japan as the AV Famicom a month and a half later, switching the front-facing cartridge slot for a more traditional top-loading position. Like the NES before it, it was designed by Lance Barr, and used controllers with a rounded form factor evocative of the SNES pads while remaining compatible with the original blocky NES controllers. The NES-101 might have cost less at the time, but its lower availability has made units more expensive on the second-hand market. At the complete other end of the price scale, however, is the Nintendo M82, a games store kiosk used from the console's US launch that could hold 12 NES carts at a time for potential buyers to flick through, with the option to impose time limits on each user. It never received a home release, obviously, and the units are incredibly expensive on the second-hand market.

In November 2016 Nintendo released the NES Classic Edition, a miniature replica of the NES featuring 30 built-in games including *Super Mario Bros. 3*, *Donkey Kong*, *The Legend of Zelda*, *Mega Man 2* and *Metroid* (Japan received a Famicom Mini instead). With four save states per title, HDMI output and 60Hz gameplay, the 'NES Mini' was an instant hit, selling 2.3 million units between its release and first discontinuation in April 2017. But with demand still high and aftermarket prices doubling the NES Classic Edition's RRP of $59.99/£49.99, a fresh run of the minis came out in 2018, pushing total sales to 3.6 million and kickstarting a market for downsized 'classic' consoles – versions of the SNES, Mega Drive, PC Engine, PlayStation and more followed.

Discounting the 19.3 million sales of the Famicom, the NES sold around 42 million units before its Western discontinuation in August 1995 – putting it way ahead of the Master System's high estimate of 13 million globally (over 20 million including Tectoy's Brazilian variants), the Atari 7800's 3.5 million, and even the Atari 2600's 30 million. Nintendo had expanded its empire like no other video gaming company before it, and while the NES isn't wholly responsible for reviving the North American gaming market after the collapse of 1983 to 1985 – a period that saw Magnavox exit the industry, Activision dramatically downscale, and arcade revenues plummet – its redesign and savvy marketing absolutely contributed to making video games an attractive pastime again, something to buy into with confidence. From the Official Nintendo Seal on its games, promising that this wasn't a knock-off but an all-new experience, to the solid build quality of its hardware, the NES simply played differently. It eclipsed all predecessors, and the gameplay of *Super Mario Bros.*, *Final Fantasy*, *Metroid* and *The Legend of Zelda* became genre blueprints that are still followed to this day.

NES: Five Must Plays

The Legend of Zelda (1987)
Initially released in Japan on the Famicom Disk System in 1986, *The Legend of Zelda* is an early masterpiece of design from celebrated developer Shigeru Miyarnoto, who both directed and produced this adventure through the fantasy realm of Hyrule. The first cartridge game to include a battery to preserve save files, the debut Zelda was an epic of its time with eight main dungeons to conquer and an overall play time of around ten hours. While it took certain cues from earlier games – its open-world layout and use of items to unlock new areas recalls *Adventure* on the Atari 2600 – *The Legend of Zelda* popularised a new breed of action game, where the player was free to go their own way, at their own pace. With 6.5 million copies sold, this is the sixth highest-selling NES game of all time, and the third-highest discounting carts that were bundled with new consoles.

Contra (1988)
This super-challenging run-and-gunner was a hit for developers Konami in arcades in 1987, and the next year the Japanese studio brought the experience home with the NES version actually benefitting from changes made to better suit the 8-bit hardware. As a result, this isn't a compromised arcade port, like so many others of the time, but feels instead like a game made exclusively for the NES. Also known as *Probotector* and *Gryzor* on other platforms and in select territories, *Contra*'s demanding difficulty could be eased somewhat through the use of what became known as the Konami code: enter up, up, down, down, left, right, left, right, B, A and then pressing Start on the title screen would see players start with 30 lives instead of three. You'll probably need them.

DuckTales (1989)
Developed by Capcom, this platformer tie-in to the Disney TV show was made by developers who'd previously worked on Mega Man games – and that quality shines through across five levels that can be taken on in any order. Three difficulty levels are available, so less-experienced players can control Scrooge McDuck, on a quest to make even more money than he already enjoys a dip in, with reduced damage – but be warned that there are still plenty of spikes and pits to lose lives to. Unlike Mario, Scrooge can't simply jump onto enemies to defeat them – instead he attacks with his cane, which can also be used like a pogo stick to reach higher platforms and ropes.

Super Mario Bros. 3 (1990)
Another NES essential spearheaded by Shigeru Miyamoto, *Super Mario Bros. 3* is in many ways a perfect sequel, taking what players knew from previous Super Mario titles and expanding on the formula, twisting expectations and guaranteeing surprises. Two-dimensional side-scrolling platformers

have looked back at this game ever since as a pinnacle of its time – and it's still one of the very greatest examples of its genre. While its 8-bit visuals couldn't match those of the SEGA Mega Drive that launched in its immediate wake, the smooth gameplay and testing difficulty curve of *Super Mario Bros. 3* meant that Famicom players at its 1988 Japanese launch – and later NES players in the States (1990) and Europe (1991) – were hooked regardless of rival machines offering more arcade-quality experiences. Such was the early 1990s success of *Super Mario Bros. 3* that its gross revenue exceeded even that made by 1993's hit movie, *Jurassic Park* – so if you want to isolate a single moment that marked gaming's arrival as the biggest entertainment medium in the world, it's probably the release of this game.

Kirby's Adventure (1993)

Today, Kirby is a major character among Nintendo's array of colourful franchises – but he and his series debuted much later than Mario, Metroid, Zelda and Donkey Kong. This colourful platformer is the second game in the Kirby series after the Game Boy exclusive *Kirby's Dream Land* came out in 1992, and it's the game that established Kirby's ability to copy an enemy's abilities when he inhales them. Where *Kirby's Dream Land* was meant to be a relatively easy game, suiting younger audiences and shorter handheld play sessions, *Kirby's Adventure* turns up the heat somewhat – it's definitely not a *hard* game, but anyone coming to it in 1993 expecting a breeze based on its cute aesthetics would have been surprised. As a late NES release, *Kirby's Adventure* really squeezes the most out of Nintendo's 8-bit hardware and is a delight to both play through and simply watch as someone else floats through its levels.

NES Collector Spot

NES collector Henry Walkley from Guildford, UK, shares his thoughts on Nintendo's breakthrough console, and his personal favourite games.

'The NES was love at first play. I was blown away. I got more into the NES with every game and attachment I discovered, but nothing could beat the first time I saw it turned on.

'The first NES game I played was *Castlevania II: Simon's Quest*, at a friend's house. The NES we bought came with *Super Mario Bros.* and *Duck Hunt* on a double cartridge – but then the first game I paid for was my own copy of *Simon's Quest*. My other favourite games include *The Legend of Zelda*, *Gradius*, *Section-Z* and *Double Dragon*. I have so many great memories of other games, like the Super Mario trilogy, but those plus *Simon's Quest* probably make up my top five.

'My collection happened naturally but very slowly. We couldn't afford to buy lots of games when I was younger, so I would borrow and lend with friends at school to find titles I liked, and then my brother and I would wash cars to buy them. It wasn't until I started earning, in the late 1990s, that I could afford to collect properly. Over the years it's built steadily into what it is now. I'd say *Castlevania III: Dracula's Curse* is probably my most prized game in my collection. Before the internet it was very hard to find copies of games, because we were limited to print adverts in magazines like *C&VG*. As soon as eBay became popular, this was the first game I sought out – and even then, finding a PAL version set me back a fair amount.

'The NES Mini offers a nice remembrance of childhood, or a quick dip into "how games used to be", but an original NES is something different. It's the same reason people like old teddy bears, or feel nostalgic looking at photos taken decades before they were born. These old things still have life. They remind us of the past, but they also give a depth and humanity to it – someone was there, someone played this. It's a window to another world.'

SEGA MARK III

Manufacturer: SEGA
Released: October 1985 (Japan)

At a cursory glance, it's entirely forgivable to mistake the Mark III for its predecessor, the second model of SEGA's SG-1000. Both are primarily white and have thin, rectangular designs of almost exactly the same proportions with a top-loading cartridge slot beside a bright yellow pause button. Edge closer and differences come into focus, like a card slot and front-facing controller ports, but it's not the surface-level refinements that made the Mark III a superior successor to SEGA's console before it – it was what the company had changed under the hood.

The Mark III included backwards compatibility with SG-1000 games, whether they were on cartridge or SEGA's cheaper My Card format, and the older systems' controllers too – but it was a far more powerful console. If you put its games side by side with the best the Famicom could offer at the time, visuals wise at least, the Mark III is leagues ahead of its competition. Increased onboard RAM – 8KB to the SG-1000's 1KB and the Famicom's 2KB – meant the Mark III could display double the colours of its main rival and produce smoother-scrolling gameplay, while an optional FM Sound Unit provided enhanced audio from the console's Texas Instruments sound chip. Its retail price of ¥15,000 – just over £90 – was a match for the SG-1000's launch RRP, representing good value; and SEGA initially pushed its Mark III-specific My Card releases as a wallet-friendly way to build a collection of games, although storage limitations saw the company revert to cartridges exclusively by 1987.

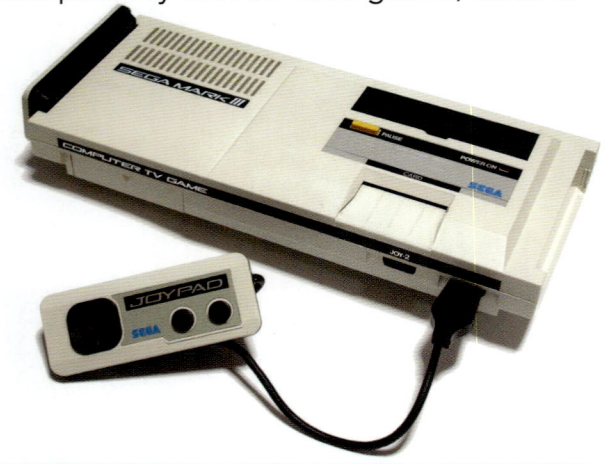

It was clearly a massive step forward from the SG-1000, and in another timeline where Nintendo hadn't secured games from huge developers like Capcom and Konami as exclusives, the Mark III might have overtaken the Famicom to claim top spot in the Japanese market. History instead tells of sales of around 1.7 million in Japan for the Mark III and SEGA's SG-1000 systems combined by 1989 – not even half of what Nintendo's Disk System add-on had achieved

42

in the same market. As terrific as SEGA's hardware was, the games simply weren't of the standard the Famicom could offer. Where Nintendo could call on popular third-party studios for software, SEGA was largely stuck with its own games, many of which were rushed through development; and while Nintendo had recognisable characters like Donkey Kong and Super Mario, SEGA had Fantasy Zone's Opa-Opa and Alex Kidd, Sonic the Hedgehog still a few years away. In Japan at least, they never stood a chance.

But just as Nintendo had redesigned the Famicom for North America and elsewhere, creating the NES, SEGA recognised there was an opportunity to properly take its hardware global, which it hadn't managed with the SG-1000. SEGA of America was founded in 1986, and work began on repackaging the Mark III for Western markets. Its primary colour changed from white to black, and the shape altered so that the console's plastic casing sloped upwards to the cartridge slot. The joypads retained the same basic form – D-pad, two face buttons, no dedicated Start or Select – albeit with minor aesthetic adjustments and a colour change to match the new console; and the optional FM sound chip became integrated. How true it is that the name Master System (see page 46) was chosen by throwing darts at a board full of potentials is, we may never know for sure, but SEGA's chairman at the time, Isao Okawa, ultimately approved of the moniker.

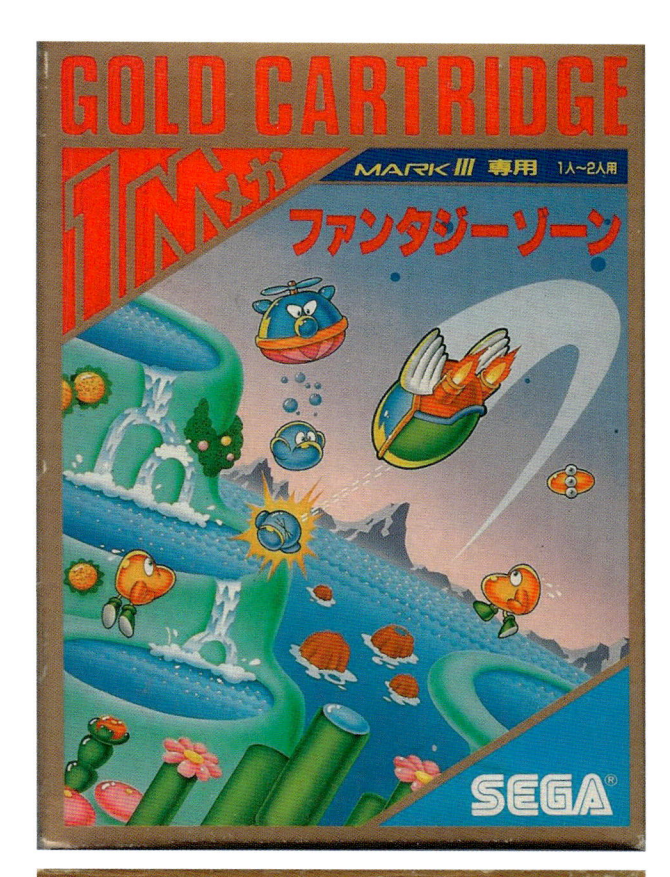

And so, SEGA had its own take on the NES, ready to compete in the revitalised North American market. But the company would soon realise its most engaged and eager 8-bit audience wasn't in the States at all, but on the other side of the Atlantic Ocean.

ATARI 7800

Manufacturer: Atari, Inc (released by Atari Corporation)

Released: May 1986 (North America), 1987 (Europe)

Atari's 5200 console of 1982 had failed to meet the commercial precedent of the VCS, and it was swiftly decided that another new system was necessary if the company was to stand up to the early 1980s competition coming from ColecoVision and Intellivision. As the failing 5200 faced discontinuation, Atari entered a new era in 1984 – owners Warner Communications sold its home computing and game console divisions to Commodore founder Jack Tramiel (pictured, right), who subsequently established Atari Corporation to manufacture all-new products under the famous brand.

His first move was to produce a cutting-edge but budget-friendly home computer range, the Atari ST (the first model of which, the 520ST, was nicknamed the Jackintosh due to similarities with Apple's machines of the time). With the North American market for games consoles in dramatic recession and Atari itself having millions of dollars wiped from its revenues in 1983, this felt like a safer bet than coming out with a successor for the underperforming 5200. Nevertheless, a successor had been developed, albeit under previous Atari management.

Atari, Inc – as the company was called prior to Tramiel's purchase – had commissioned General Computer Corporation to design a next-gen gaming system. GCC had previously created an enhanced version of Atari's own *Missile Command* arcade game, and an enhancement kit for Namco's *Pac-Man* called *Crazy Otto* that was later sold by Midway as a full sequel, *Ms. Pac-Man*. This small team knew arcade games inside out – and Atari was banking on that knowhow translating to home consoles. But the 5200's slow sales combined with the North American market collapse saw Tramiel shelve the new system, which had been originally slated for a 1984 release and named the 7800 ProSystem (2600 and 5200 added together, reflective both of its status as a superior console to the one that came before it and its backwards compatibility with all Atari 2600 cartridges, a feature the 5200 was criticised for not incorporating).

The 7800 had been revealed to the press in May 1984, with a launch line-up of 13 games featuring *Pole Position II*, *Centipede*, *Ms. Pac-Man*, *Galaga* and *Food Fight*. But when Tramiel bought Atari's home gaming division in July of that year, he put the brakes on its release – and it wouldn't be until May 1985 that a disagreement over which Atari should pay GCC for their work, Inc or Corporation, was settled, with Tramiel ultimately footing the bill. He now found himself in a position where he *had* to sell a new console – mountains of 7800 stock were collecting dust in warehouses – and so it was that in May 1986, two full years after its formal announcement, that Atari's new home system earned a full release in North America, with European distribution following the next year.

GCC had created something very special for 1984, with the 7800's custom MARIA graphics chip capable of producing visuals closer to the arcades than either Atari before it. But by the time of its full rollout in 1986, North American gamers had been spoiled by the Nintendo Entertainment System for several months – and side by side, there was little the 7800 could offer that the competition from Japan couldn't trump.

44

Nintendo's games were brighter and sharper, they sounded significantly better, and the NES joypad was intuitive and responsive in hand, whereas the 7800's choice of a palm-held joystick with squishy side-mounted triggers seemed archaic, too similar to the 5200's poorly received controllers. (Notably, European 7800 consoles were sold with NES-like control pads instead.)

But Atari had a couple of advantages over the NES. Firstly, the 7800's introductory RRP was just $79.99 in the US, with *Pole Position II* included, whereas the Deluxe Set NES bundle was a whole 100 dollars more. Over time the Atari console would go up in price a little, as the 1984 stock was sold off and replaced with newly manufactured units, and the NES RRP would come down, but at launch there's no doubting that the 7800 represented a more wallet-friendly option than Nintendo's dominant system. Secondly, the backwards compatibility with the Atari 2600 – no add-on adapter necessary – made the 7800 a natural new-gen step for anyone with Atari's original console at home and a decent handful of games. No need to throw that all away as you upgraded to a new console, as this one would still play your favourites.

Unfortunately, Nintendo's head start and stranglehold over third-party developers of note, who'd signed exclusivity deals to produce games only for the NES, meant that any advantages the 7800 seemed to have proved fairly trivial in the race to be number one in North America. While the 7800 could claim to have a huge library of software, far larger than Nintendo's, if you take away all those 2600 cartridges only 59 exclusives are left, many internally developed by Atari and including several enhanced versions of very old-feeling experiences. There certainly were some excellent games made just for the 7800, like the side-scrolling rail shooter *Alien Brigade* and the bizarre but utterly brilliant sports sim and beat 'em up crossover *Ninja Golf*. There just wasn't enough of them.

Ultimately the 7800 was a second consecutive flop for Atari, selling less than 10% of Nintendo's 1.1 million NES sales from May 1986 to February 1987. It was even beaten into third spot by another rival from Japan, as SEGA's Master System managed to move 125,000 units in the States from September 1986 to February 1987, according to *Computer Entertainer* magazine. Sales of the 7800 did pick up – a million units were sold by June 1988 – but a worldwide total of around 3.5 million by the time of its 1992 discontinuation, as Atari cancelled its 8-bit range to concentrate on the upcoming Jaguar, pales in comparison to SEGA and Nintendo's performances. While Atari had been the force to be reckoned with at the beginning of the 8-bit era, as the 1970s gave way to the '80s, the middle of the decade saw them slip away dramatically against their Japanese competitors – and the 1990s would deliver a knockout blow.

Atari 7800: Play One Game

Alien Brigade (1990)
This side-scrolling rail shooter, made internally at Atari, plays a lot like Taito's *Operation Wolf* – except its enemy soldiers are actually your former comrades, now possessed by evil aliens. Problematically, it's not just these infected fallen friends who dash onto the screen, but also escaping allies and prisoners, who you mustn't shoot. While *Alien Brigade* is playable with a standard Atari joystick, the real fun is to be had using the XG-1 light gun – which was available as a standalone purchase or bundled with the XEGS console. If you want to check it out today, *Alien Brigade* is included on the Evercade's *Atari Collection 1* and playable via 2021's Atari VCS.

MASTER SYSTEM

Manufacturer: SEGA

Released: September 1986 (North America), June 1987 (Europe), October 1987 (Japan), 1989 (Brazil, Korea)

The story of the Master System is one of failure in then-traditional console markets, success in emerging ones, and *amazing* longevity in South America. Despite initially seeing a release in North America, with SEGA hoping to challenge Nintendo and Atari in the territory, this 8-bit powerhouse, which sold itself on being the closest thing to having the arcade experience in your own home, effectively flopped both there and in Japan, with sales falling well short of the NES and Famicom. SEGA had an amazing machine, with specs outstripping the NES – 8KB of RAM to the 2KB on Nintendo's console, and a palette of 64 colours gave games a bolder, brighter look – but the NES had a substantial head start, had locked many developers into exclusivity deals, and the huge appeal of Mario had driven the system to the top of countless birthday lists.

Due to Nintendo's stranglehold on third-party developers, SEGA only had support from two studios, Activision and Parker Brothers, for the US release of the Master System. It therefore had to produce several conversions of its own arcade games and all-new experiences built specifically for the new console, and a lot of these were hurried to completion. Speaking to sega-16.com in 2006, Mark Cerny – the founder of SEGA Technical Institute and subsequently a developer of several Sony consoles – recalled the tight-turnaround times of this period while working out of SEGA's Tokyo HQ: 'They had one room with about 40 people in it, trying to make essentially all the games needed to launch the Master System. A typical project was one or two programmers, three months. The pressure was very, very high.'

With just the motorcycle racer *Hang-On* and light gun shooter *Safari Hunt* as launch titles, the Master System debuted in the States with an RRP of $200, around $20 more than the NES, and by the end of 1986 SEGA had shifted between 125,000 and 250,000 units in the territory – putting them ahead of Atari but horribly behind Nintendo's 1.1m sales of the NES in the same period. Before 1986 was out, SEGA would release some notable titles to support the console – *Alex Kidd in Miracle World* appeared in December, its titular protagonist becoming a company mascot in the pre-Sonic era; *Astro Warrior* was a well-received vertical shooter and *Rambo: First Blood Part II* turned heads with its large sprites and incessant action; and arcade hits *Fantasy Zone* and *The Ninja* somewhat delivered on that coin-ops-at-home promise. But it wasn't enough, and after 114 releases the Master System was discontinued in North America in 1992, with October 1991's *Sonic the Hedgehog* – this Ancient-developed 8-bit version is distinct from the earlier Mega Drive release, featuring different levels and music – the final game officially released for the console in the region.

Japan had pulled the plug even sooner, SEGA ending official production of its 8-bit home consoles in 1991 (the Game Gear, essentially a battery-hungry handheld Master System, lived on until 1997). The Master System had earned a release there in October 1987, replacing the Mark III, but a million units sold represented a drop in the Famicom's ocean-sized commercial success, leading SEGA to focus on 16-bit hardware. SEGA's fortunes in Europe were very different, however, with the Master System benefitting from poor regional distribution of the NES and representing an attractive alternative to, or often complement for, the popular home computer market, dominated in the mid-1980s by the ZX Spectrum series and Commodore's 64 and Amiga ranges.

US distribution rights for the Master System had gone to Tonka, a company renowned for its toy trucks but not video games. The decision backfired, with Tonka choosing to not localise a number of Japanese games for the US market and basically admitting defeat to the NES. SEGA would not make the same mistake in the Europe, partnering with Mastertronic in the UK, a company with years of software experience and established connections to major retailers, and Ariolasoft in France and Germany, which had a fine track record with home computers. After overcoming inventory headaches that saw retailer pre-orders unfulfilled in late 1987, Mastertronic was able to give the Master System an edge over the NES, but the company was struggling financially. Virgin swept in, and the newly named Virgin Mastertronic subsequently controlled much of the Master System's European distribution, taking over France and Germany from Ariolasoft in September 1988.

The Master System's UK year-one line-up put the console's US debut to shame, with *Space Harrier*, *OutRun*, *Rocky* and *Wonder Boy* appearing alongside a number of titles already released elsewhere, including *Alex Kidd in Miracle World*. Many British buyers had either *Hang-On* or *Alex Kidd* built into the console, as well as the 'hidden' bonus of *Snail Maze*, and with an RRP of £99 the Master System was as much as £50 cheaper than the NES bundles on sale at the time. By 1990 SEGA's 8-bit console was the biggest-selling system across Europe, driven by a focused promotional campaign that positioned it as the more grown-up alternative to the NES – an attitude that would carry over to marketing for the Mega Drive. Nick Alexander, the first CEO of SEGA Europe, spoke to sega-16.com in 2008: 'We decided to market the Master System at an older, cooler, teenage user. Nintendo's marketing was aimed more at a family audience with pre-teen kids.'

A redesigned Master System II came out in 1990, later models of which included *Sonic the Hedgehog* as a built-in game, and the console (range) wasn't phased out in Europe until 1996 – meaning it shared stockist shelf space not only with the Mega Drive and its add-ons, and the Game Gear, but also SEGA's 32-bit Saturn. It'd received 269 game releases in the territory, with total console sales surpassing eight million. With peripherals including 3-D Glasses (compatible with eight games), a light gun (the Light Phaser, usable with 13 games), and the back-to-front Control Stick (why, SEGA, *why*?), the Master System felt like an expandable, adaptable console that deserved better than its pitiful sales in the States and Japan. Its success in Europe is a suggestion of what could have been elsewhere.

But discontinuation in North America, Japan, Europe and Australia – where it enjoyed modest success – didn't see the Master System completely retired. Brazil had been largely overlooked by Nintendo in its global promotion of the NES, with no official representation in the region until 1993 leading to clone consoles like the Dynavision II and Gradiente's Phantom System becoming popular ways to play the likes of *Super Mario Bros.* on imported or pirated cartridges. SEGA adopted a different strategy and partnered with Tectoy (also known as TecToy and Tec Toy over the years, but this book will stick with Tectoy) in 1989, allowing the São Paulo-based company to distribute the Master System in Brazil, and later throughout Argentina and Uruguay. With no proper competition, SEGA immediately became the dominant force in the Brazilian console market, and it's estimated that of the Master System's total global sales of around 20 million, some eight million are Tectoy-distributed systems and updated variants of the original hardware.

Because Tectoy didn't stop at simply selling the Master System, and subsequently the Mega Drive, in Brazil – the company produced its own versions of SEGA's 8-bit console, including a handheld unit called the Master System Super Compact, which could be used wirelessly with televisions or connected using RCA cables. Released in 1994, the Super Compact was only ever made available in South America, and three editions were available, each with a different built-in game: *Sonic the Hedgehog*, *Alex Kidd in Miracle World*, or the football (of the soccer variety) title *Super Futebol II* – which was just 1990's *World Cup Italia '90* given a localised name.

The Super Compact – and its pink-coloured Master System Girl model – still used game cartridges; so too Tectoy's Master System III Compact, which was the region's name for the redesigned Master System II that SEGA sold in other parts of the world as a cheaper option for 8-bit latecomers. What *didn't* was 2007's Master System 3 Collection console, which was modelled on the shell of a Master System II but lacked cartridge support, featuring instead 131 built-in games. Tectoy's hardware of the very next year, the Master System 3, completely altered its look to something more in keeping with a sleek piece of modern tech, albeit still loaded with 8-bit games – *Shinobi*, *Sonic the Hedgehog* and *Golden Axe* being among the best-known inclusions. It was succeeded by the Master System Evolution in 2009,

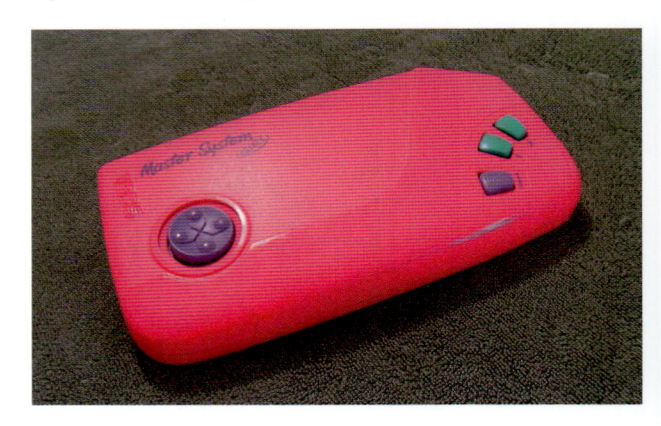

48

and at the time of writing Tectoy's ongoing product lines mean that the Master System isn't discontinued in South America.

As well as Tectoy's many redesigns of the Master System, the console also found a small foothold in South Korea, where it was branded as the Samsung Gam*Boy (and Gam*Boy II, when the Master System II was released, with later models named the Aladdin Boy), and it was sold in China by Hiroshima Trading. A very special version of the Master System was installed in Japanese hotels, called the Game Box 9. This coin-operated unit plugged into a TV and could have up to nine cartridges inserted at any one time for on-screen selection. A Western model was produced called the Master System Kiosk that had space for 16 cartridges and four controller ports, and it was mostly used in game stores.

Master System: Five Must Plays

Psycho Fox (1989)
The Master System was home to some wonderful platformers, and *Psycho Fox* is one of its very best. The left-to-right gameplay feels instantly familiar, but what sets this apart is how its protagonist can change into different forms – from a fox to a tiger, a hippo, and a monkey – each of which offers different abilities.

Wonder Boy III: The Dragon's Trap (1989)
The Dragon's Trap also stars a player character than can change forms – but for much of the game this is beyond their control, as they're cursed (by dragons, funnily enough) to appear as various anthropomorphised figures including a lizard, a fish and a mouse. Thankfully, these transformations can later be selected, allowing access to specific areas – only the fish-like character can explore underwater, for example. Weapons and armour can be upgraded in shops, and the game has a non-linear structure that encourages exploration and experimentation. The game was remade for PC, PlayStation 4, Xbox One and Nintendo Switch as *Wonder Boy: The Dragon's Trap* in 2017, giving it enhanced visuals and non-password save functionality plus the option to experience the game with its original 8-bit graphics and audio.

Sonic the Hedgehog (1991)
The 8-bit *Sonic the Hedgehog* isn't a port of the Mega Drive release but a standalone game built from the ground up, featuring unique levels and music. First released on Master System and subsequently SEGA's handheld Game Gear console, despite the latter platform being the game's primary target (many Master System games appear on the portable device due to their architecture similarities), this version of the blue blur's debut was made by Ancient, a studio established by Yuzo Koshiro, best known for his soundtracks for *Streets of Rage 2* and *The Revenge of Shinobi*. Koshiro's sister, Ayano, directed this *Sonic* and worked on its art, while he developed original musical themes and adapted some from the 16-bit game. The pair's mother was also involved, making this very much a family affair. While not as famous as the

Mega Drive's *Sonic the Hedgehog*, the Master System game is fast, colourful, and just as good as its 16-bit cousin.

Master of Darkness (1992)
This action-platformer set in Victorian London is SEGA's 8-bit take on Konami's popular Castlevania series. Assuming the role of the brilliantly named Dr Ferdinand Social, the player must initially track down Jack the Ripper, who in the game's story has been killing his victims in an attempt to resurrect Count Dracula. The game's creepy, Gothic-textured stages are populated by zombies, skeletons, ghosts and angry chaps with guns, making for a curious but absolutely compelling mix of gritty backstreet combat and supernatural silliness. Boxed and complete second-hand copies of *Master of Darkness* command a pretty penny, so if you see this one kicking around your local charity shop, grab it.

Road Rash (1994)
EA's *Road Rash* was a huge hit on the Mega Drive in 1991, but the motorcycle racer with added kicks and punches arguably impresses even more on the 8-bit Master System as its converters at Probe Software managed to push the console to its fullest. Running this version side by side with the Mega Drive game shows just how incredible their efforts were as the immediate differences are minimal. It lacked the two-player mode of the original, but its bold and smooth visuals more than made up for that. If you were ever after a game that showed how the Master System could blow the NES away visually, this is it.

Eighties Video Nasties
Two very odd video game consoles of the 1980s used neither game cards nor cartridges, but VHS cassette tapes. The first, released in 1987, was the Action Max, made by Worlds of Wonder – a company founded by former Atari sales president Don Kingsborough in 1985, and probably most famous for its line of Teddy Ruxpin toys. In 1986, Worlds of Wonder developed a toy gun game using infrared technology, Lazer Tag, and worked with Nintendo to help sell its NES to retailers. These two projects merged, somewhat, in the company's one and only games console.

The Action Max was used in conjunction with a video cassette recorder, the player tasked with using the console's light gun to shoot at flashing targets on screen. The tapes would play the same every time, but your score would depend on accuracy and being able to hit the right targets. With a retail price of $99, the Action Max might have appeared to be a decent-value alternative to the NES and other consoles on the North American market at the time. But with the low-interactivity gameplay across its five VHS cassettes basically being identical whatever the action on screen – covering fighter jet dogfights, deep-sea adventures, haunted house ghost busting, helicopter battles, and police training (all of these videos can be found on YouTube) – and the challenge only ever about achieving a high score, this was a system of super-limited longevity.

Powered by C batteries as standard – respecting the fact that a lot of households wouldn't have a spare power socket with the TV and VCR already plugged in – the Action Max took a few cues from an unreleased prototype system called the Control-Vision, developed by future Digital Pictures founder Tom Zito (who'd release *Night Trap* and other full-motion video games for SEGA's Mega-CD) and supported by Axlon at its concept stage, a company overseen by Atari co-founder Nolan Bushnell. But while the Action Max *did* see the light of day, its sales were so low (reportedly only 10,000 units) that it was swiftly taken off the market, despite striking TV ads that claimed that 'if it were anymore real, it wouldn't be a game'. With its Nintendo deal over and Lazer Tag suffering from negative press after a teenager was shot and killed by a sheriff's deputy who mistook the toy for a real gun, Worlds of Wonder declared bankruptcy in 1988 and its popular products were picked up by other companies. The Action Max was not one of them.

In 1988 another VHS-based console hit the North American market: the View-Master Interactive Vision, from the View-Master Ideal Group, Inc. This 'two-way television system that makes you a part of the show', according to its packaging, was aimed at a very young audience, with four of its seven cassettes based on *Sesame Street* and two on *The Muppets*. But it's more interactive than the Action Max as players can use the unusually shaped controller to select from two audio channels at select points of each tape, leading to different dialogue through the speakers if not outcomes on the screen. With a design resembling some sort of modern art museum, the Interactive Vision is an odd-looking device that definitely wasn't aiming to complement a household's VCR, and it reportedly sold as few as 5,000 units. But with score overlays and even some rudimentary mini-games, there's a cute charm to the Interactive Vision that would likely still appeal to younger players today.

Even SEGA dabbled in VHS games in 1988, its interactive video titles on Mega-CD still a few years off. It designed and distributed the Family Driver system, which was subsequently sold as the Video Driver by Tyco in the US, GIG in Italy, and Action GT in the UK. Only five games/cassette tapes were released across all four territories it was sold in, all following the same drive-along formula, the player using a small steering wheel controller to move a toy-sized car from side to side in front of the VHS footage playing on screen. Sensors mounted on the TV set would read where the toy car was in relation to the footage and score you accordingly out of 100 at the end of each tape – so when it tells you to stay in lane, *you stay in lane*. 'Real driving excitement', proclaimed its British packaging, but please, kids of the '80s: don't go from playing this straight to your dad's Ford Escort, as people will get hurt.

Semi-related, one console of the 1980s – albeit one that, like Control-Vision, never officially made it to release – used another type of video format. The Halcyon, manufactured by RDI Video Systems, used LaserDisc technology and aimed to bring interactive, film-quality experiences akin to *Dragon's Lair* and *Space Ace* – both produced by RDI – into the home. This behemoth of a console, named after the computer Hal from the movie *2001: A Space Odyssey* (and featuring a creepy AI voice that spoke to the player), came in three parts – the LaserDisc player and the control unit, as well as a chunky keyboard – and its games could be played using voice-recognition software. A January 1985 release window was the plan, but an RRP of $2,500 and low mainstream interest in the LaserDisc format put retailers off, and only a handful of Halcyon units are known to exist as well as two games, *NFL Football* and *Thayer's Quest*.

PC ENGINE

Manufacturer: NEC Home Electronics

Released: October 1987 (Japan), August 1989 (North America, as the TurboGrafx-16), late 1989–1990 (limited European distribution)

With SEGA's first few consoles failing to keep pace with the Famicom and Epoch retiring from the market, you might assume that Nintendo enjoyed complete dominance over the Japanese console scene in the second half of the 1980s. But that wasn't the case as, in 1987, NEC released its first video game system, developed in conjunction with renowned studio Hudson Soft: the PC Engine. This diminutive machine, slimmer than the NES-like control pad it was boxed with, had an 8-bit CPU at its heart but also contained a pair of custom-built 16-bit graphics processors, which made its visuals pop and sizzle like neither of its main competitors, the Famicom and Mark III/Master System, could dream of achieving. This doesn't exactly make the PC Engine the world's first 16-bit console (that's the Intellivision), but graphically it's sometimes hard to tell its games apart from equivalents on the Mega Drive.

By the late 1980s, Nintendo's exclusivity deals had started to reach their ends, and huge Japanese developers like Konami and Namco found themselves able to produce titles for other consoles. These partnerships, alongside Hudson Soft's existing array of gaming series – including Bomberman, Adventure Island and Star Soldier – would soon give the PC Engine a software library that could challenge that of the Famicom. Even SEGA released games for NEC's system in the period prior to the Mega Drive's launch, including *OutRun* and *Shinobi*, illustrating how if they couldn't mount a charge against Nintendo themselves, they'd happily support the company that could. (And, of course, profit in the process.)

NEC already had games industry experience before working with Hudson Soft on the PC Engine, with its PC-88 and PC-98 home computers market leaders in Japan. Hudson Soft, on the other hand, had tried and failed to move into hardware, having seen a graphics chip deal with Nintendo come to nothing, but remained eager to produce a home console that supported its credit card-sized HuCard format for games – a type of ROM media that'd previously been used, extremely limitedly, on the MSX as Bee Cards. HuCards were an evolution of the Bee Card, initially capable of holding 2Mbit of data (this was quickly increased to 4Mbit, with 1993's PC Engine port of *Street Fighter II: Champion Edition* coming on a 20Mbit card), and they slid into the front of the PC Engine in a slot that would later be used for expansion cards, used alongside CD-ROM peripherals, the first of which released in late 1988.

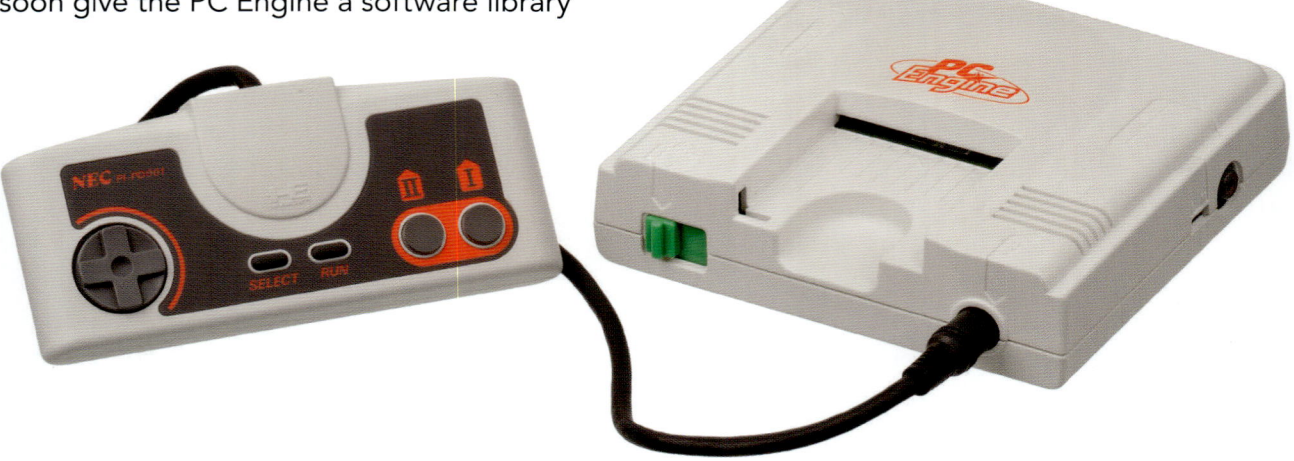

CD-ROM games were huge for the PC Engine, with over half of the 660-plus games released for the console being on CD rather than HuCard. Speaking to *BEEP* magazine in 1987, around the time of the PC Engine's launch, Hudson Soft's then company director Shinichi Nakamoto expressed how the team behind the machine were already looking ahead to CD-ROM technology: 'Right now we're devoting a great deal of effort into the development of software tools for creating CD software. You could fit 540 HuCards on one CD. Every Famicom game that has ever been created could fit on a single CD, and you'd still have extra space. Using CDs would give us the ability to have real music, and voice acting too. Graphics would be better, with more depth and even bigger sprites. So yes, we're in the middle of planning it all.'

That first add-on, the CD-ROM², arrived at the end of a fantastic year for the PC Engine. At its launch in October 1987, it raced to 500,000 sales in its first week, and in 1988 NEC sold more of its consoles than Nintendo did Famicoms. It was a temporary triumph, and overall sales of the PC Engine top out at just over eight million, substantially lower than the 19.3 million of the Famicom – but domestically it stayed ahead of the Mega Drive, which would ultimately sell fewer than four million units in its homeland. Nevertheless, the performance of the PC Engine in Japan puts pay to any perception of the 1980s and '90s console wars being waged only between Nintendo and SEGA, as in that region it was a three-way contest for several years. Interestingly, Nintendo hadn't seen the PC Engine as a rival worth worrying about, with Hudson Soft's executive manager Toshinori Oyama recounting to the GSLA (via shmuplations.com) in 2003: 'I heard that president Hiroshi Yamauchi of Nintendo gave the idea his blessing. "Sure, if Hudson wants to make a new console, they should give it a shot." Nintendo and Hudson didn't see themselves as rivals. The market seemed big enough for everyone.'

The North American market was a different beast though, and following the precedent of the SEGA Mark III and Nintendo Famicom, the PC Engine was redesigned and rebranded for the States. Speaking to *Retro Gamer* magazine for a feature republished on nintendolife.com in 2019, the former president of Hudson Soft's US arm John Greiner recalled how players were excited for the next step in games hardware. 'The US market was stirred into a fevered state by fans wanting a true gaming upgrade from the 8-bit era,' he said. And sure enough the redesigned console leaned into those graphics processors for its marketing pitch, coming out as the TurboGrafx-16, its HuCards rebranded as TurboChips, in August 1989.

Bulked out into a supposedly futuristic shape, adding two-step turbo switches to its TurboPro controller and dressed in black rather than the PC Engine's traditional white, the TurboGrafx-16 was built to impress. But the redesign process had stretched on for too long, and by the time the console was available in the test markets of New York and Los Angeles it found itself no longer just up against the NES and flagging Master System and Atari consoles but also SEGA's newly launched Genesis – the rebranded Mega Drive debuted in the States in August 1989. This was a genuine 16-bit console, and players in the territory quickly realised it offered experiences the

TurboGrafx-16 couldn't; and that it came bundled with the well-known arcade game *Altered Beast*, while the fact TurboGrafx-16 included the lower-profile *Keith Courage in Alpha Zones* only furthered the immediate appeal of SEGA's newcomer. With retailers desperate for 16-bit consoles, NEC readied some 750,000 units for the TurboGrafx-16's launch, far too many than proved necessary.

Greiner recalled to *Retro Gamer*: 'NEC over-ordered units, and this proved fatal as they committed tremendous financial resources to create the hardware, which ultimately handcuffed them in marketing spend.' With SEGA's promotional machine in overdrive, its early 1990s campaign of 'Genesis does what Nintendon't' becoming legendary, and Nintendo's reputation high even before the advent of the Super Nintendo, the TurboGrafx-16 was in trouble, with that sales figure of 750,000 units only reportedly being achieved in March 1991 – although other accounts put total North American sales of the console at only just over 600,000. 'Arguably, the TurboGrafx-16 had better games,' said Greiner of its failure to rival the Genesis, 'but a number of missteps took place when it came to hardware styling, box art, pack-in (games) and release schedule. Marketing and understanding the US gamer mentality was always a challenge for NEC.'

The TurboGrafx-16 struggled on in North America until 1994, not even a sub-$100 price point tempting too many players, and NEC opted to not properly release the console to retail in Europe at all. But that isn't to say it never had plans to, as European models were manufactured (as many as 200,000 of them) and sold in the UK, France and Spain in the early 1990s. This console retained the TurboGrafx name and console shape but dropped the '16' (perhaps wary that its 16-bit claim had been seen through) and changed its colour to a dark grey. In the UK it was distributed via mail order by Telegames; and an *unofficial* model, the PC Engine Plus, was re-engineered from Japanese consoles by a British company called Mention. Factor in a healthy import scene and the PC Engine enjoyed some awareness among more enthusiastic players in Europe, gaining something of a cult reputation but never coming close to even its sales in the US. In South Korea, the TurboGrafx-16 received another aesthetic overhaul, coming out as the curvier Haitai Vistar 16 – a system that's now exceptionally rare to come by – and an unlicensed model with SNES-like controllers called the Super Engine II was sold by Sunpronic in the Czech Republic in 1993.

Following the Japanese success of the PC Engine's CD-ROM^2 add-on, which had been remodelled as the TurboGrafx-CD in the States, NEC released a higher-spec successor in 1991, the Super CD-ROM^2. The PC Engine's 'crazy amount of connectors' – to quote Nakamoto from 1987 – made increasing the core system's capabilities relatively easy, further expansions including the RAM-boosting Arcade Card. All of these upgrades led to some staggering-looking games, such as Konami's cyberpunk graphic adventure *Snatcher* and Compile's Gundam-influenced side-scrolling shooter *Spriggan Mark II*, while its port of the Neo Geo fighter *Fatal Fury 2* appeared almost indistinguishable from the original thanks to the Arcade Card.

The base console received a Japanese makeover in 1989, the newly monikered PC Engine CoreGrafx featuring an updated CPU within its grey shell; and a totally remodelled version called the PC Engine Shuttle came out in the same year, although this lower-cost option, bundled with a curvier control pad with turbo switches, was incompatible with NEC's CD-ROM peripherals.

The PC Engine family didn't stop there, though, with a laptop-styled variant, the LT, releasing in Japan in December 1991. Featuring a built-in screen and speakers and no way to connect to a TV, you might think this was supposed to be portable – but the LT couldn't be powered by batteries, only the mains, making its on-the-go appeal somewhat compromised. Perhaps NEC didn't want to eat into the market share of its *actual* handheld PC Engine, the PC Engine GT, which had come out a year earlier in Japan and the US (where it was called the TurboExpress) and used the same HuCards as the main console. Its colour screen and TV tuner adapter made it something of a competitor for SEGA's Game Gear. But that's still not everything: 1989's PC Engine SuperGrafx offered an upgraded but expensive experience, and 1991's PC Engine Duo combined the original console and its CD-ROM extra in a single unit and was sold in the US as the TurboDuo the following year. More on both of those consoles later in these pages.

In 2020, the PC Engine did get an official European release as Konami – which became the major shareholder in Hudson Soft in 2005 and merged the company into its operations in 2012 – put out an even-smaller version of the Japanese 'upgraded' model as the PC Engine CoreGrafx Mini. This high-definition plug-and-play system included over 50 built-in games from across the Japanese and North American libraries, featuring both HuCard and CD-ROM titles, and was bundled with a faithfully proportioned controller. This mini console was meant to be simultaneously released in Japan, in white, as the PC Engine Mini, and in the US it was modelled after the TurboGrafx-16, albeit a lot smaller, but complications arising from the COVID-19 pandemic saw its international rollout staggered. As a relatively affordable introduction to the world of the PC Engine and some of its very best games, this mini can't be beaten.

PC Engine: Five Must Plays

PC Genjin (1989)
Known as *Bonk's Adventure* in the US and *PC Kid* in Europe, *PC Genjin* is a platformer starring a character that was, for a time at least, something of a mascot for the PC Engine. It's your classic left-to-right formula, but Bonk doesn't jump upon the prehistoric baddies populating each level, preferring instead to headbutt them to death. Subsequently ported to the NES, Amiga and Game Boy, this is a very silly but very satisfying game that probably should be held in as high regard as many of the better Mario and Sonic titles. Like the other PC Engine must plays here, it's included on the PC Engine Mini.

Splatterhouse (1990)
While it's not as gory and brutal as the 1988 arcade original, the PC Engine version of Namco's *Splatterhouse* remains a cult classic of the console's library. This horror-themed side-scrolling beat 'em up casts the player as the masked Rick, who rampages his way

through all manner of monstrous baddies in an attempt to rescue his girlfriend from whatever unspeakable evil lies at the heart of the West Mansion. Taking cues from a host of horror and slasher movies, *Splatterhouse* is just about as subtle as its title, but never tips over into extreme content just for the sake of some cheap shocks. This is a challenging game that'll keep you coming back for more, and not simply for the gore.

Seirei Senshi Spriggan (1991)

Developed by Compile, the Japanese studio behind the Puyo Puyo and Aleste series, *Seirei Senshi Spriggan* is one of the PC Engine's finest shoot 'em ups – and the console has its share of those particular games. Beautiful in motion, full of bright and bold graphics and blessed with an exceptional soundtrack (assuming you can hear it over all the blasting), this is a game that makes the most of its CD-ROM format. *Seirei Senshi Spriggan* might not be one to test true bullet hell die-hards – but for more casual shmup players and PC Engine newcomers, it's sure to leave a huge impression.

Akumajō Dracula X: Chi no Rondo (1993)

Known outside of Japan as *Castlevania: Rondo of Blood*, the story of this entry in Konami's long-running series directly precedes the events of the much-acclaimed (and oft-imitated) *Symphony of the Night*, released for PlayStation in 1997. For that reason alone, it's become an essential for fans of all things Castlevania; but for anyone else it remains a great game in and of itself. The player is Richter Belmont, who enters the castle of Count Dracula, armed with his Vampire Killer whip, to rescue his love, Annette. In an interesting twist to gameplay, Richter can rescue his young relative Maria Renard from the castle, and then the player can use her instead – her attacks hit harder but she takes greater damage, but her double-jump ability makes her a popular choice with players wanting to make progress faster. *Rondo of Blood* was remade twice for other platforms: as *Castlevania: Dracula X* on the Super Nintendo in 1995, and *Castlevania: The Dracula X Chronicles* on the PlayStation Portable in 2007.

Bomberman '94 (1993)

Hudson Soft's Bomberman series was already a local multiplayer sensation by the time of this title's release in late 1993, and the '94 iteration might just be the best of its 1990s games. The gameplay follows the classic formula of blow everything up but yourself, and the PC Engine's multitap peripheral allows five human players to participate at once. The game got a Mega Drive port as *Mega Bomberman*, but that restricted the multiplayer fun to four.

ATARI XEGS

Manufacturer: Atari Corporation

Released: November 1987 (North America)

Atari's 8-bit family of home computers debuted in the late 1970s, but by the mid-1980s were starting to look pretty tired beside Atari's own ST and the Commodore Amiga. Something of a final roll of the 8-bit dice, 1985's 65XE computer had a similar look to the ST but was less advanced and more a lower-budget introductory model for curious consumers. In 1987, with Atari's 7800 console struggling to gain much of a market share against the dominant

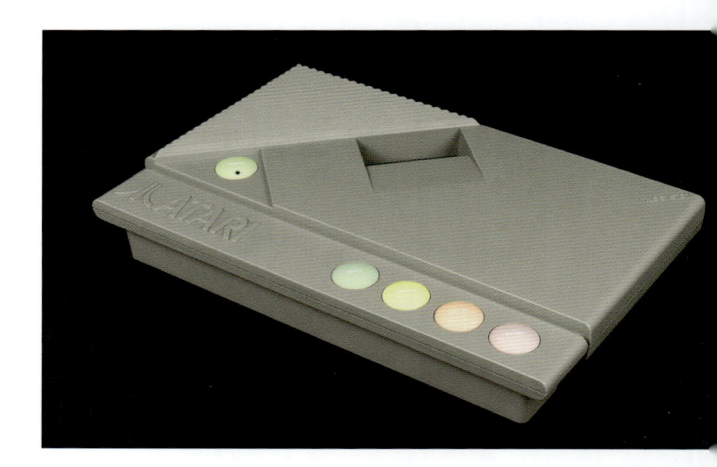

NES, the Corporation looked for a way to generate greater profits with a new games system, based on older technology and therefore cheaper to manufacture. The result was the Atari XE Game System, or XEGS.

Internally essentially an 8-bit computer identical to the 65XE, with 64KB of RAM and 256 on-screen colours, the XEGS was marketed primarily as a console but could be used as a fully functioning computer with a keyboard add-on, which was included in the 'deluxe' option of its two launch bundles. Leaning more into the console side of things, it also came with the XG-1 light gun and a CX40 joystick – the same model that was packed with Atari 2600s, just in grey – and had *Missile Command* built in. The light gun title *Bug Hunt* was also included in the box, and backwards compatibility with a decade's worth of Atari computer cartridges meant the XEGS had an instant library of hundreds of titles. Thirty-two XEGS 'exclusives' were released too, but these were simply repackaged versions of games that could be played across the 8-bit computer line.

Every sale of the XEGS made Atari a profit due to its low manufacturing costs, so low total sales of somewhere around 100,000, most of which came in the first few months on sale, didn't directly damage the bottom line. But the console was marketed at the same time as the Atari 7800 and the Jr model 2600, undoubtedly leaving consumers confused as to which system was the right one to opt for, assuming they weren't simply walking out of the store with a NES. All support for Atari's 8-bit consoles was stopped in 1992, but the XEGS had been dead in the water for a few years prior to its makers formally pulling the plug.

There's an interesting footnote to the brief XEGS story, though. Its unique design, all diagonal lines and pastel colours, was echoed in an unfinished concept console known as the Atari Mirai, of which only between 50 and 100 shells (as its insides are empty) are thought to have been made, probably sometime in 1988. Only brought to the wider world's attention in 1996 when Atari Corporation closed, the Mirai – its name means 'Future' in Japanese – uses the same colourful round buttons as the XEGS and really does look like an aesthetic evolution of the 1987 system; but its wide cartridge slot has led to the suggestion that it was intended to play SNK arcade games at home (the Neo Geo AES/MVS technology was in development at the time, and the companies had an established working relationship too). An alternative theory posits that it's a console variant of the Atari ST – although that seems unlikely after the poor reception to the XEGS.

Another theory is that this is a forerunner to the so-called Super XE console, a 16-bit prototype that never proceeded as Atari was instead aiming to distribute the Genesis in North America (which also didn't happen when Jack Tramiel realised the costs involved), while some former Atari employees have stated that the Mirai was simply an independently conceived and internally designed idea that went nowhere. It's impossible to find irrefutable accounts on this one, but hopefully the truth will come out in the future.

MEGA DRIVE

Manufacturer: SEGA

Released: October 1988 (Japan), August 1989 (North America, as the Genesis), August 1990 (South Korea, as the Super Gam*Boy), September 1990 (Europe, Brazil)

SEGA was hurting from seeing its Mark III home console fail to rival Nintendo's Famicom in Japan, but if there's one business area it traditionally excelled in, it was the arcades. Its 1985-released System 16 arcade board was proving successful, powering the likes of Shinobi, Fantasy Zone and Golden Axe. While these would all receive well-received conversions for SEGA's 8-bit hardware in time, the proposition of putting genuine arcade gaming in people's homes was too tantalising to ignore. Long had home video games promised 'arcade perfect' experiences yet fallen short – but SEGA might just be able to pull it off. The company's president at the time, Hayao Nakayama, joined forces with Hideki Sato, who'd played a key role in the development of the SG-1000 and Mark III, to work on a somewhat secretive side-project to the ongoing promotion of the Master System: the adaptation of the System 16 board for home play.

Sato had some big ideas. He wanted the console, at the time known as the Mark V, to be backwards compatible with the Master System – which it would be, albeit via the use of the Master System (or Power Base) Converter – and support a wealth of peripherals including a disc drive and keyboard, a printer and a modem. Online functionality would eventually land on the Mega Drive, with both 1990's Japan-only Mega Modem, mostly used for business applications, and in the US with the SEGA Channel, which launched in 1994 and gave users a selection of downloadable games, cheat codes and more. But with SEGA's R&D team now fully on board, headed up by Mark III team leader Masami Ishikawa, there was only one true goal for SEGA's next console: disrupt the Japanese market and show Famicom owners what the future of gaming really looked like.

Inevitably, the console – which reportedly found its Mega Drive moniker among some 300 suggestions – couldn't *exactly* replicate the System 16, but its Motorola 68000 processor was a genuine 16-bit CPU, marking SEGA's machine as a more-advanced proposition than NEC's briefly-Famicom-beating PC Engine. Its Yamaha YM2612 sound chip produced music that echoed the electronic beats of global dancefloors, and its palette of 512 colours (exceeding the NES's total of 56) meant games-makers could realise graphics more vibrant than any console that'd come before. The Mega Drive controller added both an extra button to the Master System's pair, its row of A, B and C looking very futuristic beside contemporary pads, and a dedicated start button – no need to reach for the console itself to press pause anymore. The D-pad – or 'D Button' as it was in Mega Drive instruction manuals – assumed a circular shape, and the ergonomic feel of the pad, officially called simply chart on release and was the second biggest-selling game of 1988 in Japan come the end of the year. The game went one better in 1989, taking the number one spot, and at the time of writing its total sales across all platforms are around 24.4 million, putting it inside the top 40 highest-selling games of all time. Against that, what chance did SEGA really have?

Nakayama accepted that the Mega Drive was, as quoted in Read Only Memory's *Sega Mega Drive/Genesis: Collected Works* book of 2014, 'far inferior to the (Famicom) in terms of diffusion rate and sales in the Japanese market'. But just like the Master System before it, he knew there was an international audience that might feel differently: 'In the US and Europe, we knew SEGA could challenge Nintendo. We aimed at dominating those markets, hiring experienced staff … and revitalising SEGA of America and the ailing Virgin Group in Europe.'

SEGA of America had been set up in 1986 by David Rosen, whose Rosen Enterprises Ltd had been part of the merger in 1965 that led to SEGA existing in the first place. It was Rosen who was charged with laying the groundwork for the Mega Drive's North American launch. He brought in Michael Katz from Atari's Game Division as CEO to strengthen the company's industry experience in the States, but distribution remained a question mark. After its poor handling of the Master System, Tonka was out of the equation, and Rosen – quoted in *Collected Works* – remembers 'seven or eight distribution companies after that', none of whom maintained an interest.

One of these companies was Katz's previous employers, and he spoke to *Retro Gamer* about that interaction. 'It would have gotten Atari back in the game with a 16-bit system,' he told the magazine. Atari boss Jack Tramiel thought the deal too expensive and wanted to focus on the Atari ST computer instead. In the console market, Atari would instead skip straight from the 8-bit 7800 and XEGS to the 64-bit Jaguar in the early 1990s, with catastrophic sales results. Some reports suggest that the Mega Drive's North American name,

the Control Pad, left the square-edged equivalents of the 8-bit era looking totally outdated. Add in a sleek, almost sci-fi shell surrounding the Mega Drive's impressive internal tech, with an off-centre cartridge slot and large 16-bit branding, and there was no denying that this was a console for a new generation of players.

The problem was that a lot of players in Japan really liked their Famicoms and PC Engines and weren't especially moved by SEGA's new machine. Sales were slow in the territory, with only 400,000 units sold between the console's launch on 29 October 1988 and the end of the year – for comparison, the PC Engine had achieved half a million sales in its first week. Also hindering early adoption was the fact that Nintendo's *Super Mario Bros. 3* released for the Famicom just a few days before the Mega Drive hit stores, the iconic platformer debuting on 23 October. Nintendo was preparing its own 16-bit console, which would eventually release as the Super Famicom (Super Nintendo outside of Japan), but needed to keep its 8-bit range topped up with fresh games, and they didn't come much bigger than *Super Mario Bros. 3*. It shot to the top of the software

Genesis, emerged from discussions with Atari, specifically from employee Steve Ryno; although Rosen, quoted in *Collected Works*, remembers things differently: 'I came up with the name "Genesis" because I felt this would be a new beginning for SEGA. At first the Japanese management didn't care for the word, but I insisted on it.' This wouldn't be the last time SEGA in Japan at first disagreed with proposals from the US, but let the stateside team do what they wanted anyway.

Why the name change? Rosen says he simply disliked it, and there was no way that an earlier moniker of Tomahawk could stay, but there was also a manufacturer of computer storage devices in North America called Mega Drive Systems Inc, so from a trademark perspective it would have been hard for SEGA to sell its Mega Drive in the same market. Nomenclature discussions settled, the Genesis released in North America on 14 August 1989 at an RRP of $189, supported by the launch games *Altered Beast*, *Last Battle*, *Space Harrier II*, *Super Thunder Blade*, *Thunder Force II* and *Tommy Lasorda Baseball*. While the latter title bore a famous American baseball player on its cover, and *Last Battle* had its *Fist of the North Star* tie-in elements removed for the US release, these were all Japan-made games – and America didn't take to them as SEGA would have hoped. *Ghouls 'n Ghosts*, *Super Hang-On* and *The Revenge of Shinobi* followed before the year was out, all great games but similarly unable to break through to the US mainstream.

But by January 1992, the Genesis had a 65% market share in the States, so clearly something changed the console's fortunes. Except, it was *two* things, really. Firstly, while he was replaced by former Matchbox CEO Tom Kalinske in 1990, having failed to achieve SEGA of Japan's expectation of a million Genesis consoles sold, Katz had pursued some deals with a range of high-profile sportsmen, leading to the likes of *James 'Buster' Douglas Knockout Boxing* and *Joe Montana Football* coming out in late 1990 and early 1991 respectively. He'd also arranged a partnership with American studio Electronic Arts (EA), who'd soon bring both *John Madden Football* and *NHL Hockey* (released elsewhere as *EA Hockey*) to SEGA's system, and later the wildly popular and series-establishing *FIFA International Soccer*. This star power was crowned by *Michael Jackson's Moonwalker*, released to great sales and critical acclaim in August 1990. 'The sports titles brought in a broader … older demographic than Nintendo – they appealed to teenagers and adults,' Katz said, as quoted in *Collected Works*. But SEGA needed something to rival Mario's appeal to younger players – and they'd get it in 1991.

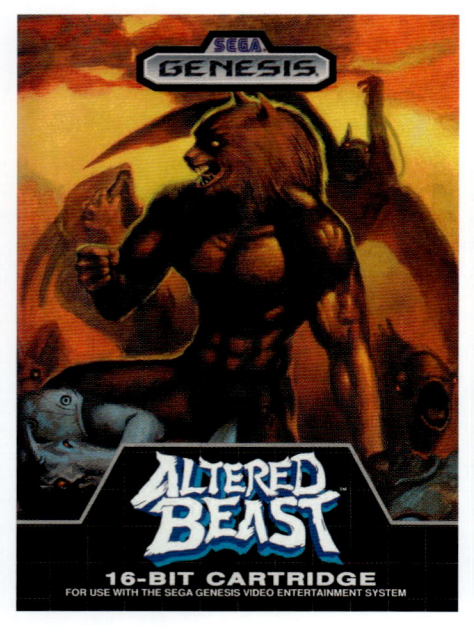

The story of Sonic the Hedgehog is worthy of a book all of its own (indeed, there are a few out there), but to summarise: SEGA of Japan was incredibly keen to develop a mascot to challenge Mario, especially in America, but one that was harder, faster and stronger than the plumber and his Mushroom Kingdom pals. Attitude was everything. After a few false starts and some development from sketched versions of a character dubbed Mr Needlemouse, they arrived at Sonic. A smoothly side-scrolling platformer played at high speed was already the target game to launch this new icon with, and the red-sneakered superstar-to-be slotted perfectly into its brightly coloured levels and loop-the-loops. But Katz had his doubts about Sonic's stateside chances, likewise his successor, so Kalinske turned to SEGA of America's marketing department to run some playtesting. With *Sonic the Hedgehog* ready to go, the game was shown to specially selected crowds, known fans of Mario games, around the United States – and around 80% of players who saw *Sonic the Hedgehog* wanted to play it instead of Mario. The doubts faded away and *Sonic* released in the States on 23 June 1991, before anywhere else in the world.

Now confident of *Sonic the Hedgehog* giving the Genesis the edge in the North American market, not just over the NES but the imminent Super Nintendo due in August 1991, Kalinske moved to replace the game that came with new Genesis purchases, *Altered Beast*, with *Sonic*. What's more, he wanted to reduce the RRP of the console, with *Sonic*, to $149. Japan was hesitant, if not livid at the proposals, but he got his wishes – and the Genesis started to take off. In 1991, SEGA sold 3.1 million Genesis consoles in North America. In 1992, that number rose to 7.6 million. Aggressive marketing – 35 TV adverts were produced in 1992 alone, many of which targeted the kind of American teenager who tuned into MTV – kept SEGA's sales ahead of those of its greatest competitor. The term 'blast processing' was thrown into the mix, both meaning nothing whatsoever yet *everything* to SEGA kids who wanted to one-up their Nintendo-owning friends. After using the 'Genesis Does What Nintendon't' tagline in earlier TV and print ads disparaging the NES, SEGA ran with the slogan 'Welcome To The Next Level' in 1992, painting the SNES as a deeply inferior console. It wasn't, as so many of its dazzling games made clear, but advertising spoke louder than any tech specs and throughout the first half of the 1990s SEGA ruled North America.

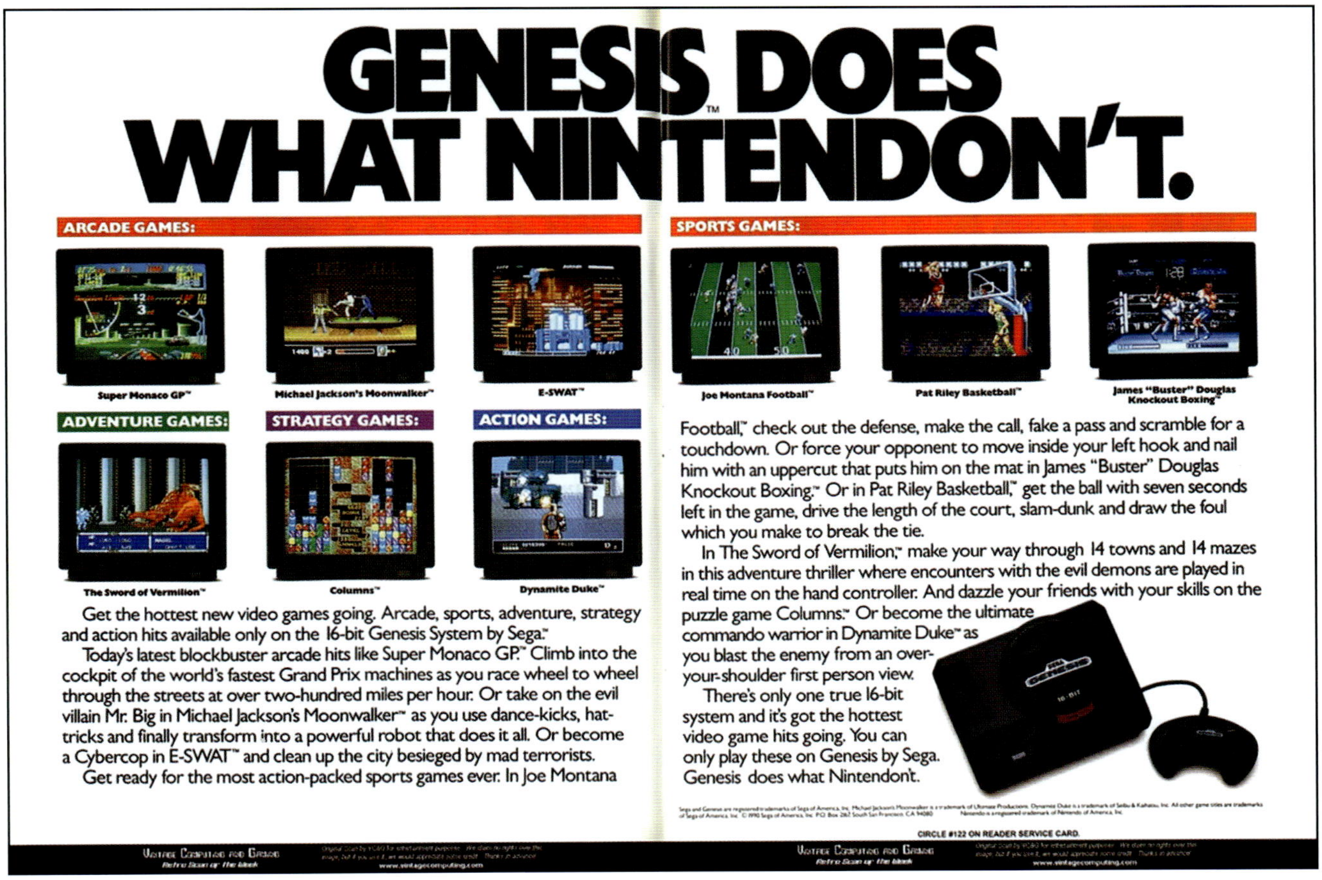

In Europe too, the Mega Drive – no need for a name change here – proved popular, with many Master System owners seeing it as a natural next step up from their 8-bit consoles, a degree of brand loyalty already established. SEGA Europe, which Virgin Mastertronic now was, also adopted a boisterous and colourful TV advertising strategy to set the console apart from its competitors, 1992's 'Cyber Razor Cut' promo proving exceptionally memorable for anyone in the UK. But on a global level, one of the most notable examples of SEGA targeting a more grown-up audience than Nintendo, and successfully so, came in September 1993 with the home release of the arcade one-on-one fighter, *Mortal Kombat*. Midway's game had been an enormous coin-op hit thanks to its gruesome finishing moves, 'fatalities', where the victorious player could rip out their opponent's heart or punch their head clean off – but on the SNES port these shocking specials were heavily censored, and the game's blood splashes replaced with what nobody believed was actually sweat. But on the Mega Drive? All the gore of the arcade, right there in your bedroom. It reportedly sold five times more copies than the SNES version, despite Nintendo's release being the superior port in several other areas.

'It looks like we're dominating on both sides of the Atlantic,' Kalinske told Spanish magazine *TodoSega* in 1993 (via sega-16.com). By then the revised, costs-reduced Mega Drive II – a squared-off design with a top-loading cart slot positioned centrally – was the default model on shelves worldwide. 'I don't think a new console will debut until 1995,' Kalinske told the interviewer when pressed about a reported 32-bit machine called the Saturn, before adding that he believed the newly released (in Europe, anyway) Mega-CD add-on would become 'the best CD-ROM format on the market'. He was wrong on both points, but the Mega Drive was *the* console in the West for a solid chunk of the 1990s and would become SEGA's best-selling console (range) ever at just over 30 million units worldwide.

The Mega Drive also followed the Master System to significant successes in Brazil, where several new versions of the console were released in the 21st century by official licensee Tectoy (as Tec Toy). In 2016, with the Xbox One and PlayStation 4 on sale worldwide, the Mega Drive was still selling in the region of 150,000 units a year in Brazil – and the Tectoy total in the territory stands at around three million. Elsewhere, the Mega Drive was sold by Samsung in South Korea as the Super Gam*Boy and later the Super Aladdin Boy (Samsung also sold localised takes on the Mega Drive II); and Dendy distributor Steepler sold an unlicensed Mega Drive clone in Russia known as the Pro 16 Bit. In India, SEGA agreed an official distribution deal with Shaw Wallace Electronics for the Mega Drive II, but a high RRP saw it sell in only low quantities.

As well as traditional console forms, the Mega Drive was incorporated into a PC in 1993. The Amstrad Mega PC was sold in Europe and Australia, had a sliding front panel that allowed access to either the disc drive or Mega Drive cartridge slot (switching to one essentially put the other to sleep), and came with its own deliciously off-white Control Pad, although you could also plug in regular black controllers. The Mega Jet, released in Japan in 1994, was a handheld variant a little like the Master System Super Compact and based on a rental device previously used on Japan Airlines. It required a TV and AC adaptor to use, which rather restricted its appeal, but was reworked into a proper portable console in 1995, the Nomad, which had a backlit screen and six-button layout. This play-anywhere device was exclusive to the North American market, where it sold around a million units. The concept of a portable Mega Drive was great – the Nomad just released too late in the console's lifespan for it to be commercially viable globally.

The Mega Drive's been on quite the journey since its official discontinuation (everywhere except Brazil) in 1997. In 1998, Majesco picked up the licence to sell the Genesis 3 in North America, an incredibly lightweight and low-budget redesign of the console that was incompatible with the Mega-CD (SEGA CD, in the region) and 32X add-ons and wouldn't play select game cartridges. The Genesis 3 was bundled with SEGA's official six-button controllers, introduced in 1993 and essential for fighting titles like *Eternal Champions* and *Super Street Fighter II* (indeed, this controller is known as the Fighting Pad 6B in Japan). More recently, SEGA released the Mega Drive Mini in late 2019 – aka the Genesis Mini in the US – which featured 42 built-in games within a shell perfectly resembling a miniaturised Mega Drive. A second Mega Drive Mini based on the Japanese Mega Drive 2 design was announced in June 2022 containing over 50 games, including a number of Mega-CD titles and never-before-released bonuses. That, and frequent releases of Mega Drive game compilations for contemporary consoles, and the addition of Mega Drive games to the Switch Online subscription service in 2021, goes to show that SEGA's 16-bit hit is a system with a legacy sure to live on for many more years.

Mega Drive: Five Must Plays

Streets of Rage 2 (1992)
If SEGA's original *Streets of Rage* of 1991 was an attempt at matching Capcom's belt-scrolling sensation *Final Fight* that fell slightly sort, then this sequel is absolutely the game that trumps it all ends up. Arguably the greatest home console beat 'em up of all time, *Streets of Rage 2* packs a serious punch with crunchy combat, dazzling visuals with hefty sprites, an array of awesome special moves spread across its four playable characters, and a soundtrack (primarily) by Yuzo Koshiro that tapped into the dance scene of the time to produce some truly memorable melodies. *Streets of Rage 2* remains the benchmark that all games in the genre since have aimed to be measured favourably against, including even 2020's exceptional series comeback of *Streets of Rage 4*.

Sonic the Hedgehog 2 (1992)
The second 16-bit Sonic game is where SEGA's hedgehog really found his groove. It's faster and more challenging than the game that came before it, its levels more detailed and dangerous, it looks sumptuous throughout, and it introduces a two-player mode thanks to the addition of Sonic's equally zippy friend, Tails. The game arrived amid a flurry of hype, with its makers declaring its North American release date of Tuesday, 24 November be known as 'Sonic 2sday'. A $10 million budget was committed to advertising *Sonic 2*, but with more than 7.5 million copies sold – making it the second highest-selling Mega Drive game ever after the original *Sonic*, which was bundled with consoles – no doubt SEGA felt it was money well spent.

Gunstar Heroes (1993)
This run-and-gunner is the debut game from the celebrated studio Treasure, makers of such acclaimed shooters as *Ikaruga* and *Sin and Punishment*, and undoubtedly one of the Mega Drive's most critically acclaimed releases. It won a number of game of the year awards in 1993, reviewers praising its intensity, eye-popping visuals and chaotic two-player mode. Several re-releases have ensured *Gunstar Heroes* has stayed playable on modern platforms – a sublime stereoscopic version featuring new gameplay modes on the Nintendo 3DS is worthy of

singling out – but running this triumph on original hardware is a thrill every Mega Drive fan should experience. While original copies of *Gunstar Heroes* fetch high prices today, the game was included on the Europe-only *Classic Collection* cartridge of 1996, alongside *Altered Beast*, *Flicky* and *Alex Kidd in the Enchanted Castle*. Mercifully, copies of this compilation don't sell for three-figure prices … yet.

The Story of Thor (1994)
Known as *Beyond Oasis* in North America, this Ancient-developed action-adventure game is as close as any SEGA release came to copying, politely, the mechanics of Nintendo's Legend of Zelda series. (1995's *Soleil*, aka *Crusader of Centy*, might also have a case.) There's an overworld to explore with little in the way of player hand holding, and shrines (note: *not* dungeons) to dive into in search of magical spirits. *The Story of Thor* might play in a largely familiar fashion, but its plot is great, its sound and graphics excellent, and its reputation has only grown in the years since its release. Don't expect much depth, but if it's colour and excitement you're after in your role-players, dig this one out.

Comix Zone (1995)
Set within the panels of a comic book, this beat 'em up still looks astounding today. You control Sketch Turner, who's magically teleported into the pages of his own comic by its villain, Mortus, who takes his place in the real world and draws enemies into the game to battle Turner. It's a very original set-up, and SEGA brought in comic creators and artists from DC and Marvel to bring its world to life. But the challenge of this one is incredibly steep, meaning that only the most dedicated player will see Turner through to one of *Comix Zone*'s two endings – one good, one not so good. Although the SEGA Saturn and Sony PlayStation were on sale by the time of *Comix Zone*'s release in August 1995, hampering the game's sales, it's no exaggeration to say that this 16-bit game outshined the visuals of several early games on those advanced consoles.

Mega Drive Collector Spot
Mega Drive collector Mike Rouse (aka Retro Gamer Boy on YouTube) from Southampton, UK – who has worked in the video games industry for over 20 years and has a wider collection of more than 4,000 games and 100 consoles – talks about his 16-bit memories and how the console's finest titles continue to inspire game developers today.

'I'm a huge beat 'em up fan, and in early 1990 I got to play *Golden Axe* at the arcade. Films like *Conan the Barbarian* were firmly ingrained in pop culture by this time, and to get to play a game that felt like it was part of this universe was exhilarating. I bought my Mega Drive the next year, saw *Golden Axe* on the shelf, bought that too, and it did not disappoint. It was the first game I ever played on a Mega Drive, and it had the graphics, sound, and gameplay I loved from the arcade original.

'The first console I'd saved up for and bought was a Master System, so when I saw the Mega Drive was coming out, I started to save up again, mostly out of brand loyalty – I loved the Master System, so why wouldn't I love this console too? When I got one, I would tell friends that I had a console as powerful as any arcade cab. It wasn't of course, but for me, there was little difference between the two.

'By the mid-1990s I had about 50 games for the Mega Drive. I acquired other consoles, like the SNES and 3DO, but none of those had a game collection like my Mega Drive. My collecting was on pause for a good five years when the PlayStation came out – the Mega Drive was always hooked up and ready to play, but it didn't get a look in during that time. But back in the Master System years I'd made up my mind that I would work in games, and in 2000 I started as a junior 3D artist at Sony PlayStation. Of course, this meant I played a lot more PlayStation games, but I also started picking up Mega Drive games again. About a year into the job, I went onto this new website called eBay and bought 53 complete, in-box Mega Drive games and about 30 Master System games for just £50. From that point on my collecting for the console started to gain some pace.

'A game I knew about but could never find when the Mega Drive was at the height of its popularity was *The Story of Thor*. It was only in 2019 when I finally added it to my collection, and I was blown away by it. It's an open-world RPG that plays more like a 2D version of *The Legend of Zelda: Breath of the Wild* than a classic 16-bit RPG. Classics like the Golden Axe series, the Streets of Rage series, and *Comix Zone* still get played constantly, while games like *Desert Strike*, *Decap Attack*, *ESWAT* and *Flashback* have a huge amount of nostalgia for me.

'I have a few rare or scarce games in my collection that I'm happy to have, like a complete in-box copy of *Lakers Versus Celtics and the NBA Playoffs*, *Alien Soldier*, and *The Pirates of Dark Water*. But I would say though that the most prized part of my Mega Drive collection is not any one game, but my complete in-box Mega Drive, Mega-CD, 32X, Power Base, and Sega Modem. It's amazing to have this truly unique gaming set-up – it's like the hi-fi system for game consoles. The console and its add-ons were ahead of their time. All that I need now to complete the console set-up is the Mega-CD Karaoke, a not-so-common device that allowed gamers in Japan to turn their Mega Drive and Mega-CD combo into a fully-fledged karaoke machine. It's an amazing piece of gaming history and I can't wait to get it in my collection.

'In the last 10 years, we have seen the pixel art style – which was a limitation of the Mega Drive's hardware – become used by some of the most successful indie titles ever released. It's not just the art that has made a resurgence but the gameplay and audio design as well. Many new indie games hark back to the classic arcade mechanics of *Streets of Rage 2* and *Thunder Force IV* and try to capture the magic of classic RPGs like *Phantasy Star IV* and *The Story of Thor*. And alongside all these new indie games inspired by the era of 16-bit gaming, there are now *new* games being made for the Mega Drive, and a number of them are up there with the best modern console indie titles. There is a resurgence in classic gaming which follows the trends we see in movies, music, and fashion. The 16-bit era would seem to be a timeless generation for gaming where people who were not born when this generation of gaming was around still enjoy and appreciate it.'

PC ENGINE SUPERGRAFX

Manufacturer: NEC Home Electronics
Released: December 1989 (Japan), 1990 (France)

Offering improved graphics and audio powered by four times the working RAM of its predecessor, the PC Engine SuperGrafx – code-named the PC Engine 2 during development – was supposed to be the natural next step for PC Engine owners to take upon its release in 1989. The sales pitch was basically: here's what you already love, only bigger (quite a lot bigger, actually) and better (technically, absolutely).

Offering full backwards compatibility with existing HuCard games and both of the PC Engine's CD-ROM add-ons, as well as older controllers, the SuperGrafx definitely could have been a contender on the Japanese market. But with development and promotion rushed in an attempt to keep pace with SEGA's Mega Drive and get out ahead of Nintendo's upcoming Super Famicom, NEC failed to properly position its new system as a standalone console, instead implying it was merely an upgraded PC Engine. Cue: a distinct absence of market excitement as genuine 16-bit consoles hit stores, and the SuperGrafx, still based around an 8-bit processor, was widely ignored.

Only five games were released exclusively for the SuperGrafx, making use of its advanced capabilities, the most notable being a terrific port of Capcom's *Dai Makaimura* – or *Ghouls 'n Ghosts* in the West. One special HuCard game, the shooter *Darius Plus*, featured minor SuperGrafx enhancements but could also be played on a regular PC Engine console. The price of these games was high, up to the equivalent of $100 per title, so too the RRP of the SuperGrafx console – at ¥39,800 (the equivalent of about £280 in 2022), it was ¥15,000 more than the PC Engine's launch price. In total only around 75,000 PC Engine SuperGrafx consoles were sold, and NEC moved back to supporting the PC Engine and its later CD-ROM variants.

NEC had planned to release a SuperGrafx-exclusive add-on called the Power Console in 1990, which featured an aircraft-like yoke suited to playing air-combat titles, flight sims and racing games. Other sticks, dials, buttons and displays surrounded this primary controller, with the Power Console coming loaded with user options enough to hopefully justify its planned RRP of ¥59,800. With SuperGrafx sales extraordinarily low however, the peripherical was scrapped. If you're keen to check out a couple of great SuperGrafx games today, both *Dai Makaimura/Ghouls 'n Ghosts* and horizontal shooter *Aldynes* are included on all versions of Konami's PC Engine Mini.

THE 1990s
A SLEEPING GIANT BECOMES A GAMING SUPERPOWER

SEGA versus Nintendo. That was the headline fight of the 1990s, the epic slugfest that defined the decade. Or was it? Because while these two Japanese gaming giants started the 1990s as market leaders, with the Mega Drive/Genesis trading blows with the Super Famicom/Nintendo, the middle of the decade threw an unseen sucker punch into the mix. Sony's PlayStation disrupted the console market, overcoming its opponents and establishing a new name at gaming's top table – the same table that SEGA would slip from as 16-bit success gave way to 32-bit slumps and a last hurrah that couldn't make up for lost time and ground. Games turned from 2D to 3D, 'arcade perfect' play at home was achieved, online gaming found a foothold, and CD-ROM put cartridges put to pasture for everyone except Nintendo.

NEO GEO

Manufacturer: SNK Corporation

Released: April 1990 (Japan), August 1990 (North America), 1991 (Europe)

SNK had been producing arcade games, and licensing them for console and computer ports, since the late 1970s. Come the mid-1980s it was really hitting its stride, with popular titles including 1986's action-platformer *Athena*, which gained a greater following upon its port to the NES, and the same year's vertical run-and-gunner *Ikari Warriors*, originally developed as a tie-in for the movie *Rambo: First Blood Part II*. It may have missed the blockbuster licence, but *Ikari Warriors* was a huge hit, earning high revenues in worldwide arcades and subsequently releasing for a wealth of home platforms. SNK even developed a few games specifically for consoles, including 1989's superbly received and series-spawning *Baseball Stars* for the NES. But with the 16-bit era of console gaming dawning, the company wanted to see if it could take its arcade expertise into the home.

Takashi Nishiyama was a man of great arcade experience. He'd directed Irem's genre-pioneering *Kung-Fu Master*, the world's first side-scrolling beat 'em up game, and later led the development of Capcom's 1987 arcade game *Street Fighter* – the precursor to 1991's genre-defining *Street Fighter II*. He was invited to join SNK, and his first project was a new arcade system that could run several different games on a single cabinet. Nishiyama envisioned a machine that arcade owners could buy the once and subsequently pay only to update the game selection. It would be a revolution for the industry, a huge money saver – and when that cabinet, the Neo Geo Multi Video System, was unveiled to the world in January 1990, it immediately had arcade operators excited. But Nishiyama and SNK didn't stop with a coin-op unveiling – there was a spot at the MVS's announcement for the smaller, distinctly home-proportioned Advanced Entertainment System.

Both the MVS and the AES ran on the same internal hardware, meaning that all new arcade games would also play on the home machine. In many areas the Neo Geo outstripped the already-on-sale SEGA Mega Drive/Genesis and the arriving-soon Super Famicom/Nintendo. It sold itself as a 24-bit system, using as it did both the 16-bit Motorola 68000 CPU and a Zilog Z80 – both present within the Mega Drive too, but the Neo Geo ran them at faster speeds. It could display over 4,000 on-screen colours simultaneously, compared to the Mega Drive's 61 and Super Nintendo's 256. The Neo Geo had another ace up its sleeve in the shape of its custom graphics chip, the Line Sprite Processor, which could in theory generate up to 380 sprites on screen at one time – way ahead of the 128 of the SNES and 80 of the Mega Drive.

But this unprecedented horsepower came at an eye-watering price. In July 1991, a year after the MVS rolled into arcades and Japanese rental options for the AES had begun, the Neo Geo's home version hit retailers at an RRP of $649.99. Included were two large arcade stick controllers (brilliant things, save for very short leads) and a game, either the sports title *Baseball Stars Professional* (a sequel to the NES release) or the shooter *NAM-1975*. The cost wasn't an accident: SNK's research told them that a select group of players was willing to cough up such an asking price, and then pay for new AES cartridges retailing for up to $200 each. And to think Sony was criticised in 2020 for selling PlayStation 5 games at $70.

Through the early 1990s the Neo Geo earned SNK a steady profit, albeit mostly because of the MVS's success. The AES remained the preserve of the few that could afford it, and SNK positioned it as the console for the most discerning (not to mention loaded) of players. 'Bigger, Badder, Better' was the tagline of one print ad featuring a vicious-looking dog tearing towards the reader; while another, more risqué ad showed a woman in lingerie lamenting that her partner now spent all his time on the AES: 'I remember when he couldn't keep his hands off me.' Anyone who wanted to carry their game progress between home and arcade could as both AES and MVS featured a memory card slot, a feature Nintendo would use much later to allow compatibility between the 2003 GameCube racer *F-Zero GX* and its arcade equivalent, *F-Zero AX*.

Street Fighter II's emergence in 1991 led other developers to release one-on-one fighters, and with MSV cabinets so widespread SNK was able to fit them with a host of on-trend titles. *Fatal Fury: King of Fighters* released in 1991, *Art of Fighting* in 1992, and *Samurai Shodown* (known as *Samurai Spirits* in Japan) in 1993. Having dabbled in all manner of genres in the 1980s, SNK became known foremost as a pre-eminent developer of fighting games, and many sequels followed these breakthrough releases. The final game released for the MVS and AES was one of these follow-ups, *Samurai Shodown V Special* coming out in July 2004, meaning that Neo Geo software support spanned 14 years even though SNK had retired the hardware in December 1997.

SNK didn't end its Neo Geo line without realising that the AES asking price was too high for many players who'd otherwise love to have these games at home. In 1994 the Neo Geo CD was released worldwide, launching at the more reasonable RRP of $399 and with games priced from $50. Slow loading times were a problem, but otherwise the hardware was an attractive alternative to the AES – plus, the revised Neo Geo CDZ (pictured above) of 1995 (only released in Japan, but region free) managed to halve the excessive waiting times. The console's games were the same as those on the MVS and AES, but the CD-ROM format made production cheaper, and its smaller control pad was more akin to what shipped with the SEGA Saturn and Sony PlayStation. However, those very same consoles offered something the Neo Geo couldn't: proper 3D gaming. Next to the fists-flying polygons of the Tekken and Virtua Fighter games, the exceptionally beautiful sprites of King of Fighters seemed flat and unappealing to some players. Neo Geo had amazing games, but the market had largely moved on – the Neo Geo CD sold around 570,000 units before its discontinuation in 1997, with AES sales estimated at around 300,000.

SNK wasn't finished though, its eyes still aimed at arcades. By 1995 the MVS was looking outdated beside cabs with 3D visuals, so SNK announced its new vision for arcade hardware: the Hyper Neo Geo 64. It eventually released in 1997, running 3D games in the Samurai Shodown and Fatal Fury series, but didn't catch on and plans to repeat the MVS/AES model with a home version of the Hyper Neo Geo 64 were scrapped. SNK hit financial trouble in 2001, leading to its closure; but company founder

Eikichi Kawasaki had set up a new business, Playmore, not long before SNK's demise, and he used it to acquire SNK's assets. Further name and ownership changes followed, and at the time of writing SNK is simply SNK again, with over 96% of its shares held by an organisation operated by the crown prince of Saudi Arabia, Mohammed bin Salman.

Several Neo Geo compilations have been released in the 21st century, as well as new hardware. The Neo Geo X, a handheld device that could be docked for TV play (a bit like Nintendo's later Switch) using a replica of the AES control stick, came out in 2012 with 20 built-in games and further titles available on five game cards sold separately. It received a mixed reception, with criticism aimed at its fuzzy TV output and reliance on physical media rather than being internet compatible for downloads. Production of the Neo Geo X was halted due to problems between SNK Playmore and the console's manufacturer, Tommo Inc, and it's now an expensive pick-up on the second-hand market.

The Neo Geo Mini followed in 2018 to mark SNK's 40th anniversary and is a lot cheaper to buy today than the X. This compact device can be used both on TVs, with Neo Geo CD-like controllers optional, or as a standalone desktop arcade cab using its integrated 3.5-inch display. It contains 40 games as standard, *many* of which are fighters, and comes in a range of models. The Arcade Stick Pro released a year later and did away with the mini-cabinet design. It includes 20 games out of the box, with another 20 unlockable, and can also be used as a controller for PC games and the Neo Geo Mini. In addition to these releases, many individual Neo Geo games are downloadable right now for modern consoles, with a large selection on the Switch eShop.

Neo Geo: Five Must Plays

Windjammers (1994)
A sort of extreme-sports *Pong* bursting with colour and energy, Data East's *Windjammers* is a competitive Frisbee game where winning means getting the flying disc past your opponent and into scoring zones. The disc can be bounced off the sides of the court, made to curve or spin wildly with a super move, and can stun opponents if it strikes them. What might not sound all that sensational on paper is actually an enthralling arcade sports experience, made all the better when played against a pal.

Neo Turf Masters (1996)
Golf isn't a sport that naturally translates to arcade play, but developers Nazca Corporation made it work brilliantly with *Neo Turf Masters*. With simple controls, large and bright sprites, and earworm-ready music, this is far from a sim-like experience with some bizarrely designed holes lining up to challenge your skill. Don't come expecting realism, but such is the mood and feel of this one that you're likely to have a great time even if you hate golf itself.

Metal Slug (1996)
Nazca Corporation's second game of 1996, the run-and-gunner *Metal Slug*, is an OTT symphony of sights and sounds, bearing deliciously detailed visuals bursting with personality and explosions enough to deafen a Hollywood blockbuster. It kickstarted a long-running series, which arguably features better games than this original release – but if you want to see how a legendary gaming franchise began, *Metal Slug* remains an absolute joy to blast through.

Blazing Star (1998)
There are many excellent shoot 'em ups on the Neo Geo, and *Blazing Star* is right up there. It's perhaps not the most testing game – committed fans of the genre could soon one-credit developers Yumekobo's horizontal thrill ride of scintillating sci-fi destruction. But for newcomers its mix of slick presentation and beautiful visuals makes it a must. If you like this one be sure to check out its predecessor, 1995's *Pulstar*, but be warned that it's far more challenging.

Garou: Mark of the Wolves (1999)
The Neo Geo has a legendary array of one-on-one fighting games, but *Garou:*

Mark of the Wolves, a follow-up to the *Fatal Fury* games, appears here over any others due to its introduction of a couple of innovative features. Players can make use of a health-regenerating Tactical Offense Position marker and move, which gives them a burst of life and power up attack damage; and counterattack opponents from a block-stunned position. Technically creative and just as hard-hitting as its Neo Geo stablemates, and with stunning artwork throughout, this fighter has remained a favourite with genre fans.

Neo Geo Collector Spot
Frazer Rhodes is from Halifax in the UK and owns a complete collection of Neo Geo AES releases. He shares his favourite games for SNK's console, his most-prized title, and his thoughts on how Neo Geo games can and should be played today.

'The early 1990s were one of the most exciting times in video game history. It was the transition from 8- to 16-bit consoles, and every week it seemed there was some new hardware coming out of Japan. With the Mega Drive and Super Famicom we were getting decent arcade conversions; but when I heard about an arcade-perfect system with the Neo Geo, I just had to find out more. It really was a no-compromises machine – it was the arcade, at home.

'The first Neo Geo game I ever played was *NAM-1975* on an Electrocoin arcade machine in Manchester. After that, in early 1992, I bought a second-hand PAL AES console which came with *Fatal Fury* and *Robo Army* for the price of £300. The first game I bought brand new from a store called Krazy Konsoles was *League Bowling*, which was £65 and worth every penny – love that game!

'The price of the games was a challenge given most came in at £120 new. However, in the UK at least there was a fairly healthy second-hand market as owners tended to buy, play and then trade back, so many games could be bought for around the £85 mark. There were two other people at my school with a Neo Geo and thankfully they were happy to swap games, which meant I got to try *World Heroes*, *Soccer Brawl* and *Art of Fighting* shortly after they were released. My neighbour and friend bought one too, which was pretty handy for swapping games.

'[I started collecting] in part because of the relatively small library of games – 117 for the home console – seemed achievable. I also got back into the system around 1997–1998, when prices were pretty much at their lowest, so games which I longed for back in the day but never got a chance to play could be picked up. With huge cartridges and premium boxes, a library of games on the shelf really does look impressive even today.

'The most I've ever spent on one game was £1,100 in 2007 for *Chibi Maruko-Chan*

72

Deluxe Quiz, a Japanese-only release which appeared in 1995 – and by today's standards, that price is a bargain. The game didn't sell many copies and is one of the rarest for the system, and it was one of a handful of titles which I needed to finish the collection. My most-prized game would have to be my copy of *Metal Slug*. Not only is it a fabulous game but it's now pretty much legendary for collectors and is highly sought after.

'My own top five games changes all the time, but today I'd go with *NAM-1975*, the first game on the system which still holds up well today; *Pulstar*, a shoot 'em up masterpiece; *Baseball Stars*, as I spent many an afternoon spent hitting home runs with a friend on this classic; *The King of Fighters '98*, the best in the series in my view; and *Metal Slug* or *Metal Slug 3* as either of them would be my favourite Neo Geo game, and they're both incredible.

'The Neo Geo was the pinnacle of the 16-bit era and a powerhouse of 2D gaming – which appeals to players today. For me it's the Rolls-Royce of consoles, and nowadays compilations are a great way for people to experience its games, that they might not otherwise have the opportunity to play. But my preference would always be to use the original hardware, because that's how I first experienced the system. You also have the theatre of the huge cartridges, the original joysticks, and I guess it was how the games were meant to be experienced. But whatever way gamers enjoy the Neo Geo game library, they are accessing some of the best games to grace a home console.'

GX4000

Manufacturer: Amstrad
Released: September 1990 (Europe)

Amstrad's line of 8-bit CPC computers (the CPC standing for Colour Personal Computer) had sold steadily since 1984 and at the end of the decade the company's founder, *The Apprentice* star Alan Sugar, decided it was time for a slice of the home console pie. The resulting system, the GX4000, would be both Amstrad's first and last console, selling as it did a wretchedly low number of units and supporting a library of fewer than 30 games, many of which were cheaper on other platforms.

With its internal specifications largely drawing on the tech used in the CPC line, the GX4000 was in some ways a superior console in comparison to the Nintendo Entertainment System and SEGA Master System. While still an 8-bit machine, its 64KB of RAM under the hood was way ahead of the NES's 2KB and SEGA's 8KB, and its colour palette of 4,096 was larger than the Mega Drive's 512. Early press coverage was optimistic of Amstrad's chances, with *ACE* magazine writing that it was superior to every 8-bit console except the PC Engine and *CVG* impressed by its graphical capabilities.

The GX4000's reliance on existing components meant that its production was relatively inexpensive, leaving Amstrad with money left over for a multi-million-pound marketing campaign including a *Star Trek*-spoofing TV advert telling of its 'lifelike picture' qualities. A launch price of £99.99 for the console and around £25 for each game cartridge was appealing against its 8-bit competition, but there were two major problems facing Amstrad's machine.

Firstly, support from developers was thin on the ground. Ocean was a big name at the time and ported *Batman* and *Navy Seals* from CPC to GX4000, but these games were far cheaper on CPC disks, and the same was true of Core Design's *Switchblade* and Atari's *Klax*. There simply weren't enough head-turning exclusives on the console. And secondly, the console market was changing, with 8-bit hardware already out of date now that the SEGA Mega Drive was available.

Alan Sugar batted away questions about how the GX4000 would fare against SEGA's 16-bit system, saying that it wasn't about tech specs or software support but what these products *did*. After which, the GX4000 proceeded to do not very much at all. Its controllers – Game Paddles, according to the console's manual – were very much in the NES and Master System guise and felt good in the hand, with firmer face buttons than SEGA's pads; but such well-made stuff was useless without good games to play, and the GX4000's total of 27 carts released says everything about its support and longevity, with discontinuation coming in 1991. CPC owners weren't persuaded to add it to their set-ups, and those already invested in SEGA and Nintendo saw nothing to tempt them away from their existing ecosystems.

With 15,000 units sold, the GX4000 isn't a product that Lord Sugar, as he's known these days, likely looks back fondly on. But as one of very few British-made consoles – preceded only by a few *Pong* clones in the 1970s and 1985's BBC Bridge Companion, which used swappable ROM cartridges but *only* played and taught variations of bridge – it has a place in history. And as a genuine curiosity of the home console market, it's something that today's retro collectors have a generous soft spot for.

SUPER FAMICOM (SUPER NINTENDO)

Manufacturer: Nintendo

Released: November 1990 (Japan), August 1991 (North America), April 1992 (UK and Ireland), June 1992 (Europe), July 1992 (Australia), August 1993 (Brazil), November 1994 (Russia)

Nintendo's market dominance in Japan and North America, with its 8-bit Famicom and NES consoles respectively, meant the company felt confident against the competition coming its way from NEC's PC Engine/TurboGrafx-16 and SEGA's Mega Drive/Genesis. As SEGA raced into the 16-bit hardware world, Nintendo patiently waited, with its own 16-bit console hitting stores more than two years after the Mega Drive's Japanese debut. It was still selling a lot of 8-bit software, and the phenomenon that was *Super Mario Bros. 3* had dented the Mega Drive's launch in late 1988, stealing press coverage and keeping players glued to their Famicoms.

And Nintendo's unpanicked position was made more comfortable by what was going on behind the scenes. While players worldwide continued to enjoy the NES, Nintendo revealed that it was working on its next console to Japanese press in September 1987, via the local *Kyoto Shimbun* newspaper. There wasn't anything to see, but company president Hiroshi Yamauchi (pictured above) already had the name in place: this next-generation console would be called the Super Famicom. While going under the radar for many, reports of this new Super Famicom would have surely alerted Nintendo diehards, ensuring that their attention wasn't stolen by the launch later that same year of the PC Engine.

Almost a year later, in August 1988, Yamauchi was interviewed in the magazine *Touch*, where he disclosed further details. The Super Famicom would use a modified WDC 65C816 as its CPU, later shown to be the Rioch 5A22 running at up to 3.58MHz (the same speed as the Mega Drive's secondary Zilog Z80 CPU but slower than its main Motorola 68000); its sound chip would be custom made in co-operation with Sony; and games would be released based on quality, not quantity, with the in-development *Super Mario Bros. 4* an early title. Yamauchi also predicted three million sales in the Super Famicom's first year, an expectation that was close to being on the money.

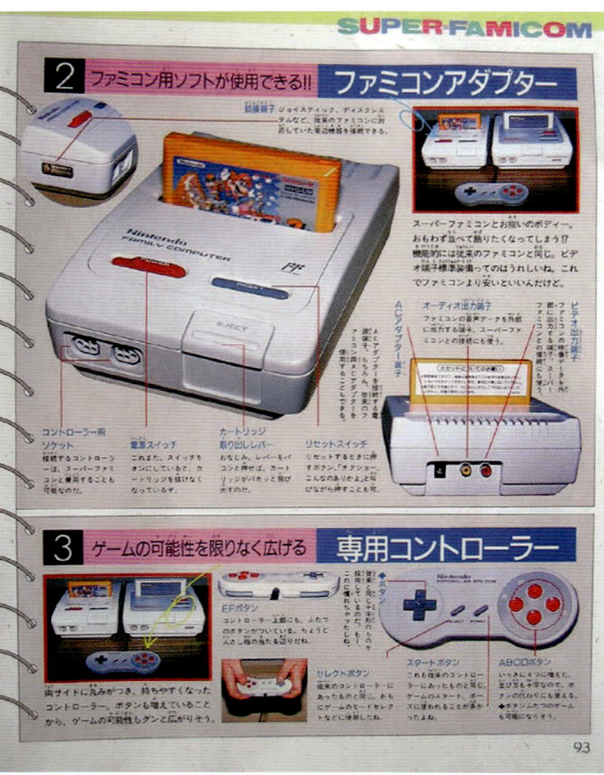

In November 1988, the console was shown to around 200 members of the gaming press for the first time, with the magazine *Famicom Tsūshin* (nowadays known as *Famitsu*) reporting on its impressive sound and ground-breaking graphical scaling and rotation abilities. Another Japanese magazine, *Famicom Hissyoubon*, noted that a third game in the Legend of Zelda series would come out alongside the Super Famicom's launch, as well as a fourth Super Mario Bros. title, while both publications ran photos of the console and its controller that, when seen nowadays, highlight clear differences from what would come out in 1990. The console shown in 1988 had a different layout with thin buttons – power, reset and a video-out selection switch allowing for Famicom Adaptor compatibility – running down the right side of the unit's top, beneath the cartridge slot, with the eject button at the very front and much smaller controller ports, while the pads themselves featured all-red face buttons marked A, B, C and D.

You read that right: a device called the Famicom Adaptor was shown with Nintendo's new machine in November 1988 (see photo, left). This wasn't a traditional plug-through adapter allowing users to run older cartridges, like SEGA's Master System Converter did for the Mega Drive, but a standalone Famicom redesigned to echo the curved look of the 16-bit console and use its controllers, which could also output into the Super Famicom beside it, allowing for a single signal to go into the user's television. This might be the only time this system was showcased, as it didn't reappear in a second press preview of the Super Famicom in July 1989, but the NES-101/AV Famicom that did come out in 1993 (with no SNES compatibility) had both red-buttoned controllers and a curvier top-loading design, which probably wasn't a coincidence. In the UK, *Computer & Video Games* magazine ran its own brief coverage of the November 1988 preview in its 'Mean Machines'

76

column (which would later evolve into a full publication), wrongly stating that the Super Famicom *would* support older 8-bit cartridges – but perhaps something got lost in translation.

By the time of that July 1989 preview, the form of the Super Famicom was almost finalised, with the power switch, eject and reset buttons lined up as they'd appear on the retail model (in Japan, Europe and everywhere else except North America and Brazil, anyway). The power switch and controller buttons remained red, but everything was almost there. Besides, it's really what's on a console's insides that counts, and designer Masayuki Uemura, who'd previously led development of the Famicom, had to navigate a wealth of input as to what that'd be like. Speaking to *Used Games* magazine in 2000, as archived by shmuplations.com, he said: 'Within Nintendo, there were a lot of divergent opinions and conversations being had. There were people who thought, "Everything's go to be super," and some … pointed out that everything came down to the quality of the software, so why not just put two Famicoms together and call it a day? People had all sorts of ambitions. Ultimately, we went with the following design principle: "The exterior will look like the Famicom, but the interior will be SUPER."'

Clearly, the final system's looks aren't especially evocative of the Famicom, but the console's specs were very much assembled to lean into the Super of its name. Its Sony-made S-SMP sound chip – designed by Ken Kutaragi, future chairman of Sony Interactive Entertainment and basically the man responsible for the PlayStation ever happening – was capable of the most glorious soundtracks, outshining anything tootling out of the PC Engine or Mega Drive, and its 64KB of video RAM enabled developers to implement pseudo-3D sprites with scaling and rotation. These Mode 7 visuals would come to be a famous feature of the Super Famicom, used in one of the console's two Japanese launch titles, *F-Zero*, and later in *Pilotwings*, *Secret of Mana*, *Super Mario Kart* and many more acclaimed titles.

Later, select Nintendo cartridges like *Star Fox* and *Super Mario World 2: Yoshi's Island* would use the Super FX chip, designed by British studio Argonaut Games, to generate 3D polygon visuals and produce advanced sprite effects, further widening the gap between the Super Famicom's incredible graphics and that of other 16-bit platforms. Fun fact: the Super FX's code name was MARIO, and 'Mario Chip 1' is written on the inside of *Star Fox* carts. Said Uemura of the Super Famicom's pronounced visual progression from its 8-bit predecessor, to *Used Games*: 'I thought, surely this alone (the improved graphics) won't justify people buying a brand-new console. But I was very wrong: the superficiality of the world can be quite cruel. Everyone jumped from the Famicom to the Super Famicom right away. We'd simply put lipstick on an old idea, but it was highly praised in any event.'

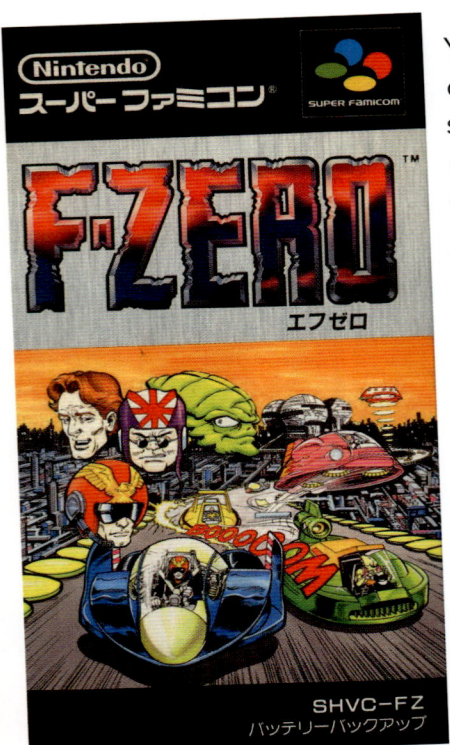

Yakuza gangs began monitoring deliveries with a view to stealing shipments, which saw Nintendo only distribute its stock after dark. A couple of weeks after the console's debut, Sharp released 14-inch and 21-inch TV sets exclusively in Japan with integrated Super Famicoms, the SF1 SNES TV. Yamauchi's hope of three million consoles sold in year one was realised too, as by the end of 1991 some 3.8 million units were in players' hands – and that was in Japan only, as another two million were sold in the United States that year.

The North American market was the natural next step for the Super Famicom – and just like the console before it, it underwent both a redesign and name change, becoming the Super Nintendo and ditching its curves for a squared-off look. Its controllers were changed too, face buttons turning two shades of purple and two of the inputs given concave fronts. While the Super Famicom had been designed with add-ons in mind – its underside expansion port would be used with the Japan-only Satellaview in 1995, which enabled users to download games, magazines and music from the internet – Nintendo of America's Lance Barr, who'd remodelled the Famicom into the NES, wasn't impressed. 'I felt it was too soft and had no edge,' he told nintendojo.com in 2005. 'We were always looking at future modular components, so you had to design with the idea of stacking on top of other components. I thought the Super Famicom didn't look good when stacked, and even by itself had a kind of 'bag of bread' look.' North American cartridges also took on a boxier form, preventing play on consoles from other territories (although many adapters were released to circumvent this region locking).

The Super Famicom released in Japan on 21 November 1990, a Wednesday, with just two games – *F-Zero* and that fourth Super Mario Bros. game, the Yoshi-introducing *Super Mario World* – but Yamauchi's promise of quality over quantity resonated with players as the console raced to over 300,000 sales in mere hours, disrupting businesses who saw workers abandon their responsibilities to try to buy one. So popular was Nintendo's new console at its launch that the Japanese government asked games companies to hold their big releases for weekends and, allegedly,

The Super Nintendo – the SNES – launched in North America on 23 August 1991 with *Super Mario Land*, *F-Zero*, *SimCity*, *Pilotwings* and *Gradius III*, a larger line-up

78

than what had been seen in Japan but still putting rich and rewarding experiences ahead of simply getting products on shelves. While the Genesis had a decent head start over Nintendo's console, having launched in August 1989, the SNES caught up across the 1990s, with between 20 and 23.3 million units ultimately sold in North America, a sizeable chunk of its worldwide total of between 41 and 49 million. While data varies from source to source, top-end estimates put the Mega Drive/Genesis at between 42 and 47 million sales – so when it comes to the 16-bit 'console war', it's probably best to call it a tie.

The Super Nintendo arrived in Europe just in time for the release of the game that would give it a considerable edge, albeit for a fleeting period, over the Mega Drive – which was selling superbly in the region. Capcom's *Street Fighter II* was an arcade smash in 1991, and between June and December 1992 its first and then-only home console port rolled out onto the Super Famicom and SNES. At the time the biggest cartridge on the console, at 16 megabits, *Street Fighter II* carried a hefty price tag of $69.99 in the US, but it was so close to the arcade game that SNES owners rushed to buy it – and those who didn't already have a SNES set about getting one. British games magazine *Mean Machines* was in awe of the port, awarding it 98%, with reviewer Julian Rignall commenting: 'If any game was ever going to sell the Super Nintendo, *Street Fighter II* is it.' And as the fifth highest-selling SNES game of all time with 6.3 million copies sold, it certainly played a huge part in the system's popularity.

Trading restrictions between Japan and South Korea saw the Super Famicom sold by Hyundai and rebranded as the Super Comboy, while toy manufacturer Playtronic picked it up in Brazil, where the design followed the North American release – the only other territory to do so. TV advertising never went quite as aggressive as SEGA's, but in the UK comedian Rik Mayall, star of the riotous comedy shows *Bottom* and *The Young Ones*, appeared regularly to promote titles like *Super Mario All-Stars*, *Star Fox* (*Starwing* in the UK), and *Nigel Mansell's World Championship Racing* (these, plus his ads for the Game Boy – games for which are SNES compatible via the Super Game Boy peripherals – are well worth finding on YouTube). In the US, a 1991 ad for the newly released console featured a pre-fame Paul

Rudd, who'd later go on to be Ant-Man in the Marvel Cinematic Universe.

SEGA released its Mega-CD CD-ROM peripheral in Japan at the end of 1991, giving the Mega Drive a little extra power visually and sonically (for all the commercial good it did) – and it had long been Nintendo's intention to also explore disc-based gaming. Having provided the SNES with its sound chip, Sony's Ken Kutaragi wanted to take the relationship between the companies further. Encouraged by Sony CEO Norio Ohga, who'd been instrumental in the development and popularisation of the compact disc format for music, he worked on creating a CD-ROM add-on for Nintendo's system. A contract was signed in 1988, with Sony instructed to develop a SNES expansion, the Super NES CD-ROM, that'd sit beneath the main console and use a new Super Disc format for its games; *and* produce a standalone all-in-one console that'd be compatible with Super Discs and SNES cartridges.

But Nintendo president Yamauchi intervened: the Sony deal conceded too much licensing control to Sony, and he wasn't prepared to progress with it. But rather than directly tell Sony that the agreement was off, Nintendo secretly struck a better deal with Dutch manufacturer Philips for the project. It only was the day after Sony revealed the prototype of its CD-ROM-and-carts console at the 1991 Consumer Electronics Show in Las Vegas that the Philips news reached Kutaragi and his colleagues. This, inevitably, carved a huge chasm between Sony and Nintendo, and in the following years not only did no Super NES CD-ROM add-on materialise, from Philips or anyone else, but Sony decided to go it alone with its console ambitions, leaving its collaborative prototype, called the Play Station, in the past. (Although, there was *something* about that name.) A later collaborative product that ran Super Famicom games, the laptop-styled HET by Bandai, was prototyped and appeared at the 1993 Tokyo Toy Show. It was cancelled soon after this showcase however, possibly because Nintendo didn't want to put another system onto the portable gaming market and risk diluting the appeal of the Game Boy.

The Super Nintendo was pushed to its fullest by both Nintendo itself and other developers through the mid-1990s, with Rare's *Donkey Kong Country* of 1994 using Silicon Graphics for its 3D-rendered visuals. Despite its release coming a few years into the SNES lifecycle, *Donkey Kong Country* is the third highest-selling game for the console (9.3m), behind only the *Super Mario All-Stars* compilation (10.5m) and the original launch title *Super Mario World* (20.6m). Further superbly celebrated SNES

80

games came out even after home consoles had already started making the move to 32-bit systems, including Square's time-travelling RPG *Chrono Trigger* of 1995 and the same developer's *Super Mario RPG: Legend of the Seven Stars* of the following year – and a redesigned SNES, the New-Style Super NES, came out in 1997 (1998 in Japan, as the Super Famicom Jr) to offer a cheap entry point for latecomers. The final official game for the Super Famicom (as it released in Japan), HAL Laboratory's *Metal Slader Glory: Directors Cut*, came out in late November 2000, a full decade after the console's launch and less than a year before the GameCube would arrive on the scene.

The Super Nintendo's official discontinuation arrived at different times in different territories. In North America the axe fell in 1999, but support remained in place in Japan until September 2003, and in the UK until May 2005. Many of the console's most well-regarded games have come out for other systems, with a range of ports – including *Yoshi's Island*, *Final Fantasy VI* and *The Legend of Zelda: A Link to the Past* – releasing on Nintendo's Game Boy Advance handheld, and many more on 3DS, Wii, Wii U and Switch via Virtual Console and Switch Online services. In 2017, Nintendo released the Super NES Classic Edition, a mini-console pre-loaded with 21 SNES titles (including the previously unreleased *Star Fox 2*), which sold five million units in six months; and in 2018 readers of *Retro Gamer* magazine in the UK voted the SNES the number one gaming system of all time. So while Nintendo's Famicom and NES inarguably transformed the company into a gaming giant, it's probably the 16-bit console that remains the fan favourite.

SNES: Five Must Plays

Super Mario World (1990)
The best Super Mario platformer, ever? Probably. The follow-up to the already incredible *Super Mario Bros. 3* isn't the most eye-popping of SNES games to play today, but its gameplay will forever feel amazing.

The new Cape Feather power-up enables Mario to fly and glide back down again, and the addition of Yoshi, who Mario can ride on, allows for fun variation across each level he's featured in. Several other refinements to a pretty much perfect formula ensure this classic of its time will always be an essential of both the SNES library and Mario series games.

Street Fighter II (1992)
Capcom's sequel changed one-on-one fighting games forever upon its 1991 arcade release, and the terrific SNES version made the console incredibly desirable the next year. With all playable characters and their signature special moves included, there's little that's compromised in this port, hence its immediate impact on the home console market. While later *Street Fighter II* iterations arguably make for more rewarding play today, going back to where it all started is hugely recommended for any fighting game fan or Nintendo enthusiast.

Super Metroid (1994)
This exploration-encouraging action-adventure game took the Metroid formula laid down by previous releases on NES and Game Boy and amped up the visual flair, the sonic uneasiness, and the all-round creepiness of the experience. Two years in the making, *Super Metroid* is an atmospheric masterclass, making full use of its hardware to put the player in the depths of the hostile planet Zebes, as protagonist Samus Aran is besieged by her enduring enemies, the Space Pirates. An inspiration on countless games over the last three decades, many of which are now classified as Metroidvanias (after this release and the similarly structured *Castlevania: Symphony of the Night*), *Super Metroid* is one of the most timeless games of the entire 16-bit era.

EarthBound (1995)
Known as *Mother 2* in Japan, Ape Inc and HAL Laboratory's quirky role-player *EarthBound* was denied an official European release until it landed on Virtual Console in 2016. Before then it was somewhat

enigmatic to those who'd never played it, looking unlike other games of its genre due to its contemporary 1990s setting and oddball tone. Once experienced, though, it proves very capable of touching the player with its storyline and overarching themes, and its streak of strange humour keeps the plot lively even when the odds at stake are massive. Dismissed by many critics at the time of its release, *EarthBound* is a game that seems to only improve with age.

Chrono Trigger (1995)
Square's RPGs for the SNES and Super Famicom are the stuff of legend. *Final Fantasy V* and *VI*, *Secret of Mana*, *Live A Live*, *Secret of Evermore* – all spectacular and worth investigating. But *Chrono Trigger* is probably the best of them all. Co-designed by Hironobu Sakaguchi, Akira Toriyama and Yoji Horii – the creators of Final Fantasy, Dragon Ball and Dragon Quest, respectively – this could have been a mess of conflicting directions and egos bumping against each other. But what came out in March 1995 was poetry: an elegiac and expansive treasure of a time-travelling adventure, now regularly cited as one of the greatest role-playing games of all time. Initially only released in Japan and North America, European SNES owners had to import this masterpiece until a Nintendo DS port came out in 2009. Said handheld version, including animated cutscenes from the PlayStation adaptation, is a great way to experience *Chrono Trigger* today, but it's much easier (and cheaper) to check out the game's widely available PC release from 2018.

Commodore's Console Woes
A huge name in home computing through the 1980s, most notably with its Amiga and C64 lines, Commodore ventured into the console world at the beginning of the 1990s. An earlier dalliance with the home gaming market, with 1982's Japan-only console-computer hybrid MAX Machine, hadn't gone well, but nevertheless Commodore would go on to make and market three systems before declaring bankruptcy in 1994 – not purely because of its poorly received gaming products, but their performances didn't help, and their final release really was a failed last roll of the dice.

First up, in December 1990, was the Commodore 64 Games System – or C64GS – which only earned an official release in the UK and Denmark at an RRP of £99.99. With tech specs virtually identical to 1982's 8-bit Commodore 64 computer and a widely disliked bundled joystick, the Cheetah Annihilator, it was even more out of touch with the console audience's tastes of the time than Amstrad's GX4000. The C64GS supported neither a keyboard nor the cassette format of the C64 itself – although the connectors for a tape player and expansion slot *are* inside, exactly where they are on a C64, just closed off by the plastic casing – with all its games releasing on ROM carts. These were more expensive than the C64's tape versions, and with the older computer already a popular gaming system few owners saw any reason to also buy Commodore's console. Fast-loading games clearly wasn't enough. As for those picking and choosing between which new games system to take home with them, nothing the C64GS offered rivalled what SEGA and Nintendo had on shelves, especially with the 16-bit Mega Drive already available.

The 1990s

Commodore had promised a lot more than it ultimately delivered, with pre-release advertising for the C64GS telling of 100 games available by the end of 1990 but only 28 coming out in total, of which only nine were exclusives. Theoretically, cartridges that played in the C64 – as the computer could support carts and discs, as well as cassettes – *should* have worked in the C64GS; but these games were largely developed with keyboard controls in mind, rendering them essentially unplayable on the joystick-only console. Press enter to continue? Good luck with that.

Technically outdated and effectively pointless given the greater flexibility of the computer it was based on, the C64GS sold somewhere between 2,000 and 20,000 units, with unsold machines reportedly converted into C64 computers. *If* sales were nearer the lower end of that range – it really is impossible to know for sure – it'd surely make the C64GS the world's worst-selling commercially released console. Commodore didn't delay in launching a second console though, with the multimedia CDTV – capable of playing games, music, movies and more – arriving in March and April 1991, retailing for £499 in the UK and $999 in the United States. Internally based on the Commodore Amiga 500, with a built-in CD-ROM, the CDTV could be expanded to a full computer with an additional keyboard and disc drive. But just like its predecessor, it failed to find an audience.

That price tag was a nail in the CDTV's coffin before it'd had any chance to impress – but damaging its chances further was the fact that Commodore itself was working on a CD-ROM peripheral for the Amiga 500, which released in 1992 as the Amiga A570 and could run all CDTV software. Bundled with a slim remote control that doubled as a game pad, with a classic D-pad and double face button layout, the CDTV may have seen greater market penetration at a cheaper RRP, appealing to those without an Amiga 500, and Commodore certainly thought it still had potential after its lacklustre launch and low sales (between 25,000 and 50,000) as development began on a costs-reduced CDTV-II. But that was canned, focus switching instead to a brand-new console based on yet another Commodore home computer.

The Amiga CD32 launched in Europe in September 1993 and looked every inch the modern gaming system, with its unusually shaped but undeniably sleek controller, top-loading CD-ROM drive (made by Sony) and chunky reset button. With 32-bit proudly plastered across its shell, this was a new-generation machine that stole a march on the SEGA Saturn and Sony PlayStation, beating both of those 32-bit consoles to market by over a year (although it released a few months after another so-called 32-bit

83

machine, the Japan-only FM Towns Marty). Technically comparable to the Amiga 1200 home computer and using the same Advanced Graphics Architecture (AGA) chipset, the CD32 could be expanded with a keyboard and disc drive to do everything the 1200 could – but as its design and controller made clear, this was first and foremost a video games console, and Commodore was feeling confident about its chances.

And why not? After all, the CD32 could do things the 16-bit systems of the time could only dream of with its 2MB of RAM and 3D visual capabilities (although these would be outshined by the PlayStation soon enough). And unlike the CDTV, the CD32 released at a far more competitive price point of $399 in the US and £299 in the UK, complete with two bundled games – in Britain, this made it cheaper than SEGA's Mega Drive CD-ROM add-on, the Mega-CD, which had launched that April for £369. And this was no mere peripheral – it was a full-on standalone console with pin-sharp picture quality, CD-quality sound and some great developers, like Team17 and Core Design, on its side.

Marketing in the UK featured comparisons between the CD32 and 16-bit hardware, showing how advanced Commodore's system was, and a celebrity endorsement was secured with radio DJ and TV presenter Chris Evans – riding high at the time due to his hosting role on Channel 4's *The Big Breakfast* – putting his hugely recognisable face behind the console. Commodore's cheekiest move was posting a massive billboard advertising the CD32 up outside SEGA's west London office, proclaiming, 'To be this good will take SEGA ages' – a play on SEGA's own tagline of 'To be this good takes SEGA'. While it never had the same level of visibility in the US, advertising materials claimed that the CD32 'beat' not only the Mega-CD but also the 3DO, Atari Jaguar and Philips CD-i. (Reader, it did not.)

Despite enjoying support from a wealth of respected developers, the CD32's games struggled to appear especially advanced when compared to their regular Amiga versions, at least in magazine screenshots. Players expected to be wowed, but games – *great* games, no doubt, in and of themselves – like Sensible Software's *Cannon Fodder*, David Braben's *Frontier: Elite II* and Adventure Soft's *Simon the Sorcerer* didn't scream next-generation gaming with their looks. Nevertheless, the CD32 outsold the Mega-CD in the UK through 1993, ultimately selling a high estimate of between 75,000 and 100,000 units across its limited markets. But it was nowhere near enough. Commodore was struggling financially before the console's release, largely in North America where the CD32 made next to no impact at all, and its commercial performance came nowhere near to reversing the company out of the red. The CD32 was discontinued in late April 1994, having been on sale for just seven months, and Commodore's voluntary bankruptcy was announced a week later.

Largely forgotten by all but collectors in the years since its abrupt demise, the CD32 enjoyed a semi-revival in early 2022 as Retro Games Ltd's THEA500 Mini console – a plug-and-play device shaped like a tiny Amiga 500 and pre-loaded with 25 games – released with a controller shaped almost exactly like the one that came with Commodore's final console. The Mini also supports emulation for the CD32 – and, indeed, the whole Amiga range – meaning that owners could run the entire CD32 library on it. It's a morally and legally dubious area, but it's an option – and probably the best one for players nowadays as original (and working) CD32 consoles are hard, not to mention expensive, to come by.

PC ENGINE DUO

Manufacturer: NEC

Released: September 1991 (Japan), October 1992 (North America)

An all-in-one combination of the PC Engine and its Super CD-ROM² add-on, the PC Engine Duo offered newcomers to NEC's range the chance to get plenty of bang for their buck in a sleek and stylish single unit. With its HuCard slot hidden away when not in use and a top-loading CD-ROM drive, this new system was far tidier than having the original console and its similarly sized peripheral stuck together (and *much* easier on the eye than the American TurboGrafx-16 with its CD-ROM drive plugged into its rear, which must be one of the ugliest fusions of hardware in console gaming history).

And with the PC Engine a popular platform in Japan, it was warmly welcomed, selling close to two million units and ultimately enjoying two later revisions after its 1991 launch: the PC Engine Duo R in 1993, which swapped dark grey casing (carried over from 1989's PC Engine CoreGrafx) for the more traditional PC engine white; and 1994's PC Engine Duo RX, which traded the two-button pad that'd always been bundled with NEC's consoles for a six-button version more suited to fighting games.

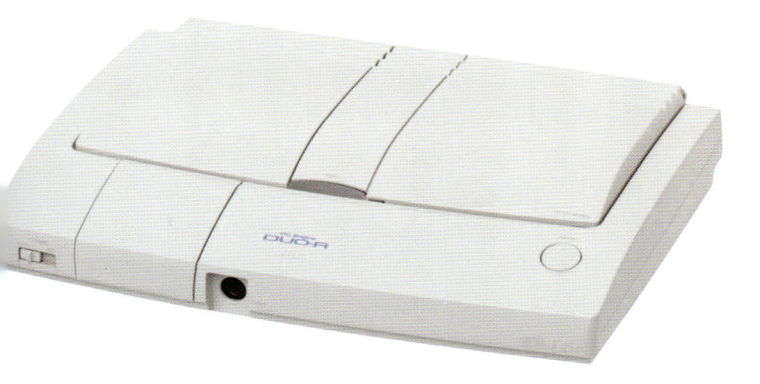

Named the TurboDuo for its North American release in 1992, NEC's combi-console struggled against the SEGA Mega Drive and Super Nintendo – perhaps unsurprising given that the TurboGrafx-16 hadn't been a huge seller beforehand. A first production run of 20,000 units reportedly didn't sell out in the territory, with leftover stock sold off via mail order and, several years later, whatever remained was listed on eBay. NEC ceased support of its consoles in the States in 1994 but remained an active presence in the Japanese market for much of the 1990s, even releasing a successor to the PC Engine and PC Engine Duo in 1994: the 32-bit PC-FX.

While its six-button pad told consumers that this was a games console, the form of the PC-FX was comparable to a tower-style home computer. With 1989's SuperGrafx quickly forgotten, NEC intended for this to be the true next step up from the PC Engine and its CD-ROM expansions and variants. But by the time of its release in late December 1994, exclusively in Japan and off the back of another aborted 32-bit console code-named 'Tetsujin' ('iron man'), Japanese players already had the Sony PlayStation or SEGA Saturn to opt for instead. The PC-FX received poor reviews from the games press of the time, criticising its lack of 3D graphics and poor software support as many third-party studios only had eyes for SEGA and Sony's 32-bit consoles.

The PC-FX's high retail price of ¥49,800 – approximately $500 at the time, and ¥10,000 more than the PlayStation – further hindered its appeal, yet NEC maintained support for the console up until its discontinuation in February 1998. By then between 120,000 and 290,000 units from a production total of 400,000 had been sold and 62 games (many of which were anime-style visual novels) released – a drop in the ocean of the PC Engine and PC Engine Duo's combined total of almost eight million console sales and over 660 titles in the same market. Bruised by this commercial failure, NEC never released another gaming console again.

CD-I

Manufacturer: Philips

Released: December 1991 (North America), April 1992 (Japan), July 1992 (Europe)

Making slightly more of a splash than the comparably marketed Commodore CDTV, the Philips CD-i was a multimedia device that could play your music CDs (including ones with added graphics capabilities, like showing lyrics on your TV), photo CDs, movies so long as you installed the sold-separately Digital Video Card expansion, and even video games. It was also a system that took an awful long time to make it to store shelves, with development of the CD-i (Compact Disc Interactive) format having commenced in 1984, led not only by the Dutch company Philips but also Sony, and revealed to the world at a 1986 conference run by Microsoft – an announcement that reportedly took even Microsoft CEO Bill Gates by surprise. Further support for the format came from Matsushita, better known as Panasonic.

And Philips' own gaming history went back even further. In 1978 the company had put out the Videopac G7000 console, which was also sold as the Magnavox Odyssey 2 as Philips had bought Magnavox in 1974, and before that had its own Tele-Games range of dedicated games consoles (not to be confused with Sears' *Pong* console, also called Tele-Games, but equally basic). The CD-i was something altogether bolder, however, its debut commercial model arriving on 3 December 1991 and immediately outpunching much of the gaming competition – at least when it came to hardware.

With a custom 16-bit CPU based around a Motorola 68000 offering some capabilities comparable to the 32-bit consoles that were still a few years from release – and a CPU that ran at 15MHz too, twice as fast as the Commodore Amiga and SEGA Mega Drive – as well as 1MB of RAM and a palette of 16.7 million colours, putting it far ahead of the Super Nintendo's 128k of RAM and 32,768 colours, this was clearly a very capable

piece of hardware, albeit one that'd taken a long while to reach consumers. However, the first CD-i to be released at retail, the front-loading American CDI 910 (labelled the 205 in Europe), was priced at $799 in the US and around £600 in the UK, which compromised any widespread appeal immediately. And while the price fell over time, what didn't pick up was the quality of games available for CD-i consoles – over 120 were released between 1991 and 1998, but few made players content with SEGA, Sony or Nintendo titles turn their heads to what Philips was offering.

The CD-i range – including a commercially released top-loading model, the 450, which took on a more traditionally console-shaped form; portable versions including 1993's Sony-manufactured Intelligent Discman; several other non-retail Philips-made lines including the 'professional grade' 600 series; and a host of models badged by other brands including Magnavox and Grundig – supported a variety of controllers, including TV-like remotes, keyboards, mice and the kid-friendly Roller Controller. But only one of them, the 22ER9021 CD-i Gamepad, really resembled a conventional gaming peripheral, with an ergonomic shape akin to a Mega Drive pad. Others were widely mocked for their unsuitability for the console's games, which ranged from sports titles to point-and-click puzzlers via full-motion video affairs and platformers, with the (typically) 450-bundled wired controller especially disliked for its central D-pad with action buttons either side.

The most infamous games to have released for the CD-i are those featuring Nintendo's Legend of Zelda and Super

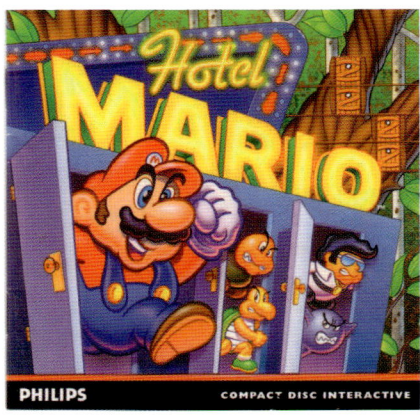

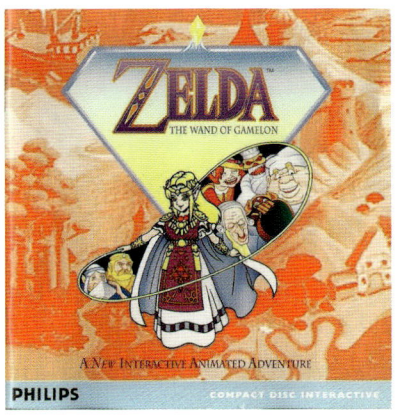

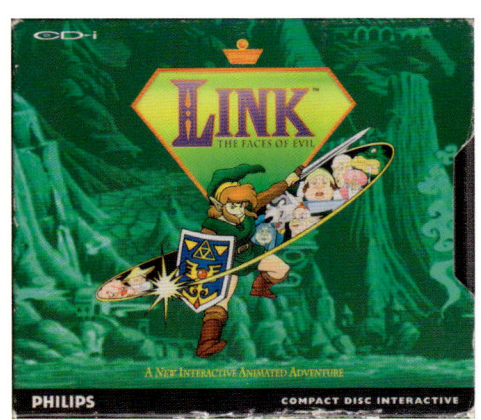

Mario characters. A 2D puzzle game, *Hotel Mario*, was released in 1994 and featured Nintendo's mascot shutting doors and jumping on or over enemies across a succession of single-screen challenges set across seven Koopaling-managed hotels. It features the usual power-ups, like Fire Flowers and Super Mushrooms, and can be played with a friend who controls Luigi. A side-scrolling platform title, *Super Mario's Wacky Worlds*, was in development for the CD-i as a direct sequel to *Super Mario World* on the SNES, but it was cancelled long before its code was anywhere close to being completed.

Three Zelda games came out for the CD-i. *Link: The Faces of Evil*, *Zelda: The Wand of Gamelon* both released in 1993, and then came 1996's *Zelda's Adventure*. The first two Zelda titles feature ropey animated cutscenes full of questionable dialogue, so too *Hotel Mario*, and these have become better known through comedic memes than via the games themselves. While often cited as some of the worst games ever made, these CD-i Zeldas aren't without any merit, and are notable for making Zelda a playable character in two out of three releases. They stand up poorly beside Nintendo's own efforts though, plagued as they are by diabolical controls and lengthy load times. They came about due to Nintendo and Philips having agreed to collaborate on a CD-ROM drive for the SNES, and while that add-on was never completed the terms of the contract allowed Philips to use Nintendo licences with nearly no input from Nintendo itself. Nowadays, these curios are only of significance to collectors as they're not much fun to play.

The CD-i was officially discontinued in 1998 with total system sales of between 570,000 and a million depending on which estimate you look at, but Philips had largely left the system on life support since a multi-million-dollar marketing campaign of 1994 failed to boost sales significantly, and it sold the CD-i games library to Infogrames in 1996. That same French studio would put out the last-ever official CD-i game, the FMV rail shooter *Solar Crusade*, in 1999, after which it was game over for Philips as a presence in the home gaming market.

CD-I: Play One Game

Burn Cycle (1994)

Stylised as *Burn:Cycle* on its cover art, this point-and-click detective game with shooting sequences and frustrating puzzles was marketed as an exclusive to draw people away from other systems and finally realise the potential of Philip's hardware. It didn't quite work out that way, but it's still the game to play first. The Burn Cycle of the title is a cyber virus that implants itself in hacker protagonist Sol Cutter's brain, and the cyberpunk-y storyline is a fun mix of ridiculous dialogue and high-stakes tension as the game only gives you two hours to reach its (good) conclusion before Cutter's mind self-destructs. The gameplay isn't much – steer your cursor to shoot guards, to go into a different room, line up puzzle pieces, it's all fairly basic. But visually, this game sizzles with creativity. Some will see it as an aesthetic mess, others a masterpiece of outré ambition dressed up in dreamscape vibrancy. *Burn:Cycle* also released for PC and Mac in 1995, but versions for PlayStation and Saturn were cancelled, making the CD-i its sole console home.

MEGA-CD

Manufacturer: SEGA

Released: December 1991 (Japan), October 1992 (North America), March 1993 (Australia), April 1993 (Europe), October 1993 (Brazil)

SEGA's Mega-CD – known in North America as the Sega CD – was its makers' retaliation against NEC's CD-ROM² add-on for the PC Engine and the Super Nintendo, which had emerged offering superior graphical capabilities when compared to the Mega Drive. This CD-ROM add-on sat beneath the Mega Drive in its original configuration – the Mega Drive II would receive its own Mega-CD II, which slotted beside it – offering a look very similar to hi-fi separates. As well as games, the Mega-CD could play audio compact discs and CD+Gs, the same visuals-enhanced releases that would run on the Commodore CDTV and Philips CD-i. Unlike those systems however, SEGA's first venture into the world of CD-ROM technology brought with it a host of terrific games.

Despite the Mega Drive's stateside success as the Genesis, development of the Mega-CD was undertaken under highly secretive circumstances in Japan, with SEGA deciding not to initially share its plans with the North American team. When SEGA of America did get wind of the new peripheral being developed though, there was great enthusiasm and optimism about its chances – at least once they felt there were enough games in the works with American audience appeal. In June 1991, SEGA's new product was revealed to the whole world at the Tokyo Toy Show, albeit with no actual games beside it. Nevertheless, the hardware spoke volumes.

A second Motorola 68000 CPU worked with the one inside the Mega Drive (albeit faster, running at 12.5MHz) to boost performance. A custom graphics processor allowed for effects beyond those of Mode 7 on the SNES, with even the Mega-CD's start-up screen showing off impressive scaling and rotating tricks, and polygon effects were also supported. Audio was now of CD quality, allowing game soundtracks to evolve and scripts to have full voice acting. And full motion video was supported, streamed directly from the disc, so that players could enjoy games with live-action actors, albeit only interacting with the action in fairly minimal ways. The Mega-

89

CD looked impressive – but at its launch, consumers with high expectations were left somewhat underwhelmed.

While the Mega-CD would receive games that really utilised its graphical capabilities, such as the brilliant *Sonic CD* with its 3D special stages and the polygonal fighter spaceships of *Silpheed*, Japanese launch games *Heavy Nova* and *Sol-Feace* appeared with no obvious visual enhancements over their previous 16-bit incarnations on the Sharp X68000 computer. (That said, *Sol-Feace* did take advantage of the Mega-CD's audio power and featured a sublime soundtrack.) At ¥49,800 it was an expensive addition to a Mega Drive owner's set-up too, and its launch price of $299.95 and £269.99 in the US and UK respectively also saw buyers think twice. But its positioning as an add-on and not a standalone console proved beneficial in some ways as SEGA was able to work with developers otherwise locked into exclusive deals with Nintendo, leading to an incredible, better-than-the-arcade port of Capcom's *Final Fight* that put the SNES version to shame.

Over time, the asking price of the Mega-CD fell, and its library expanded to include some genuine all-timers – although some of them now sell for silly money on the second-hand market. Konami's cyberpunk graphic adventure *Snatcher*, directed by Metal Gear Solid creator Hideo Kojima, has its one and only English-language release on the Mega-CD. The fantasy platformer *Popful Mail* and bizarre horizontal shooter *Keio Flying Squadron* are brilliantly colourful and quirky takes on their genres, and the aforementioned *Sonic CD* is one of the SEGA mascot's greatest 2D games with an incredible soundtrack to boot (in the Japanese and European release, anyway). And while the Mega-CD's FMV games were criticised for their pixelated footage and limited interactivity, games like *Ground Zero: Texas* and *Night Trap* were enjoyed by many players and have received high-definition re-releases for modern platforms.

After the costs-reduced Mega-CD II of 1993, SEGA combined the Mega Drive with its CD-ROM add-on as the Multi-Mega – aka the Sega Genesis CDX in America and Sega Multi-Mega CDX in Brazil – in April 1994. This delightfully compact console was small enough to also be used as a portable CD player using batteries but had to be plugged into the mains (and a TV) to work as a games machine. Its US launch price of $399.99 was a lot though, and even SEGA itself considered the Multi-Mega something of a novelty rather than a mainline product and stopped production when another Mega Drive add-on, the 32X, was released. The Mega-CD itself was officially discontinued in 1996, with SEGA's attentions switched to the Saturn.

But the Multi-Mega wasn't the only option for buyers wanting a Mega Drive and Mega-CD in a single unit. Manufactured and initially sold by Victor (JVC) and later badged by SEGA itself, the Wondermega hit Japanese retailers in April 1992, just months after the Mega-CD's release in the region, giving consumers an attractive all-in-one option (albeit one priced above buying the two separate products). The Wondermega was redesigned in 1993, adding an infrared controller receiver and including a wireless six-button pad, and in April 1994 a lightly modified version of this model was released in the US as the JVC X'Eye.

A few months later, in September 1994, Japan received another exclusive Mega Drive-and-Mega-CD combo in the shape of Aiwa's boombox-styled CSD-G1M, one of the rarest Mega Drives ever released. This looks just like a regular piece of stereo equipment until you lean in and see that it has a cartridge slot beneath its single cassette deck, with the top-loading CD player running the CD-ROM games. The CSD-G1M also came with its own controllers, blue three-button pads bearing both Aiwa and SEGA branding. At the time of writing, the one CSD-G1M on eBay is on sale in Belgium for 3,500 euros, and that's with a damaged speaker. One for the dedicated collector only, then.

Mega-CD: Play One Game

Sonic CD (1993)

Sonic CD is simply one of the greatest games to ever feature SEGA's blue blur of a mascot. Its time-travel mechanic, which sees Sonic race into the past or future of levels to destroy machines his arch enemy Robotnik has put there, was criticised by some for slowing the pace of the game down – but taken as a different kind of Sonic title, more about exploration than speed, *Sonic CD* shines magnificently. Stages are masterfully designed, with all manner of routes to take and new obstacles and enemies added to proceedings, and the original Japanese score (changed for the North American release) is one of the best you'll hear coming out of any 16-bit hardware. *Sonic CD* sold 1.5 million copies worldwide, making it the Mega-CD's best-selling game, and has been ported to several other platforms in the years since its release. In 2022 it was one of the four Sonic games featured on the *Sonic Origins* compilation, which represents the easiest way to play it today.

Rarely Sighted Systems

The mid-1990s saw SEGA and Nintendo challenged by Sony, whose PlayStation of 1994 laid the foundations for a phenomenally successful series of systems that continue to be huge sellers to this day. Atari was in the mix too, with the Jaguar and its CD add-on, and the 3DO managed to slice off a tiny portion of the market for itself. But these were far from the only consoles taking their shots, trying their luck, and, in the cases of the below-collected systems, ultimately ending up somewhere between failure and irrelevance.

Which isn't to say there's anything especially bad about the FM Towns Marty, which was produced by Fujitsu exclusively for the Japanese market and released in February 1993. With its AM386 processor running at 16MHz and 2MB of RAM under the hood, this was a diminutive powerhouse capable of a palette of over 16 million colours and running both CD-ROM and 3.5-inch floppy discs formats. (The same size discs you used in your old Amiga or Atari ST, but don't go sticking your copy of *Superfrog* into one of these.) Backwards compatible with the games of the FM Towns home computer, upon which its internal architecture is based, and for many considered the world's first 32-bit console, the FM Towns Marty really could have been a contender in Japan *if* its launch price had been lower, a lot lower, than a staggering ¥98,000 – nearly four times the initial RRP of the Super Famicom and PC Engine.

Despite strong support from developers like Psygnosis, Taito, Namco, Electronic Arts and even SEGA – ports of *Columns*, *Turbo Outrun* and *Galaxy Force* appeared on the console – the Marty just couldn't convince enough people that it was worth its asking price, and total sales reached a high estimate of 75,000 units prior to discontinuation in 1995, well below Fujitsu's hopes of a million in year one. This number includes sales of a revised model, the grey-shelled FM Towns Marty 2, which released in 1994 at a lower price. But given that price was still ¥66,000, it made little difference to the machine's chances. A third version of the console was made for cars and included GPS compatibility. This bizarre idea was 1994's Car Marty MVP-1, and it did everything its home console predecessor could do *plus* direct you home from the supermarket. It also cost around ¥250,000 for everything you needed to make it work to its fullest, so you can already imagine how popular it proved to be.

The Bandai Playdia, released in September 1994, is another Japan-only console that barely registered with players elsewhere in the world. It only played FMV games, many of which were aimed at children and featured Bandai-owned franchises like Sailor Moon, Ultraman and Dragon Ball Z. Compatible with a single infrared controller that was neatly stored away in the console – no multiplayer here – the Playdia was a short-lived system as Bandai's attentions turned to something rather grander.

Designed by future-iPhone-makers Apple and running on the Mac OS 7 operating system, the Pippin was a computer-console hybrid first licensed by Bandai, who built, distributed and marketed Apple's 'advanced technology' (so says the box). It launched in Japan at ¥64,800ß, branded as the white-shelled ATMARK, and in the United States in June 1996 as the black-shelled @WORLD ('At World'), for a price of $599. Both versions featured a distinctive controller, shaped like a boomerang and featuring a trackball at its centre.

Despite the huge RRP – twice the cost of a brand-new PlayStation – Bandai's expectations were big. It predicted 300,000 Pippin units sold in North America and 200,000 in Japan in the first 12 months. But by the end of 1997 only around 42,000 systems had been sold, and only 20 games released. Norwegian company Katz Media also licensed the Pippin technology, producing the Katz Media Player 2000 in 1997. But Apple cancelled the Pippin platform that very same year, laying off over 4,000 employees and leading to Katz Media filing for bankruptcy in 1998. Bandai suffered heavy financial losses of some ¥26 billion, around $214 million, but survived thanks to the success of its Tamagotchi digital pet range, which had launched in late 1996. It even released another console range, the handheld WonderSwan, in 1999, which sold steadily until 2003.

The Pioneer LaserActive reached Japanese stores in August 1993 and debuted in North America the very next month, taking the multimedia machine concept to a new level. Out of the box it would play LaserDisc movies (and a

92

selection of LaserDisc LD-ROM games), compact discs and karaoke software, but its singularly neat trick was its expandability with special region-free modules – available at extra cost – that enabled it to play Mega Drive and PC Engine games. The Mega LD PAC module came bundled with a specially branded six-button pad and allowed for use of both Mega Drive/Genesis cartridges and Mega-CD discs, while the LD-ROM² PAC opened up the PC Engine library across HuCard and CD-ROM formats. But these were expensive add-ons, costing $600 each, and with the LaserActive itself retailing for $970 Pioneer only sold 40,000 base units before discontinuing the platform.

Other low-selling and rarely remembered consoles of the decade include the Memorex VIS (Visual Interactive System), arguably more a featured-stripped Windows PC than a console proper. The VIS was made by Tandy Electronics and sold only in the US by RadioShack in 1992, with a focus on educational software. Its sales only reached a top estimate of 15,000, almost certainly because of its limited distribution and high RRP of $699, later reduced to $399 for all the good the discount did.

Gaming giant Capcom put out a console of its very own in 1994, only in Japan, but the CPS (Capcom Power System) Changer was restricted to mail-order sales only and exclusively used arcade motherboards for its games. Eleven games were made available for it, which meant plugging the boards into a special adaptor, including *Street Fighter II: Champion Edition* and *Knights of the Round*, and a chunky fight stick helped it feel like the arcade experience at home. The CPS was Capcom's take on the Neo Geo AES, but it never caught on in the same way due to the odd way in which it was marketed and sold, and how the games weren't conventional cartridges, and Capcom quietly dropped it in early 1996.

In October 1995 the China-only Super A'can console was released, but its 16-bit specs and cartridge-based design (it even looks like an American Super Nintendo) made it immediately behind the times. It was discontinued in April 1996 with sales totalling no more than 20,000, losing its makers Funtech – a subsidiary of the semiconductor company UMC – over six million US dollars, which saw the company closed. Also released in 1996, the simplistic Casio Loopy was ostensibly aimed at the female market, as the Super Lady Cassette Vision had been in the mid-1980s. Mercifully a lot less pink than said older system, the Loopy's most unusual feature was an integrated thermal printer, allowing users to print out stickers made using its small library of ten games (including the fantastically named *Bow-Wow Puppy Love Story* and *I Want a Room in Loopy Town!*). It sold, at most, 200,000 units between release and its discontinuation in 1998.

3DO INTERACTIVE MULTIPLAYER

Manufacturer: Panasonic, Goldstar, Sanyo

Released: October 1993 (North America), March 1994 (Japan), June 1994 (Europe), December 1994 (South Korea)

In 1991, nine years after founding the software publisher Electronic Arts and having previously been the director of marketing and strategy at Apple, Trip Hawkins (pictured below) needed a new challenge. He found it not with a new video game series or a specific piece of gaming hardware, but with a concept of a gaming standard, like VHS or CD, that could be used by countless manufacturers to underpin their own consoles. He founded The 3DO Company and set about developing a system of industry-leading spec that could be sold to others for production and marketing.

The hardware for the 3DO Interactive Multiplayer was designed by a team led by David Needle and RJ Mical, who'd worked on Commodore's Amiga line of computers and co-created the colour handheld Lynx console released by Atari (but not originally made for them – but that's a story for another book). A 32-bit ARM60 CPU was installed, alongside a custom co-processor, 2MB of RAM and 1MB of VRAM. The 3DO could generate up to 16 million pixels per second and supported 16-bit stereo sound and compact disc audio. After two years of development, Hawkins and his colleagues had themselves a monster in comparison to the 16-bit consoles of the time – and there were a few suitors ready to license their design and take it to market.

First out of the blocks was Panasonic, whose FZ-1 R.E.A.L. 3DO released in the US on 4 October 1993 for a recommended RRP of $699. Stockists immediately saw a problem with this, adding their own discounts of up to $100 to encourage sales. Hawkins himself would later state that it was never the intent for the 3DO to be marketed at such a price – but the deal that The 3DO Company struck with its partnered manufacturers meant that they were paid a fee on every single console sale, which pushed the price above SEGA and Nintendo systems that were more often sold at a loss knowing that their games would make the money back. As a hardware manufacturer primarily, Panasonic needed to also profit on each 3DO sale, hence the exaggerated asking price. Over time, the cost of a new 3DO did come down – models from South Korean company GoldStar (the GDO-101 Alive, GDO-101M and GDO-203P Alive II) and Sanyo (the Japan-exclusive

IMP-21J TRY) launched at lower prices, and Panasonic's own costs-reduced redesign of 1995, the FZ-10, could be found for around $300 – the same price as a PlayStation.

Just as interesting as the names that did sign up to the 3DO are those that didn't. Hawkins met with Sony and said that they'd seriously considered licensing the technology in the same way that Panasonic had. At the time, the PlayStation was far from being finalised, and Hawkins says that they came close to signing a deal. Ultimately Sony chose to stick with what its R&D department was working on – had it not, the history of console gaming would have looked very different. SEGA was also on 3DO's list of potential partners, and SEGA of America CEO of the time Tom Kalinske did meet with Hawkins in Tokyo but felt that the complexity of the product and its high cost didn't fit his plans. Like Sony, SEGA would release its own 32-bit console, the Saturn, not long after the 3DO's emergence. Another company, the telecoms giant AT&T, was in line to produce the 3DO for the American market, but its model never got past the prototype stage.

Over 200 games would release for the 3DO between its release and discontinuation in late 1996, but at launch there was only the one when ten had been promised: *Crash 'n Burn*. This violent arcade racer is notable not only for being the only thing to play at the time, but also for being the first game made by Crystal Dynamics, a studio that'd later make games for the Tomb Raider franchise, develop the Gex series, and produce several Legacy of Kain titles. Even with its high price and slow software support, the 3DO was attracting admirers: it was named *Time* magazine's Product of the Year for 1993 and the games industry got very excited around every conference preview. The games media wasn't universally positive though – while optimistic coverage ran in early issues of *EDGE* magazine, *Electronic Gaming Monthly* actually named it the worst console of 1993. More contemporary assessments of the 3DO have flip-flopped between naming it one of the most underrated systems of its era and one of the worst of all time.

Across its multiple models, the 3DO range sold more than a million units, its highest-selling game being the later pack-in game *Gex* (again, Crystal Dynamics with the bundled title). An advanced-spec follow-up system known as M2 (pictured below) was planned and prototyped, initially as an expansion to the original 3DO and later a standalone console. Panasonic signed an exclusive deal to take it to market and sought a partnership with SEGA to firm up its position – but the project was cancelled in 1997 after developers got cold feet, sceptical of the hardware's actual capabilities, and the proposed SEGA partnership collapsed. In promoting the 3DO, Hawkins spoke of how he saw CD-ROM being the dominant format in the five years after his console range's release, and he predicted that SEGA and Nintendo would be scrambling to keep up with companies like his. And he was certainly right about one thing.

3DO: Play One Game

Road Rash (1994)

The 3DO has its share of stinkers – a wretched port of *DOOM*, the bizarre rocker-trapped-in-VR shooter *Virtuoso*, and the adults-only romantic 'comedy' *Plumbers Don't Wear Ties*. But the console's unique 1994 version of EA's motorcycle scrapper *Road Rash* is sublime, its digitised sprites popping loudly and lashing out with plenty of weight against a soundtrack featuring bands like Soundgarden and Therapy?. In a change to previous series entries' gameplay, including the already highlighted Master System version, this *Road Rash* featured branching routes in each race, and both bikes and riders have their own health bars. While *EGM* had been incredibly critical of the 3DO in 1993, the magazine went out of its way to praise *Road Rash*, with it earning several of its game of the year awards. The game was subsequently ported to the American Sega CD, PlayStation, Saturn and PC, and the digitised sprites returned for the Mega Drive/Genesis-exclusive *Road Rash III* in 1995.

ATARI JAGUAR

Manufacturer: IBM

Released: November 1993 (North America), June 1994 (Europe), August 1994 (Australia), December 1994 (Japan)

A powerhouse that never had its full potential realised as developers failed to truly harness its capabilities, the Atari Jaguar represents the final console that really used 'bits' as a marketing measurement of quality. TV and print adverts for the system asked consumers to 'Do The Math', suggesting that the 16-bit SEGA Mega Drive/Genesis and 32-bit 3DO were nothing in comparison to the 64 bits of high-intensity gaming action the Jaguar could deliver. But the Jaguar was home to far more games that looked like 16-bit titles than ones bursting with new-generation sights and sounds, and its games industry legacy is a mix of reassessments deeming it underrated and unfair mockery at its design and peripherals.

The Jaguar was one of two consoles in development for Atari Corporation in the early 1990s. The company's CEO Jack Tramiel had stepped away from the business, leaving his son, Sam, in charge. Atari's home computers were selling well enough, but Sam still saw a place for the brand in the console market, despite the relative failures of the XEGS and 7800 and a 16-bit system, the Super XE, never making it past prototyping. Atari reached out to a British company, Flare Technology, whose Flare One system was widely admired among hardware developers and would have been used in the Konix Multisystem console, had that machine ever made it to market. Its next notable project, Flare II, would be bought by Atari and used as the basis for both of its console projects: the 32-bit Panther and the 64-bit Jaguar. Both the Panther and Jaguar used a 16-bit Motorola 68000, much like the one found inside the Mega Drive, alongside custom graphics and sound chips. In the Panther these were called Otis and Panther, while in the Jaguar Tom was a 32-bit graphics processing unit with a 64-bit blitter (a memory management coprocessor) and 64-bit object processor, and Jerry a 32-bit digital signal processor with CD-quality sound. The 68000 inside the Jaguar was meant to be used to manage Tom and Jerry and not as the primary CPU for software – but as the games library for the console expanded, it became apparent that many developers were focusing on this older component for 16-bit ports (games like *Cannon Fodder*, *Pinball Fantasies* and *Theme Park*) rather than making the most of the Jaguar's 64-bit power.

The Panther was cancelled in 1991, despite development kits being at several studios and production of games under way, leaving the focus entirely on the Jaguar and its 64 bits. Not that everyone in the games media accepted the console as a 64-bit system, what with Tom and Jerry ultimately being 32-bit processors. But just as on-paper inferior hardware had outperformed superior competition before the Jaguar's release, its emphasis on the horsepower under the hood wouldn't count for much when the games available lacked the appeal of those on SEGA and Nintendo consoles, as well as the 3DO and PlayStation.

The Jaguar debuted in North America on 23 November 1993 for $249.99, less than the 3DO, and initially performed modestly at retail with test-market sales in New York and San Francisco totalling around 17,000 units. The console's pack-in game, the polygon-graphics shooter *Cybermorph*, didn't look especially advanced when placed beside the Super Nintendo's Super FX chip-powered *Star Fox*, which had come out at the start of the year (it later transpired that the game had been developed at first for the Panther, somewhat explaining its shortcomings), and the three other launch titles – *Raiden*, *Dino Dudes* (aka *The Humans*) and *Trevor McFur in the Crescent Galaxy* – all featured 2D gameplay akin to that seen on older consoles. Not the best first impression, and while sales did pick up in North America, the Jaguar's Japanese launch was disastrous, with only around 5,000 units sold in the territory. Europe was a different story however, with demand reportedly incredibly high for the Jaguar in the lead up to Christmas 1994. As many as 250,000 units were requested for the region – but manufacturer IBM, who'd been brought on in a $500m deal to produce the consoles, could only deliver 50,000 before the end of the year, leaving consumers and retailers disappointed.

The Jaguar's regular controller was divisive, much larger and less obviously ergonomic than competing systems' pads, but it has enjoyed some hindsight appreciation in more recent years. Its D-pad and three-button layout is standard (a six-button Pro Controller followed in 1995), but the 12 numerical keys allowed for some handy quick-access options unavailable on other consoles and come in very handy for tense shooters like the Jaguar's (really rather good) port of *DOOM* and its much-hyped-at-release exclusive *Alien vs Predator*, both of which arrived in late 1994. There were other celebrated titles released for the Jaguar that did make use of Tom and Jerry, including *Tempest 2000*, *Iron Soldier* and *Wolfenstein 3D*, but so many other releases appeared the same at first glance as 16-bit versions, leaving players unimpressed by this supposed 64-bit titan.

In 1995 the Jaguar received a CD-ROM drive – cruelly compared to a toilet, but you can see why – which only received 13 official games and did little to boost the console's flagging sales. A local area network adapter called the JagLink only supported a measly three games, but at least Jaguar owners could buy it. Not so much a long-promised virtual reality headset for the Jaguar, which was scrapped alongside a dedicated modem for online play and a standalone hybrid console, the Jaguar Duo, that combined cartridge and CD-ROM compatibility in the same way as SEGA's Multi-Mega. (Speaking of SEGA, the Japanese giant purchased $40m of shares in Atari Corporation in 1994, for all the good it did.) Also planned at one stage was compatibility between the Jaguar and Atari's Lynx handheld, which would have served as a second screen on select games, becoming a motion tracker for *Alien vs Predator*.

There were clearly lots of good ideas surrounding the Jaguar, but few of them came to anything, and with total worldwide sales by the end of its discontinuation in 1996 sitting at around 150,000, despite several price cuts, its commercial struggles were obvious. The PlayStation disrupted the market as few predicted, with Atari and SEGA both guilty of publicly underplaying its potential, and the Jaguar was killed off with tens of thousands of units unsold and only 63 cartridge games released. A 'Jaguar 2' console, code-named Midsummer (its twin chips named Oberon and Puck, after Shakespeare's *A Midsummer Night's Dream* characters) and offering backwards compatibility for its predecessor, was planned but never properly prototyped, and the Atari name and all its properties were bought by Hasbro Interactive in 1998. The Jaguar remained Atari's final home console until 2017 when the *new* Atari VCS was revealed, a microconsole that (at the time of writing in mid-2022) has only received a very limited release in select markets.

But 1996 wasn't quite the end for the Jaguar. Hasbro relinquished its rights to take a licence fee from anyone developing games for the console or its CD-ROM add-on, leading to many post-discontinuation releases and a strong homebrew scene. The moulds used to create the console's shell were sold to Imagin Systems in 1997, which used them to produce a dental imagery device called the HotRod camera. The same shell was used by Retro VGS's Retro Chameleon game console in 2015 when it appeared on crowd-funding platforms Kickstarter and IndieGoGo, but the console – which later carried the Coleco name – raised only a fraction of its $1.95m target. It was cancelled before a planned 2016 release having become embroiled in controversy: a public showcase of the console at the New York Toy Fair revealed it to be New-Style Super NES hardware poorly hidden behind a Coleco-branded Jaguar-style case. Whether or not it was ever going to be a genuine system or was simply a scam that failed, nobody can be sure – but Coleco withdrew from the project when a functional prototype couldn't be produced and independently assessed, and that was the end of the Chameleon.

Jaguar: Play One Game

Alien vs Predator (1994)
It's not as smooth or satisfying to play as *DOOM* is on the Jaguar, but this first-person shooter based on the popular sci-fi franchises is a hugely atmospheric and tense experience, even with its jerky animations and inconsistent collision detection. Developed by British studio Rebellion, *Alien vs Predator* allows the player to be an acid-for-blood xenomorph, a Predator hunter or a human marine, each of whom have their own campaigns. The game sold well, with high estimates of 85,000 units (representing an attachment rate of over 50% for Jaguar owners), and a CD-ROM sequel was in discussion prior to the Jaguar's discontinuation. But while that second game never materialised for Atari's hardware, Rebellion did put out *Aliens Versus Predator* for PC in 1999, and further AvP titles for the PlayStation Portable and home consoles in the 21st century.

SATURN

Manufacturer: SEGA

Released: November 1994 (Japan), May 1995 (North America), July 1995 (Europe)

A console that kept its code name right through to its release, SEGA's Saturn is where the Japanese company, which enjoyed such successes in Europe with the Master System and in North America with the Mega Drive/Genesis, came somewhat unstuck. And the misfortune that befell SEGA in the mid-1990s was almost entirely of its own making, independent of the competition from the Sony PlayStation and Nintendo 64.

Saturn development hit its stride in 1993 led by Hideki Sato, who'd overseen the creation of the Master System and Mega Drive. That year, SEGA partnered with Hitachi to produce a new CPU for its new console. Named the Super-H RISC Engine, or SH-2, the Saturn would use two of these in tandem alongside six other processors including two handling video display and two sound. Originally using only one SH-2 processor, SEGA added a second to give the Saturn greater 3D graphics capabilities in response to learning of Sony's PlayStation. Sato would later say that the PlayStation specs he saw were incorrect, but nevertheless the dual-SH-2 set-up did allow the Saturn to pull off polygonal visuals that one processor alone would have struggled with. But this architecture was not popular with SEGA of America, whose Tom Kalinske wanted to form a partnership with computer hardware firm Silicon Graphics.

That didn't happen, but Silicon Graphics did ultimately join forces with SEGA's biggest rival to develop the Nintendo 64.

The Mega Drive had been comprehensively beaten by the Super Famicom in Japan, but when the time came to launch the Saturn in SEGA's home territory on 22 November 1994, it went exceptionally well. Its launch price of ¥44,800 was competitive in the CD-ROM-based console space – far less than the ¥79,000 launch RRP of the 3DO and the ¥98,000 of the FM Towns Marty – and the initial shipment of 200,000 units sold out within a day, driven by the Saturn's high-quality port of the hugely popular arcade game *Virtua Fighter*. SEGA didn't resupply retailers until 3 December – the same day that the PlayStation launched in Japan, and for less money than the Saturn – but despite this brief period of unavailability and the fresh competition from Sony, SEGA's new console ended 1994 with between 500,000 and 840,000 units sold – far ahead of the PlayStation's 300,000. Six months into 1995 and the Saturn's Japanese sales had passed a million. Hitachi also released its own HiSaturn-branded consoles in Japan, including the Game & Car Navi model, which was semi-portable with an optional flip-up LCD screen and could be powered from a vehicle's cigarette lighter socket.

It was in mid-1995 that the Saturn made its entrance into the North American market – but this was a far rockier process than what had happened in Japan. In early 1994,

SEGA president Hayao Nakayama was worried about the competition facing the Genesis in the States and Canada, especially the potential of the newly released Atari Jaguar. Knowing that the Saturn wouldn't be on sale there until 1995, he told SEGA of America to respond with something to inject longevity into the 16-bit console – and this is how the 32X came to be.

A mushroom-shaped add-on for the Genesis (and Mega Drive, obviously) that slipped into its cartridge slot but necessitated its own power supply, the 32X – which lost its 'Mars' code name before release – effectively turned a 16-bit machine into a 32-bit one. It ran on the same SH-2 CPUs as the Saturn, albeit with them running slower, and used cartridges rather than CD-ROMS (although a handful of disc games were made that needed the Mega-CD and 32X add-ons to run). Released in November 1994 in North America, and the next month in Europe and Japan, the 32X raced to 650,000 sales – but that pace slowed when it became obvious that SEGA was more focused on the Saturn and couldn't split itself between two 32-bit platforms at the same time, so why buy the one that wasn't going to be supported. The 32X was phased out in 1996 with total sales of around 800,000, and a standalone console capable of playing both Mega Drive and 32X cartridges, called the Neptune (pictured above), never made it past prototyping.

With the 32X already causing consumer confusion outside of Japan, SEGA made a far greater misstep on 11 May 1995 at the inaugural E3 games industry conference in Los Angeles. Encouraged to get ahead of PlayStation in the North American market, SEGA of America brought the release date of the Saturn forward and Kalinske announced its immediate availability on stage at E3 for a price of $399, bundled with *Virtua Fighter*. Not a bad price, and while the game wasn't as big in the US as it was in Japan, this represented a decent pitch. What wasn't so good for SEGA was its choice of who to let in on their big secret before revealing it to the world. Only select retailers had been sent some of the Saturn's initial stock of 30,000 units, including Toys 'R' Us and Babbage's (the chain that would later become GameStop), and those left in the dark were incensed. One, KB Toys, responded by announcing that it would no longer stock SEGA products.

But then came greater damage, this time not of SEGA's own doing. The PlayStation was due to get its North American release date announcement at the same E3, and

Sony Computer Entertainment president Steve Race wasted no time when it was their turn in the spotlight to stick the knife in. He walked up and spoke three words: 'Two nine nine.' The PlayStation wouldn't be out in North America until September, four months after the Saturn, but its US$299 price point was a huge blow. SEGA responded, reducing the Saturn to the same price in October 1995, but it was too late – by the end of the year Sony had sold 800,000 PlayStations, double the amount of Saturns in the territory. This must have stung Kalinske, who had said in *EDGE* magazine's April 1995 issue that he hoped that the PlayStation would 'turn out to be another Betamax', and that Sony's games 'don't make any sense… I think we're ahead of them in the software line-up area'.

Any price drop was hard for SEGA to take, as it was already making a loss on every Saturn sold. 'For each Saturn sold, we lost about ¥10,000,' Sato said in a 2018 interview conducted as part of a SEGA oral history (translations later published on sega-16.com). 'The goal was to recoup the losses from software royalties. However, if software sales are weak, for each console sold, we're ultimately losing ¥5,000 to ¥6,000. What's going to happen from the business perspective? We're going to stop selling consoles.' And that's precisely what SEGA did, slowing down hardware distribution to lower these losses. 'Even though there were people who wanted to buy the console, SEGA didn't want to sell it,' Sato continued, 'because the more they sold the more they went into the red.

'With recognisable SEGA series that were popular in North American and European markets absent on the Saturn – there was no new mainline Sonic game, no Streets of Rage, no Phantasy Star – it struggled to replicate its Japanese success overseas despite a series of great arcade conversions including *Virtua Cop* and *Sega Rally*. While at home it achieved 5.75 million sales in total, almost two million more than the Mega Drive sold in the region, by the end of 1996 the Saturn's stateside sales were 1.2 million, well behind the PlayStation's 2.9 million. And by 1997 the global picture for SEGA was looking bleak – PlayStation owned 47% of the worldwide console market, Nintendo 40% now that its N64 was available, and SEGA had just 12%. At the end of 1997 SEGA posted its first net loss since 1988, finding itself ¥39 billion short of breaking even. The axe fell on the Saturn in Europe and North America in 1998, with Japanese support continuing until 2000. Its lifetime total sales reached 9.25 million – less than 10% of the PlayStation's global sales of over 100 million.

Bernie Stolar, who arrived from Sony Computer Entertainment America to take up the position of president of SEGA of America in 1998, was dismissive of the Saturn on several occasions, stating: 'I thought the Saturn was a mistake as far as hardware was concerned.' But while external developers did struggle to make games for the Saturn and its multiple CPUs, in the right hands it could do wondrous things. Its twin SH-2s could produce more polygons per second than the PlayStation, and those with a background in 3D games could make it sing. One such person was Yu Suzuki (pictured below), the director of SEGA arcade games like *Virtua Racing* and *Virtua Fighter*, and producer on *Daytona USA*. He even prototyped the 3D open-world adventure game *Shenmue* on the Saturn before its development switched to the Dreamcast.

Nevertheless, 3D games had been an afterthought, which further compromised the Saturn's chances as player tastes shifted from sprites to polygons, with Sato telling online magazine Beep21 in 2021: 'In the beginning I wasn't thinking of 3D capabilities for the Saturn – but additionally, the game developers at

SEGA had basically no knowledge of 3D game development. The only developers who had real experience with 3D were Yu Suzuki and AM2 (arcade R&D team) with the Virtua series.' Sato wasn't oblivious to another factor in the PlayStation's triumph over the Saturn though, saying in 2018 what Kalinske couldn't in 1995: 'It was obvious that the PlayStation had the better games. No matter how much effort SEGA put in on its own, it wasn't going to be enough.' And even before the Saturn's release, the chairman of Sony Computer (now Interactive) Entertainment Ken Kutaragi cheekily asked Sato if SEGA would consider abandoning hardware and making games for the PlayStation, offering them preferential treatment. SEGA said no, feeling positive about what its 32-bit system. But one console later, one failure later, the decision to stick or twist would effectively be taken from them.

While the Mega Drive has enjoyed countless game compilations and two mini-console releases in the 21st century, and many Dreamcast games have been made playable on other platforms, the Saturn and its library has remained largely locked to the mid-1990s. And as more time passes between those games' releases and today, the greater the interest grows in revisiting them. But in a 2022 interview with Japan's *Famitsu* magazine, SEGA hardware producer Yosuke Okunari confirmed that there were no immediate plans to make a Saturn Mini, in the mould of the popular Mega Drive products. Citing the difficulty of emulating Saturn software and the expense of the components needed to create such a mini-console, Okunari suggested (perhaps jokingly) that even if SEGA could make such a thing, its retail price might rival that of the PlayStation 5 and Xbox Series X. Therefore, anyone wanting to play the best of the Saturn today has little choice but to buy an original console and spend a lot of money on individual games. For now, anyway.

Saturn: Five Must Plays

Virtua Fighter 2 (1995)
SEGA's sequel to its 3D fighter of 1993 used motion-capture technology to make its combatants move more fluidly than before, and it translated its arcade success of 1994 to its Saturn port the following year. Two new characters were added, each fighter's move set was expanded, and texture mapping was used to make the game pop in a different way to the clean polygons of the original game. Director and producer Yu Suzuki spearheaded development of a new operating system for the Saturn, the SEGA Graphics Library, which enabled the home version to be as close as possible to the arcade experience. Critics and players alike were impressed, and *Virtua Fighter 2* for Saturn was the third highest-selling game in Japan in 1995 and won several game of the year awards.

Sega Rally Championship (1995)
Another brilliant Saturn arcade conversion that showed that it really could rival the PlayStation for 3D visuals, *Sega Rally Championship* is AM3's coin-op classic turned into a home-console stunner. Whereas the initial Saturn version of *Daytona USA* had disappointed, *Sega Rally* did quite the opposite with reviewers praising its high-speed visuals and power-sliding fun. Scores of over 90% were commonplace and the Saturn release went on to sell 1.2 million copies – thankfully making it one of the cheaper games to buy nowadays.

Nights into Dreams (1996)
The Saturn didn't receive a proper, mainline Sonic game – but SEGA's Sonic Team did produce *Nights into Dreams*, a free-flowing

102

action game where the aim is to fly through rings within a tight time limit. You do this as the character Nights, but the game's real protagonists are Elliot and Claris, teenagers who find themselves trapped in a dream world. They merge with Nights to navigate dreams, defeat bosses, and ultimately foil the plans of the big baddie Wizeman, who aims to destroy both this realm and the real world. A festive-themed spin-off, *Christmas Nights*, was released at the end of 1996, and *Nights into Dreams* received a sequel on Nintendo Wii, *Nights: Journey of Dreams*. *Nights into Dreams* is also one of few Saturn games to receive a remake, as it did on the PlayStation 2 in 2008, and high-definition release of the original came out in 2012 on PC, Xbox 360 and PlayStation 3.

Die Hard Arcade (1997)

This polygonal beat 'em up might carry the Die Hard licence in Europe and North America, but it's really just a reskin of a terrific Japanese brawler called *Dynamite Deka* (*Dynamite Detective*). Don't be surprised then when John McClane comes up against a grenades-tossing firefighter-gone-bad, a Mexican wrestler and spider-shaped robots on his way to rescuing the US President's kidnapped daughter, because this doesn't follow the plot of any of the movies. It's a brief but rewarding game, best played with two players where co-operative combos can be used on bad guys, and its quick-time event sequences are fun, with instant replays showing your fist connecting with your adversary's face.

Panzer Dragoon Saga (1998)

A role-playing spin-off from the earlier shooter titles in this series, *Panzer Dragoon Saga* is both one of the Saturn's most celebrated games and one of the most expensive to find today. Mixing real-time and turn-based combat with open-world adventuring (often on the back of a dragon) and a storyline that sees protagonist Edge battle a sinister artificial intelligence supported by a handful of allies, *Saga* was SEGA's response to the PlayStation's *Final Fantasy VII*. Its popularity at the time didn't match Squaresoft's worldwide hit, with sales so poor that SEGA held something of an internal inquest, but critics were wowed by *Saga*, awarding it countless high scores. Several of its developers at SEGA's Team Andromeda studio, which disbanded after its release, would go on to create another rail-shooter-style Panzer Dragoon title in the shape of 2002's *Panzer Dragoon Orta* for Xbox – and while demand for a *Saga* re-release or remake grows every year, so far nothing has been announced.

PLAYSTATION

Manufacturer: Sony Electronics

Released: December 1994 (Japan), September 1995 (North America, Europe), November 1995 (Australia)

'Do it.' Rarely have words from employer to employee been so direct, and so forceful, as when Sony CEO Norio Ohga told company engineer Ken Kutaragi to press ahead with his proposal for a radical, CD-ROM-based gaming console, designed and made exclusively by the Japanese technology giant. Previously, Sony's upper management had been wary of video games, considering them toys or a fad that'd pass soon enough. This was the attitude even while they were publishing games, via Sony Imagesoft, for platforms like the NES, standalone console that'd run both the Super Famicom's cartridges and the CD-ROM games, which would come on an all-new disc format that Sony was calling the Super Disc. At the 1991 Consumer Electronics Show in Las Vegas, Sony proudly revealed its all-in-one console, the Play Station, for the first time – a blocky yet boldly designed system with a cartridge slot on the top, a CD tray at the front, and specially branded SNES-style controllers. It successfully merged Sony and Nintendo aesthetics, and the conference was buzzing with excitement for what it was seeing. Sony was on a high – but the very next day news emerged that Nintendo was backing out of the partnership, choosing instead to pursue its CD-ROM ambitions with the Dutch company Philips.

Nintendo's reasoning was that Philips was giving them a better deal, as the Super Disc format rights were entirely Sony's, and they'd also profit the most from sales of the Play Station console. For Nintendo president Hiroshi Yamauchi this was a double threat: firstly, to Nintendo's revenues on the co-operative venture; and secondly, it'd position Sony – until then seen as a lowly player in the gaming market – as a potential rival of great strength, another SEGA to compete against at retail. Naturally, Kutaragi and his team were confused and bruised, and then outright incensed. There had to be retribution.

And it wasn't only Sony's Japanese divisions who wanted to strike back at Nintendo, as Sony America went to SEGA of America in the aftermath of the backstabbing to discuss a potential teaming up. SEGA president Hayao Nakayama wasn't into the idea, however, with SEGA of America CEO of the time Tom Kalinske later telling IGN in 2013: 'We went to Nakayama and the Board at SEGA, and they turned me down. They said, "That's a stupid idea, Sony doesn't know how to make hardware. They don't know how to make software either. Why would we do this?" That is what caused the division between SEGA and Sony and caused Sony to become our competitor.'

Burned by both Nintendo and SEGA, Kutaragi got his green light for Sony to

Game Boy and Mega-CD; manufacturing MSX home computers in Japan; and as they were working with Nintendo on a CD-ROM peripheral for the Super Famicom/SNES. But when the deal with Nintendo collapsed, and Kutaragi (pictured above) – who'd been instrumental in the design of the sound chip for the SNES – told Ohga of the opportunity, not simply for Sony's bottom line but also to strike back against a reneging Nintendo who'd very publicly hung them out to dry, he had but one clear instruction: 'Do it.'

Now, the exact exchange between Kutaragi and Ohga might have gone slightly differently to the account above, but what the former took into that meeting and how the latter responded to it is in no doubt. Sony had signed a deal with Nintendo in 1988 to collaborate on two projects: a CD-ROM add-on for the then-in-development Super Famicom, and a press ahead with its own system. Initially conceived as something that still used CD-ROM and SNES cartridges, with up to 200 prototypes of this design produced, the reception to the likes of the Philips CD-i and Commodore's CDTV told Kutaragi that whatever Sony came out with needed to be substantially different, genuinely cutting edge, and capable of pushing video gaming as a medium to a new level of cultural appreciation. As Nintendo's deal with Philips fizzled out, leaving only some ropey Nintendo licence games on the CD-i as tangible evidence of there ever being a partnership, and SEGA's *Virtua Fighter* showcased how real-time 3D graphics were going to wow gamers going forward, a new concept came into focus: the PlayStation-X.

On 27 October 1993, Sony formally announced that it was entering the home console market with its own system. Soon after, on 16 November 1993, Sony Computer Entertainment was formed and started negotiating exclusive deals with third-party developers – as unlike Nintendo and SEGA, Sony wasn't set up to make its own games. The likes of Namco, Capcom and Konami were convinced by what this new PlayStation-X, or PSX, was promising: a 32-bit CPU capable of complex 3D visuals, a maximum of 360,000 flat-shaded polygons per second, 16.7 million colours, 24 sound channels and full-motion video of a quality far ahead of other CD-ROM consoles. And while Sony could have followed Commodore, Philips and more down the multimedia route, it had only one aim: to be a video gaming juggernaut powerful enough to shake up the international market shares of SEGA and, more importantly, Nintendo.

Sony's closest competitor in terms of both technical specifications and release timing would be the SEGA Saturn, and in some respects this rival system outshined the PlayStation, which lost its 'X' before reaching retail. The Saturn's polygon potential was greater than the PlayStation, with some 700,000 per second possible with its two main CPUs optimised. The Saturn could also run incredibly detailed 2D sprites effortlessly, whereas the PlayStation's architecture featured no dedicated 2D graphics processor. But Sony knew that talk of processors and chips was even more boring to players in the mid-1990s than which console had the most 'bits', and that it was the quality of the games that'd make PlayStation's reputation.

'We looked at the business models of all of the companies in the [gaming] space, or that had tried to get into the space, and we asked ourselves: could we do this better?' said Sony Computer Entertainment's Kaz Hirai to the gaming TV channel G4, in a show looking back at Sony's debut console around the time of the PlayStation 2's launch. Phil Harrison, now vice president at Google

The 1990s

and at Sony between 1992 and 2008, added to the same PlayStation documentary: 'We knew in order to be successful we had to capture the hearts and minds of the developers and the publishers equally.' And that's exactly what PlayStation achieved, successfully signing up Namco's incredible arcade game *Ridge Racer* as a launch title and buying acclaimed UK studio Psygnosis to make the likes of *Wipeout* and *G-Police* for PlayStation first and foremost. Not that Psygnosis was instantly impressed by its new owners, with the company's co-founder Ian Hetherington telling *MCV* in 2015 that the PlayStation was 'not fit for purpose when we got involved with it', adding: 'The thing that made PlayStation cool, beyond any shadow of a doubt, was *Wipeout*.'

Several console-selling exclusives, 'killer apps' if you will, would land on PlayStation in quick succession. *Wipeout* in 1995, featuring music from the Chemical Brothers and Orbital, was followed by Namco's exciting arcade fighter *Tekken 2* in 1996; Squaresoft's 10-million-selling role-playing game *Final Fantasy VII*, previously in development for Nintendo consoles, came out in 1997; Konami's stealth-action masterpiece *Metal Gear Solid* in 1998; and the same studio's survival-horror classic *Silent Hill* in 1999. This regular turnover of exceptional titles saw the second half of the 1990s dominated by the PlayStation, which moved ahead of the Saturn in sales through 1995 and couldn't be caught by the Nintendo 64 when it came out in 1996. By the time of its discontinuation in March 2006, as Sony switched focus to the PlayStation 3 while maintaining support for the PS2 and PlayStation Portable, the original PlayStation had sold more than 102 million units, over three times the sales of the N64 and ten times the Saturn.

But when the PlayStation launched, there was no certainty that it'd succeed in the way it did. Its strategy of aiming for older players, those ready to leave the mascots of Mario and Sonic behind, was a risk – Harrison would tell G4, 'Everybody wants to be 19 – if you're 12, you want to be 19, and if you're 25 you really want to be 19 again, so 19 was the communication tone of voice.' That was a new way of thinking for games marketing, specifically focusing on young adults. Launch sales in Japan of 300,000 by the end of 1994 were good but some way short of the Saturn's, with players in the region more confident of SEGA's hardware than Sony's despite the PlayStation launching for ¥39,800, ¥5,000 less than its rival.

In the gaming press, *Next Generation* magazine commented that the PlayStation's CPU was average at best, and Japan's *Famitsu* awarded the PlayStation a score of only 19/40. But again, Sony's hardware was only half the story – it was the games that'd turn the tide in Japan. The release of *Final Fantasy VII* in 1997 helped PlayStation sell a massive 4.4 million consoles in one year, overtaking the Saturn in the process. It then rubbed salt in the wound in 1998, adding 6.1 million sales in 12 months, more than the Saturn would sell in Japan in its entire lifetime.

In North America, the famous E3 of 1995 – where Sony announced the PlayStation would go on sale for $299, $100 less than the Saturn – gave the console a head start that it would never let slip. And in Europe the PlayStation similarly forged ahead, outselling the Saturn by three to one in the UK in its first few months, and in 1997 over 50 British night clubs opened dedicated PlayStation rooms, further emphasising that this machine wasn't a kid's toy. Refusing to rest on any laurels, Sony refined its PlayStation hardware, adding an improved disc drive (some early models had to be turned upside down to work after a lot of use), evolving its audio- and video-out options at the rear of the console, and offering greater control within virtual 3D spaces with an all-new pad, 1997's Dual Analog Controller. This twin-stick model would set a new standard for games consoles, with most subsequent systems echoing its design, and was further revised in the DualShock, which added vibration feedback to the player's on-screen actions. As for those famous face-button symbols, the controller's designer, Teiyu Goto, told *Famitsu* in 2010: 'The triangle refers to viewpoint – I had it represent one's head, or direction. Square refers to a piece of paper, [representing] menus or documents and I made it pink. The circle and cross represent yes or no decision making, and I made them red and blue respectively.'

As well as its new versions of the standard PlayStation, Sony released the Net Yaroze in 1997, a development kit that anyone could purchase, allowing them to create their own games and share them – sometimes online, sometimes via magazine demo discs. These systems resembled regular PlayStations but were black rather than grey and could be connected to the user's PC. A redesigned PlayStation, sold at a reduced price (just $99 in the US) and featuring a slimmer, curvier and brighter shell, arrived in July 2000 just a few months after the release of the PlayStation 2. This smaller console, known as the PS One, sold exceptionally well, outperforming the PS2 in 2000 and offering users the option of attaching a dedicated flip-up LCD screen to the unit, effectively making this a semi-portable system (you still needed access to mains power, making it comparable to the PC Engine LT).

What *was* portable, however, was the Japan-only PocketStation, an official PlayStation-compatible memory card released in 1999 that featured a tiny 32x32 pixel LCD display so users could play mini-games while on the move. This was Sony's first handheld console, *ish*, not 2004's PlayStation Portable. Further official peripherals for the PlayStation included the odd-looking Analog Joystick, which only released in Japan; the local multiplayer-enabling Multitap allowing four pads and memory cards to be used in one of the console's controller ports; a mouse, used for a healthy selection of games including strategy and first-person shooter titles; and a link cable for connecting two consoles.

With some 7,900 games released (including regional variants, updated versions and special editions) and those total sales of over 100 million, the PlayStation (including its PS One revision) is indisputably one of the most successful and important games consoles ever released. When SEGA's vastly superior Dreamcast released in 1998, it couldn't do much to dent its appeal, and even Nintendo had to concede its place as the world's leading gaming manufacturer in the late-1990s as Sony's machine gobbled up an incredible 47% of the global console market. The combined might of the PlayStation and its successor, the PS2, was a huge factor in SEGA's decision to cease operations as a hardware manufacturer, and both the PS2 and PS4 ultimately overtook the PlayStation – these days commonly referred to as the PS1 – in sales, showing that Sony's achievement was no fluke. A dedicated mini version of the PlayStation, the PlayStation Classic, was released in late 2018 with HD output, two controllers and 20 built-in games, and remains available to this day.

'I remember the then-chairman of Nintendo saying that if we ever got to a million units, he would resign, as he clearly knew nothing of the games business,'

Harrison recounted to G4 in the channel's PlayStation documentary. 'It took him a few more years to get around to it, but I thought it was a great statement.' Add to that a comment from Nintendo's Shigeru Miyamoto – 'The claim that Sony… would be able to sell as much hardware as Nintendo sounds uncertain,' he told *EDGE* magazine in 1995 – and you can clearly see an attitude that really encapsulates the story of PlayStation, in the 1990s. First seen as a company to be discarded as a partner and then largely ignored as a commercial competitor, Sony proved every detractor wrong, ending the decade in such a strong position that to this day the PlayStation brand is probably the strongest of any in the home gaming market. It rose from insignificance to rule over the old guard in a way that few could have predicted when the drama of CES 1991 was unfolding, or when CD-ROM gaming on consoles was struggling to find a foothold. In the 2020s, the PlayStation brand motto is 'Play Has No Limits' – and looking back at that first console it's easy to see how its makers regarded any boundaries, any expectations, as only there to be broken. From 'do it' to 'done it', and so much more.

Playstation: Five Must Plays

Ridge Racer (1994)
Namco's phenomenal arcade racer was converted to the PlayStation with incredible attention to detail, essentially rebuilt from the ground up to become a hugely desirable launch title for all the console's major markets. Fast loading times (thanks to the game loading into the console's RAM before the title screen – that's why there's a game of *Galaxian* to keep you occupied) combined with great responsiveness, music and texture-mapped visuals made it a critical and commercial hit, although the absence of a two-player mode was a missed opportunity.

Resident Evil (1996)
Resident Evil was developer Capcom's spiritual follow-up to its own creepy horror game for the Nintendo Famicom, 1989's *Sweet Home*. Known as *Bio Hazard* in Japan, it follows a team of special police agents into a spooky mansion full of zombies and mutated creatures, later revealed to be infected with the T-virus. Hugely atmospheric and mixing tense action with brain-tickling puzzles, *Resident Evil* was an early essential for any PlayStation owner – and while it's received superior sequels and a brilliant remake in the years since, there's still something compelling about taking this ground-breaking original for a spin.

Castlevania: Symphony of the Night (1997)
A rare PlayStation classic that sets its action in two dimensions rather than full 3D, Konami's 13th Castlevania release turned out to be its luckiest, as slow initial sales gave way to widespread critical acclaim and unanimous contemporary praise (the result: original PS1 copies sell for big money nowadays, but thankfully it's playable on other platforms). Players must explore every inch of the game's setting, Dracula's castle, hunting for items to unlock further progress and backtracking to previously inaccessible areas in a style comparable to The Legend of Zelda's dungeon design. It, alongside *Super Metroid*, is responsible for the popularisation of the so-called Metroidvania sub-genre of action-adventure games, its non-linear structure hugely influential on countless games released in its wake. Interestingly, development of *Symphony of the Night* began for SEGA's 32X, leading one to wonder how that add-on's fortunes may have differed had it released for it and not the PlayStation.

Final Fantasy VII (1997)
Another PlayStation hit that began life elsewhere, with development starting on the Super Famicom and testing carried out on the Nintendo 64 before makers Squaresoft elected to partner with Sony, *Final Fantasy VII* might be the most important role-playing game of all time. With its epic story of greedy corporations and environmental disasters, dramatic turn-based battles and stirring music that fully immerses them in the drama, it won several game of the

year awards and boosted sales of the PlayStation by several million. Declared by some to be the best game of all time when it was released, it achieved over ten million worldwide sales to become its platform's second highest-selling game after *Gran Turismo*. The first part of a full remake of the game was released for PlayStation 4 in April 2020, with its second chapter due out for the PlayStation 5 in 2023 or 2024.

Metal Gear Solid (1998)
Directed, produced and written by Hideo Kojima, *Metal Gear Solid* is its primary creator's love letter not only to stealth games but also cinema, as it plays out in the manner of a Hollywood blockbuster with several in-engine cutscenes and strong voice acting. Called a 'sneak 'em up' in some quarters of the games press, it often left the player with no weapons, necessitating smart navigation of its stages to proceed. Inarguably an incredibly influential title, *Metal Gear Solid* is also fun to play today even if you've little interest in its more convoluted sequels, and its fourth wall-breaking elements are as timeless as the appeal of video gaming itself. Be sure to have a DualShock in hand for this one.

Playstation Collector Spot
Duncan Aird from Cardiff in Wales explains how he went from a FIFA game in the late 1990s to a PlayStation collection running to over 1,000 games, and why the PlayStation Classic failed to truly represent what the console was all about in miniature form.

'The very first PlayStation game I ever played was, in a rather uneventful reveal, *FIFA: Road to World Cup 98*. My closest friend had a PS1 before me and was a big FIFA guy (still is), so I'd go team up in his kitchen against the CPU. The game didn't blow me away, but what did was the audio in it. Anybody who's played *FIFA 98* will undoubtedly be a fan of Blur's 'Song 2' from the opening intro. The commentary during the matches was shockingly smooth and natural for the action on screen, at least to my nine-year-old ear, and the voices themselves were clean and clear. So, for my next birthday, it was a no-brainer what I was going to ask for.

'The PlayStation was love at first play, undeniably and without hesitation. I'd played several of my friend's N64 games before, but after playing a PlayStation game with full CD quality soundtracks, voice acting, and what felt like more in-depth gameplay was brand new for me at the time. So for my 10th birthday in 1998 I was gifted *the* PlayStation from my parents. But I wasn't sure what games I wanted with it. Before this the greatest extent of my home console gaming was playing *Super Mario World* on a Virgin plane ride thanks to Nintendo's Gateway System. So, like any child would in this position, I asked for one of everything – leading to the first PS1 game(s) I ever picked up being *Gex 3D: Enter the Gecko*, *V-Rally*, and *FIFA 98*.

'The love I have for this console is so unconditional, so unequivocal, that those very same games from the 10th birthday still sit proudly on my shelf today – the precise copies. The entire console holds a special place in my heart, from a nostalgia and technological perspective, and my heart has never wavered from the PS1. Not since that day. And that was a huge benefit when it came to building a collection, as it has been incredibly rare for me to ever sell any PS1 games after picking them up. Unless they're sealed (a form of collecting that does not interest me, personally) or in a genre I'm fully aware I will never play properly.

'From 1998 until around 2010 my collection grew rather naturally, grabbing handfuls of PS1 games every month or so – often choosing new PS1 titles over buying healthy food during my university years. By the time graduation came around I had 200 or so games to my name – a lot, to be sure, but by no means an obscene collection. After university though, disposable income became grander and things quickly spiralled out of control in late 2014. However, the peak really hit in 2016 between Halloween and Thanksgiving where my collection grew from 400 PS1 games to 600 – an average of around seven games per day. By 2018 the tally was officially over 1,000.

'Through pure chance I avoided the beginning of the retro price boom, which really got stupid in late 2016 and early 2017. Before then car boot sales and charity shops were good pick-up spots, and eBay hadn't been riddled with worldwide resale prices yet. To build the collection I have today would be a shocking amount of money, but a very high percentage of my PS1 games were picked up for between £1 and £10 over those years, with only the most special or specific of titles convincing me to hand over more significant cash. Five years ago, *Castlevania: Symphony of the Night* would set you back around £150–200 (as mine did), but now it sells for over £500 regularly. I feel very fortunate to have started collecting when I did.

'When it comes to most-prized items in my collection, there are three things: my 'Blockbuster PlayStation Challenge' disc, an ASCII Sphere 360 controller, and a copy of *Chaos Break*. The Blockbuster Challenge Disc was found in a bundle of 15 or so ex-rental discs and was simply another random disc in the wallet, like any of the other games. I later learned it was never intended for sale and was for the UK Games Tournament 1997 where selected stores would hold contests to see who could get the fastest lap time on *Rage Racer*, and the 28 fastest times nationwide went on to compete in the finals in London. The controller is simply one of the most ludicrous accessories I've seen for a home console. The thing has a giant ball on it and is designed to give full 360-degree 3D movement using the ball alone. It works, it's pretty dumb, but it's incredibly niche and bizarre – I love it. *Chaos Break* is a beautifully bleak survival horror game, and while not the rarest or most expensive game on the platform, it is incredibly difficult to find now in perfect condition. Back pre-2016, before (British second-hand games retailer) CEX put retro games into their official pricing system, each store would just throw on whatever price felt right. My copy of *Chaos Break* was found for the princely sum of £15 and is in such perfect condition I'd not be surprised if nobody before me ever played it.

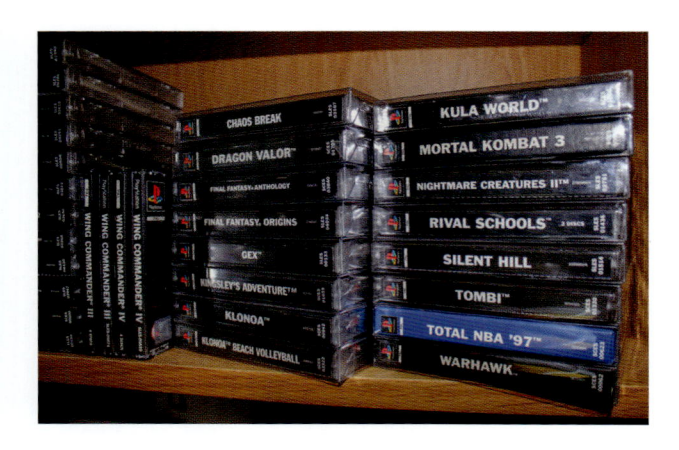

'I have so many personal favourite PS1 games. The Spyro the Dragon trilogy games have a very special place in my heart. *Kingsley's Adventure* doesn't get the love and recognition it deserves as a superb 3D action game – and it's still exclusive to the PS1. *Ape Escape*, as one of the first games to fully utilise the DualShock's two joysticks. *Tombi* and its sequel are fantastic platformers, and it's a travesty they're not more readily available. *Nightmare Creatures* still horrifies me, and it and its sequel should be put alongside *Silent Hill* and *Clock Tower* as one of the best horror games of the era. There are lots more – which is illustrative of why the PlayStation Classic was doomed from the start (and I say this as somebody who owns one and loves it). The original PlayStation's greatest strength, which I do believe still holds up, is the breadth of experiences in the library. This is what doomed the PlayStation Classic: everybody who grew up with the PS1, or was into the console at any point previously, was going to find the included games limited. If you ask ten PS1 fans for their ten favourite games, you'd be unlikely to find any crossover aside from the heaviest of hitters.

'The original PlayStation is a not only a glimpse into how still-running franchises were shaped, with many holding strong to this very day, but into such a wide pool of titles which only exist on the PS1. Not all of these franchises began life on the system, of course, but many evolved into the form we know and love now because of the PlayStation: Metal Gear Solid, Final Fantasy VII, Gran Turismo, Tekken, Tomb Raider, Crash Bandicoot, Resident Evil, Tony Hawk's Pro Skater, Oddworld, Silent Hill (RIP), Grand Theft Auto – and these aren't hidden gems buried in the console's library, they're only some of the most obvious contenders. And the spate of remakes we've seen in recent years just goes to show what a huge impression these PS1 games left on players.'

NINTENDO 64

Manufacturer: Nintendo

Released: June 1996 (Japan), September 1996 (North America), March 1997 (Europe, Australia)

The story of the Nintendo 64 doesn't begin with the Japanese gaming giant whose name is slapped across the front of the console, but with American computer hardware and software manufacturer Silicon Graphics, Inc (SGI). Known for its incredibly sophisticated 3D graphics workstations, used to create the CGI dinosaurs of *Jurassic Park*, SGI was keen to move into the home console market and had developed a new CPU based on the 64-bit MIPS R4000 microprocessor used in its

Indigo, Indy and Onyx systems. It used only a quarter of the power of its previous designs and could be sold for $40 per unit instead of up to $200. It seemed ideal for mass usage in a commercial consumer product, and this led the company's founder, Jim Clark, to make a series of proposals to video game console manufacturers who might be interested in using their new technology. SGI met with SEGA, who reportedly found flaws with the chips they were presented with, and some accounts suggest The 3DO Company also passed on a deal.

Undeterred, SGI revised its design and in early 1993 Clark flew to Japan to speak with Nintendo president Hiroshi Yamauchi – and this meeting went rather better. On 20 August 1993, reports surfaced that SGI was about to announce a partnership with Nintendo to, as *United Press International* put it in their coverage, 'compete with upstart 3DO Company in the potentially lucrative field of leading-edge video game machines'. The news pushed SGI's stock price up and The 3DO Company's down, and three days later the alliance was made official at a press conference in San Francisco: under the code name of Project Reality, the pair would collaborate on new-generation video gaming hardware of unprecedented specs. A release date of late 1995 was given alongside a retail price of $250, and this would be a true 64-bit games console, unlike the Atari Jaguar that ran on two 32-bit processors. This wasn't the first time that Nintendo and SGI had worked together, as the American company had created an audience-reactive 3D Mario face for trade conferences (*very* similar to one that'd welcome players to the mascot's N64 launch title), but this was a huge step into the unknown for them. And that soon began to cause problems.

The Project Reality team got to work, initially using a modified Super Nintendo controller with an analogue stick and additional Z button to test how games would run on its new hardware. On 23 June 1994 the far-from-finished console was given a name: the Ultra 64. This wouldn't stick though, and after alternative names for different territories were discussed – the Ultra Famicom for Japan and the Nintendo Ultra 64 elsewhere – a decision was made to use just one, worldwide: Nintendo 64, swiftly shortened by players everywhere to N64. (In a reference to the earlier moniker, all N64 model numbers for hardware and software begin with 'NUS' – 'Nintendo Ultra Sixty-Four'.) The console's unique-looking design, curvier than the PlayStation and Saturn and with four controller ports instead of two, was revealed towards the end of 1994, without a controller but beside a ROM cartridge, confirming that Nintendo wouldn't follow SEGA and Sony into CD-ROM gaming. This prompted plenty of debate over whether or not the titles coming to the console would match the grand-scale experiences that Nintendo's major rivals were promising.

One of Nintendo's most venerated designers wasn't worried, though. Speaking to EDGE magazine for its June 1995 issue, Mario, Donkey Kong and Zelda creator Shigeru Miyamoto (pictured above) said: 'The Ultra 64 will be the cheapest hardware available in the next-generation market. And the Ultra 64 will be the most powerful new system. I think it's down to software, really. If the system does not have five or six good games at launch – and I don't put in my contribution – consumers will buy other hardware.' This emphasising of high-quality software to match the technical might of the new console echoed the comments of the then-chairman of Nintendo of America, Howard Lincoln, who'd told Billboard magazine in June 1994: 'We can turn the consumer off if we put out inferior software. That's why we're convinced that a few great games at launch are more important than great games mixed in with a lot of dogs.' This would prove something of a prophetic statement when it came to the N64's North American launch.

But despite positivity in the press, behind the scenes Nintendo and SGI were falling behind schedule. Around the time that Miyamoto's words were published in EDGE, Nintendo announced that its new console's release date would be pushed from the end of 1995 to April 1996. SGI's chips were proving unreliable and necessitated further redesigning, and this meant that third-party developers couldn't work to any finalised system specs, slowing their progress too. Eventually software development kits sent to external studios had to be completely overhauled, and even within Nintendo there were headaches. A fully functional console was only finished in mid-1995, and when the Nintendo 64 was finally shown to the public in November 1995, at Nintendo's own Space World trade show in Kyoto, its demoed launch title *Super Mario 64* was only half finished and displayed very limited texture mapping.

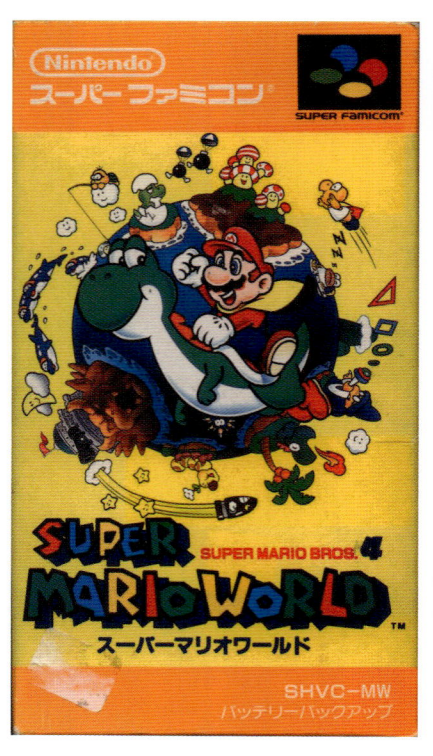

Nintendo again delayed the Nintendo 64's launch date, to 23 June 1996, citing manufacturing problems. It also scrapped its original plan to release the console in all major territories simultaneously. Speculation was rife that Nintendo simply didn't have enough games ready to launch its new system with, and sure enough its line-up was incredibly thin when 23 June came around and the Nintendo 64 was finally made available. *Super Mario 64*, *Pilotwings 64* and the virtual boardgame (and Japan-only release) *Saikyō Habu Shōgi* were all that consumers could pick from, and while the N64's price of ¥25,000 was much cheaper than what the Saturn and PlayStation had launched at, it didn't come with a pack-in game. It didn't seem to matter: the N64's initial shipment of 300,000 units sold out in a day, and three days later total sales sat at over half a million. Never underestimate the appeal of a new Mario title – especially one that that saw the plumber take his first steps into real 3D gameplay, aided by the console controller's revolutionary analogue stick (which had come a long way since Project Reality's modded SNES pads).

The Nintendo 64 controller was the result of some 100 different designs, with its first mock-up made from clay rather than drawn on a computer. A collaboration between Nintendo of America designer Lance Barr and Nintendo's R&D3 team in Japan, it underwent an incredible amount of testing before being finalised, and its self-centring analogue stick – while not specially integrated into the pad with the launch game in mind – was much welcomed by *Super Mario 64* director and producer Miyamoto, who found that it lent itself to the gameplay perfectly. But the N64 controller isn't purely built for 3D play – its M-shaped layout allows players to hold it by its left and right prongs and use the D-pad and regular face buttons for traditional 2D experiences, or by its middle and right prongs for 3D games. Some releases, like 1997's *GoldenEye 007*, allowed for two controllers to be used by a single player at once, meaning that Nintendo was offering twin-stick play while Sony was introducing its Dual Analog Controller. Situated on the underside of the N64 pad was an expansion port, used for Controller Pak memory cards and the vibration-enabling Rumble Pak.

As for the use of cartridges over CD-ROMs for games, Nintendo president Hiroshi Yamauchi would simply tell *The Nikkei Weekly* in 1996: 'People overestimate the merits [of CD-ROM].' The actual pros and cons for going for ROM cartridges over discs was fairly even, with CD-ROMs offering more storage but carts greater loading speed, but the choice really came down to money: consoles using CD drives were more expensive to produce, and using cartridges meant that Nintendo could control the manufacture of its games, adding a healthy mark-up on each one produced while avoiding the piracy that befell both the PlayStation and Saturn (not to mention many more CD-ROM systems). Forget about file sizes and loading times, then – Nintendo's decision to stick with cartridges, capping its game sizes at a maximum of 64MB rather than the 700MB of a single PS1 disc, was mostly motivated by profit.

At least Nintendo's developers knew how to make the most of that limited memory – eventually, anyway. With less capacity for showy visuals and full-motion video, gameplay had to matter on the N64, and Yamauchi knew that one game in particular had to be perfect for the console's launch. Manufacturing problems wasn't quite the real reason why the Nintendo 64 shifted from an April release date to June, as the company's president told *The Nikkei Weekly*: 'Nintendo's software team needed a few extra months to finish *Super Mario 64*. Game creators can finish games quickly if they compromise. But users have sharp eyes. They soon know if the games are compromised. [Miyamoto] asked for two more months, and I gave them to him unconditionally.'

Miyamoto himself, in interviews around the time of the Nintendo 64's release, spoke of how the console 'weeded out weaker developers at an early stage', and how that was 'necessary' in the long term. He also (allegedly, although this may be more urban gaming legend than fact as the source of the line is much debated) commented, regarding another vitally important N64 title, *The Legend of Zelda: Ocarina of Time*, that 'a delayed game is eventually good, but a rushed game is forever bad'. Whether the quote, that's been repeated time and again in reports whenever much-anticipated games experience delays, is legit or not, it certainly summarised the Nintendo philosophy of the time – as Lincoln had said, 'a few great games at launch are more important than great games mixed in with a lot of dogs'.

It wasn't a huge surprise then that Nintendo actively pulled games from the N64's North American launch on 29 September 1996. *Super Mario 64* and *Pilotwings 64* were present in the day-one line-up, but every other game that had been expected to release at the same time was removed. Arcade racer *Cruis'n USA* was held back until December, eventually launching to widespread critical disappointment. The shooter *Body Harvest* from DMA Design (these days known as Rockstar North) had to wait until October 1998 to come out in the States after Nintendo took issue with its violent content. *Tetrisphere*, *Turok: Dinosaur Hunter*, *Wave Race 64* and *Star Wars: Shadow of the Empire* all saw their debuts delayed too – but just as in Japan the tiny selection of games available for super-early adopters didn't slow sales, which raced to half a million in just over a month, helped by a very competitive RRP of $199.99, as demand from retailers took Nintendo by surprise. Nintendo of America's executive vice president Peter Main told the press that the N64 'could sell between 1.5 and 2 million units this calendar year' – a feat that wasn't achieved, but the console did pass the two million mark in the States in April 1997.

A few months later, in June 1997, Nintendo dropped the price of its N64 in the United States to $149 to maintain competitive pace with its SEGA and PlayStation rivals. And to an extent, the company's strategy in the US, underpinned by a multi-million-dollar advertising campaign, worked: with 20.11 million sales, North America was the most successful market for the console, far ahead of the 6.35 million units sold in Europe and 5.54 million in Japan. But while the States was where the most consoles were being enjoyed by players, it was only in Japan where the N64's most notable official add-on was released.

Revealed at the same 1995 Space World where punters got to play the N64 for the first time, the Nintendo 64DD was supposed to provide a substantial power boost to the main console (until cartridge sizes were expanded, anyway), with its high-speed floppy disk-based games – the 'DD' standing for 'Disk Drive' – also serving as rewritable storage in the same manner as the Famicom Disk System in the 1980s. The peripheral allowed for internet access via a service called Randnet, through which online games could be played and messages exchanges, and was supposed to, in Nintendo's own marketing words of 1997, 'allow game developers freedom to store unprecedented amounts of gaming data on a console machine'. But the 64DD was plagued by delays, with several of its proposed games ultimately making the move to conventional N64 cartridges – foremost amongst them, *The Legend of Zelda: The Ocarina of Time*, in-development footage of which had been shown at Space World 1995. The 64DD finally released in December 1999 via a mail-order subscription service and sold around 15,000 units, while only ten dedicated disks came out and Randnet was shut down in 2001. Nintendo of America passed on putting the 64DD out in the States, referencing the still-fresh failure of SEGA's 32X.

The Nintendo 64 was released in a wide array of colours on top of its default grey, with options including transparent green, orange and blue, solid gold, and a handful of Pokémon-styled designs, all of which came bundled with matching controllers. In addition to the model sold in most global markets, a China-exclusive version of the N64, the iQue Player, came out in November 2003 – over a year after the worldwide discontinuation of the N64 in April 2002. This controller-styled device stored games on a 64MB memory card and plugged directly into the television. Four limited-time demos came with each iQue unit, and complete titles (of which 14 were made available, including *Super Mario 64*, *Ocarina of Time* and *Super Smash Bros.*) had to be downloaded onto the memory card at dedicated in-store kiosks. It stayed on sale until 2016 and support was finally withdrawn by its manufacturers (also called iQue) in 2018. The console's Chinese name is Shén Yóu Jī, which translates as 'Divine Gaming Machine'.

With just under 33 million total units sold worldwide, the Nintendo 64 was one of its makers' lower-selling consoles. Nevertheless, the control the company had over cartridge manufacturing and the modest production costs associated with the system meant that Nintendo enjoyed some strong financial results during the N64's lifetime, including the posting of a $1.2 billion profit in 1998 – its highest since 1993 when the SNES was at the peak of its powers, albeit a figure inflated by Game Boy revenues. The N64's commercial success and popularity with players helped Nintendo put its quasi-3D Virtual Boy console behind it, said 1995 machine (not profiled in full here due to its portability and self-contained design) proving a total flop and selling fewer than a million units. No other Nintendo console would sell in such low numbers – but that doesn't mean that there were no further disappointments lurking in the company's future.

Nintendo 64: Five Must Plays

Super Mario 64 (1996)
Any console's launch titles are of incredible importance, but few sold their system quite as magnificently as *Super Mario 64*. With its playful tone established from the first minute, and plenty of colourful space provided to get to grips with this new three-dimensional take on the Nintendo mascot's traditional mix of warp pipes and power-ups, Mario's 3D debut rewrote the rules on what the platform genre could be. It wasn't the first 3D platformer, no, but it was the best for its time – and it's only rarely been surpassed since. Its camera can feel fiddly at times, but *Super Mario 64* remains a true joy to dip into today (easily doable via the Switch Online service), so perfect is its marriage of responsive analogue controls and exploration-rich level design.

GoldenEye 007 (1997)
Rare's James Bond tie-in, released two years after the movie that gives it both its name and narrative, *GoldenEye 007* was one of the first N64 games that really made those four controller ports on the front of the console make sense. A phenomenal local multiplayer first-person shooter, this was a perfect post-pub (or college, or work, or whatever) party game with a compelling mixture of deathmatch modes named after other Bond films. It's a blast solo too, as you guide the super spy through the story beats of the movie, eventually facing off against a very angular Sean Bean. Naturally, he dies.

Star Wars: Rogue Squadron (1998)
If making use of the N64's Expansion Pak, to boost the console's RAM from 4MB to 8MB, *Rogue Squadron* looks incredible. But even without the extra visual boost, as it's only optional in this instance, this arcade-style Star Wars flying shooter is a hoot. Five different craft are available at first, with the iconic X-wing sharing selection menu space with a snowspeeder and three other 'wing' varieties beside unlockable options, and missions follow four basic patterns: protect, rescue, reconnaissance and (everyone's favourite) search and destroy. The story's a pulpy stew of little importance to all but Star Wars super-fans – but you don't pick this one up for the cutscenes. It's all about strapping in, blasting off and taking out those TIE fighters.

Super Smash Bros. (1999)
The original franchise-crossover fighter, this is where it all began for Nintendo's mega-hit Super Smash Bros. series. Its roster is small – just 12 playable characters in total – but in the late 1990s this was the only way you could pair the most recognisable Pokémon Pikachu with F-Zero's Captain Falcon to beat the stuffing out of the Mario brothers. *Super Smash Bros.* is another N64 game where having four controllers and three friends to invite over really brings the game to life, as the on-screen chaos is matched only by the laughs you'll be having.

The Legend of Zelda: Majora's Mask (2000)
While it reuses a large array of assets from *Ocarina of Time*, released two years earlier (and to which it's a sequel), *Majora's Mask* is so very far from a recycling of what came before it – directly, or at any point of the Legend of Zelda series. Set in the world of Termina, it finds Link having to prevent the cataclysmic event of an evil-faced moon crashing down to earth in just 72 hours – which translates to just over 50 real-world minutes. Which, clearly, is nowhere near enough time to avert such a disaster – but thankfully Link has his ocarina from the previous game and can play a time-travelling melody, putting him back at the start of his

time in Termina with all that he's learned intact (and all-important masks earned retained). Unlike *Star Wars: Rogue Squadron* this game does necessitate the N64's Expansion Pak to run (worth it) – but should that not be possible in the here and now, *Majora's Mask* is also playable via a 3DS remake, and through the Wii U's Virtual Console and the Nintendo Switch Online service.

Nintendo 64 Collector Spot
Mikey Dowling from Lake Forest, California, has enjoyed a long career with games developer Obsidian Entertainment, joining in 2008 as a QA tester and assuming the role of director of communications in 2018. He's worked on titles including Fallout: New Vegas and Pillars of Eternity – but when he's not focused on modern gaming his retro love is the Nintendo 64, and he's aiming to collect every game released for the console in North America. He shares his favourites, thoughts on its Switch emulation, and what drew him to the system in the first place.

'I remember reading about the N64 in *Electronic Gaming Monthly* around the time it was announced and being interested, but I wasn't thinking I needed it right away. I was in junior high, so it's not like I was able to buy it right away. Then I saw a demo of *Super Mario 64* in Toys 'R' Us, and playing it got me hooked. I'd never played a game that let you move in that way. I kept thinking about it, and talking about it with my family, and one of my grandmothers very thankfully ended up getting the console for me on launch day.

'Keeping those boxes in good condition though? Ha! As a kid, giving me those cardboard boxes was a bad idea. I didn't care, so they all got thrashed or just trashed outright – something I frown upon my past self for, now. I actually lost a lot of my original N64 games at one point, but in 2013 I wanted to get the system again, so I got a lot from eBay that came with *Super Mario 64*, *WCW/nWo Revenge*, *Star Wars: Shadows of the Empire*, *Tony Hawk's Pro Skater* and *Cruis'n USA*. After that I started going after other lots that had games I was interested in. Later I looked into how many titles were released in North America. Only 325? That feels doable. And from there it was on, and I've been working on the collection on and off ever since.

'I now have about 45 games to go to complete my collection, but the retro market changed dramatically during the COVID-19 pandemic – something like *Super Bowling* used to be $70 or so when I started collecting, and now it's more like $800. The most I've spent on one game so far is $110, on *NFL Blitz Special Edition*. I lucked out finding *ClayFighter: Sculptor's Cut* real cheap early on, otherwise the last time I saw that game for sale it was $1,499 USD. But my most-prized game would be either *Super Mario 64* or *GoldenEye 007* for the nostalgia factors. *GoldenEye* was the game-changer – my friends and I spent so much time on it, playing one-shot kills, slappers only, and proximity mine death matches. It got wild. *Ocarina of Time* floored me when it came out, but I'm fairly certain we didn't put as much time into a game as a group as we did *GoldenEye*. The N64 and that cart travelled everywhere with my group of friends, just so we could play it whenever.

'I prefer to play on the original console than use emulation. I play using the RetroTINK, so I can use a modern monitor, but I do have a 19-inch Sony tube TB that I can use if I need to. Is that better than emulation? I think it's a personal preference, but I love that people who weren't around for the N64 have the opportunity to check out some of its games on the Switch now. If you're lucky enough to get one of the N64 remake controllers for the Switch, firstly I'm jealous of you, and secondly that's absolutely the way to play.

'My favourite N64 game ever is probably *Super Mario 64*, followed by *GoldenEye 007*, *WWF No Mercy*, *Killer Instinct Gold*, and *Star Fox 64*. But there are some significant gems on the console, even though third-party support for the N64 was few and far between as the PlayStation was cheaper and easier to develop for. Should I ever get every game for it, I might play through them all and write up some kind of blog about what was learned from the game in question, or what should be looked at by the industry as something that was forgotten or never really caught on. Or I'd just stream myself playing through every single one, so people can experience the collection with me. But for newcomers, Switch Online is great – I just wish those who play that way better luck at getting the N64 controller than I had!'

DREAMCAST

Manufacturer: SEGA

Released: November 1998 (Japan), September 1999 (North America), October 1999 (Europe, Brazil), November 1999 (Australia)

The disappointing sub-ten million sales of the Saturn left SEGA in a very tricky position regarding its hardware division. But even before its 32-bit console had launched, the company was already setting in motion plans for its successor, a system that could be produced quickly, perhaps replacing the Saturn just two years after its release. Word of this so-called Saturn 2 reached the press in early 1995, with SEGA placing responsibility for the project – focused solely on unprecedented visual power – in the hands of Lockheed Martin. Several console designs were submitted but all were rejected as SEGA looked to other partners instead, including NVIDIA and Matsushita/Panasonic, the latter of which was shopping around its M2 console – the same hardware acquired from 3DO – and hoped that SEGA would take it on. SEGA would not, as it turned out, and conversations with NVIDIA about its video card tech also fizzled out.

In late 1995 another name began circulating: Eclipse. This was said to be a 64-bit machine that either operated as a standalone console or as an add-on for the Saturn. Little is known about Eclipse but apparently some testing was carried out, with third-party developers not responding positively. In 1996, SEGA of America's Tom Kalinske announced his resignation and was replaced as its CEO by Shoichiro Irimajiri, who'd only joined SEGA of Japan three years earlier. With the Saturn now comprehensively outpaced commercially by the PlayStation and the Nintendo 64 about to pass it too, Irimajiri's first job in the States was to hire ex-IBM engineer Tatsuo Yamamoto to lead development of a new console, code-named Black Belt, with video card tech from 3Dfx, a leader in the PC market. At the same time, Hideki Sato, who'd overseen the design of all previous SEGA home consoles released globally, began work on a new console in Japan, code-named Dural, with a CPU provided by Hitachi and its PowerVR graphics processor by NEC.

Over time, SEGA's priority for its next console shifted: raw power was less important than having a machine that developers could easily work with to produce the very best games possible. The Black Belt concept was well received by studios that got to see it, and the US-based project also earned the support of new SEGA of America COO Bernie Stolar, who was desperate for the company to come out with something to succeed the ailing Saturn, which was driving SEGA's profits sharply downwards (a planned merger with Bandai had fallen apart in 1997, further damaging the company's bottom line). But as Black Belt was evolving, so too was Dural, which in 1998 was renamed Katana – and it was this Sato-helmed model that SEGA chose to take through to its final Dreamcast design, the new 128-bit console's name picked from around 5,000 publicly submitted suggestions. ('Consumers were used to the "bit wars",' Sato told *Famitsu* around the time of the Dreamcast's Japanese launch, 'so even though we knew it was a lot of nonsense, we needed to appeal to them in those terms.') *Space Channel 5* art director Yumiko Miyabe commented on the system's moniker in a 20th anniversary Dreamcast feature on gamedeveloper.com, published in September 2019: 'When I heard the name Dreamcast, it sounded enigmatic to me. It made me feel the company's spirit to challenge a new field, going beyond the conventional.'

Stolar would later tell gamasutra.com: 'I felt the US version, the 3Dfx version, should have been used, (but) Japan wanted the Japanese version, and Japan won. I lost that argument.' An argument he *didn't* lose was for the incorporation of a dedicated 56k modem, later telling theringer.com, in 2019: 'Online was most important to me, so I chose that over DVD and internal storage because my plan was to add those later.' Bing Gordon, then chief creative officer at EA, one of SEGA's most important North American partners, told gamasutra.com: '(SEGA) said they looked at 3Dfx, but decided against it. We looked at this and asked ourselves, "Why did they make these choices? It's gotta be some kind of political thing, because these are dumb choices."' After further disagreements between the parties, EA would decide not to support SEGA's Dreamcast with any of its games whatsoever, a huge shift from the relationship the two enjoyed in the years of the Mega Drive/Genesis. Instead, EA Sports-branded titles would release for the PlayStation, PC and Nintendo platforms, and later the PlayStation 2. Feeling like they'd been misled with the Black Belt project, 3Dfx filed a lawsuit against SEGA and NEC, which was settled in August 1998 with SEGA having to pay $10.5m to the claimants.

One of the most questioned design decisions of the Dreamcast is SEGA's opting for a GD-ROM drive (the 'G' is for Gigabyte, as each disc could hold 1GB), co-produced with Yamaha, instead of using DVD-ROM. From SEGA's perspective, it was a partly move against the piracy that afflicted CD-ROM games (not that illegally copied games couldn't be played on a Dreamcast, as it would still read CD-ROM discs). The company was also trying to keep costs down – costs that would have to be passed on to the consumer. While it was hoped that the Dreamcast would eventually be able to run DVD-ROMs, offering capacity of up to 8.5GB, initially it was simply too expensive to use them, with Sato telling *EDGE* magazine in 1999 that the costs were prohibitive and the 'development environment was a major problem'. The PlayStation 2 *would* use DVD-ROM, and that was undoubtedly a huge factor in its amazing commercial success, offering next-gen gaming and DVD film functionality at a time when regular DVD players were expensive. In hindsight, SEGA's passing on DVD was a major blow to the Dreamcast's chances.

Nevertheless, SEGA's aim of making the Dreamcast easy to develop for was achieved and represented a huge plus after the Saturn's troubles. Using components manufactured by third parties not only kept production costs down but meant that other companies had awareness of and expertise with what was inside the new console. Speaking to gamedeveloper.com in September 2019, Takeshi Hirai, lead system programmer on *Shenmue*, commented: 'The reason the Dreamcast was so popular both within SEGA and with other companies was ease of development. It was easy to make visuals, easy to make sound. Performance was good, and you could have the hardware and middleware talk to each other with much less interference, develop specifications, then code it all together.' Another anonymous interviewee featured in the same 20th anniversary article added: 'The Dreamcast was a much easier platform to develop for than previous ones (which) required trial and error and special tricks to get the desired visuals. We could create high-quality visuals just by using the default functions.'

On 21 May 1998, SEGA showed a still-in-development Dreamcast to the world at its own New Challenge Conference in Tokyo, announcing a November release date for Japan. Irimajiri talked attendees through the specifications of the new console, with representatives from production partners including NEC and Hitachi involved and Microsoft's Bill Gates appearing in a pre-recorded video to explain how the Dreamcast would use an adapted version of Windows CE as its operating system. This would mark Microsoft's first major step into the console world, but the company would soon take many more. Days later, SEGA of America stated that the Dreamcast would launch in that region in late 1999, with between 20 and 30 titles available day one. Further showcases followed in 1998 but the final console wasn't revealed until October, at a second SEGA Challenge Conference.

Here, many third-party developers were announced as working on games for the Dreamcast, including Konami, Capcom and Namco, and its pioneering built-in modem for online gaming was detailed in full. The console's launch price was also confirmed: ¥29,800, with a controller featuring one analogue stick based on the Saturn's 3D Control Pad (which had been bundled with certain copies of *Nights into Dreams*). One earlier design for the Dreamcast's standard control pad had been for a Nintendo Wii-like remote-style device, and SEGA hardware designer Kenji Tosaki would tell segasaturnshiro.com in June 2022 that 'it was the game developers that didn't want dual analogue 3D sticks' – an unusual stance perhaps, given how ubiquitous that layout would quickly become, but at the time PlayStation's twin-analogue controllers were only just beginning to have their potential realised.

When the Dreamcast was finally released in Japan on 27 November 1998, it quickly vanished from shelves – but not in a way that led to many smiles at SEGA. Pre-order demand was substantial, accounting for 50% of day-one sales, but production problems with the PowerVR graphics processor meant that not enough units could be sent to retailers, and all stock sold out on the first day. Later, SEGA would estimate that as many as 300,000 more units could have been sold in this brief but important window. The decision to go with GD-ROM had consumers pausing too, likewise a lacklustre launch line-up of just four games: the visual novel *July*, bizarre racer *Pen Pen Tricelon*, city-smasher *Godzilla Generations*, and *Virtua Fighter 3tb*, an updated version of SEGA's arcade hit of 1996 and 1997 that proved to be the one release that sold in any great numbers.

The much-anticipated *Sonic Adventure*, the first properly 3D experience for SEGA's speedy mascot after the Saturn's cancelled *Sonic X-treme*, had been previewed as a game arriving at the same time as its console, but it was frustratingly delayed to 23 December and released in a compromised form. 'The schedule for the title was tight,' director Takashi Iizuka told *Retro Gamer* magazine in 2018. 'There were issues we wanted to fix … and more polish we wanted to put into the title, but the position we were in made us give up on addressing everything we wanted to.' These shortcomings and glitches were fixed for the game's North American release in September 1999, with this version subsequently issued in Japan as *Sonic Adventure International*. By February 1999, around 900,000 Dreamcast consoles had been sold in Japan – a respectable result but some way short of SEGA's hopes of installing a sizeable user base before Sony's incoming PlayStation 2, which was known to be in production and was formally revealed to the world in March 1999.

With global games players now fully aware of a second PlayStation's existence, albeit with no release date or pricing details revealed, SEGA went on a marketing offensive. Senior producer at SEGA of Europe at the time, Katsuhisa Sato, recalled to terredejeux.net in 2020 'a massive promotional campaign worldwide at the launch of the Dreamcast. Everybody at SEGA was so excited about the Dreamcast launch, at that time.' In North America, Stolar told *Time* that SEGA was ready to spend $100 million on the console's promotion and the same amount again on product development. Helping the Dreamcast's stateside chances was the fact that *Sonic Adventure* was a launch game on 9 September 1999, one of 19 titles available on day one including Capcom's *Power Stone*, Namco's *SoulCalibur*, two NFL games from Visual Concepts and Midway respectively, *Ready 2 Rumble Boxing* and *Mortal Kombat Gold*. An RRP of $199 was appealing, too.

A US advertising campaign devised by the agency Foote, Cone and Belding played on the power of the console by implying that it was almost sentient, its tagline of 'It's Thinking' showing 'the quirkiness of SEGA, the irreverence of SEGA, the thumb-your-nose-at-the-other-guy that is SEGA', according to SEGA of America's president from 2000 to 2003, Peter Moore (pictured below), as told to theringer.com in 1999. He added in the same interview, regarding the Dreamcast's online multiplayer compatibility out of the box: 'I coined the phrase during that period, "We're taking gamers where gaming is going." And I knew damn well gaming was going there (online). Whether SEGA would be there to take them is a whole different story.' Strong early sales in Europe – 500,000 units sold between launch on 14 October 1999 and the end of the year at a price of £200 – suggested that SEGA's mix of modestly priced hardware, future-facing functions and impressive game library was enough to combat the looming PS2. But the pace wasn't sustained, and elsewhere in the world sales and awareness were almost non-existent. The Australian RRP of A$499 was on the extremely high side and a launch period report on gamespot.com also noted 'the complete lack of mainstream media advertising', adding: 'If you didn't know any better, you would never know the machine existed.'

By the end of 1999, 1.5 million Dreamcasts had been sold in North America, and Japanese sales were comfortably over a million. But these figures were nowhere near enough, and as the 21st century dawned, the writing began to appear on the wall for SEGA. Having slashed the price of a new Dreamcast to ¥19,900 in June 1999, SEGA found itself losing money on every console it sold in the region. By mid-2000, two million consoles had been sold in Japan – but the PlayStation 2 had released in March and sold almost a million units in just 24 hours, and it would go on to sell over ten million globally just a year later. SEGA couldn't compete, and the PS2's total Japanese sales overtook the Dreamcast's by October 2000. As soon as the PS2 began making waves in Japan, the effects were felt elsewhere. North American stockists slowed their orders for SEGA's console, making room for Sony's new machine's arrival in October 2000; and in Europe the Dreamcast had its price cut to £149.99 to combat PlayStation, only for Sony's machine to surpass SEGA's *total* sales within six months of its November 2000 launch.

Third-party developers switched priorities, the Dreamcast no longer a key platform with the PlayStation 2's growing dominance clear for all to see. And with both Nintendo's GameCube and Microsoft's Xbox set for late-2001 releases, on 31 January 2001 SEGA announced what would have been unthinkable just a few years earlier: it would be discontinuing the Dreamcast and restructuring to focus solely on software development, abandoning its production of home gaming consoles 18 years after the release of the SG-1000. SEGA of Japan laid off around a third of its workforce in Tokyo, and Moore recalled to UK newspaper *The Guardian* in 2008: 'We had a tremendous 18 months. Dreamcast was on fire – we really thought we could do it. Then we had a target from Japan … We had to make N hundreds of millions of dollars by the holiday season, and shift N millions units of hardware, otherwise we just couldn't sustain the business. So on 31 January 2001 we said SEGA is leaving hardware – somehow I got to make that call, not the Japanese. I had to fire a lot of people; it was not a pleasant day. We were selling 50,000 units a day, then 60,000, then 100,000 – but it was just not enough to get the critical mass to take on the launch of the PS2. SEGA had the option of pouring in more money and going bankrupt, and they decided they wanted to live to fight another day. We licked our wounds, ate some humble pie and went to Sony and Nintendo to ask for dev kits.'

It was the right move for SEGA, as several of its best-known series – including Sonic – began to appear on non-SEGA platforms. 'The atmosphere in SEGA of Europe wasn't so bad,' Sato told terredejeux.net. 'The development team was immediately involved in the development of PS2-compatible games, and quickly ported some Dreamcast games. So, we were quite busy after the end of the Dreamcast.' And many of those ports helped to illustrate what a terrific array of games had come out for the Dreamcast – games and series that many players missed out on by not originally picking up SEGA's hardware. *Crazy Taxi* found its way to the GameCube, PC and PS2. *Phantasy Star Online* to the GameCube, Xbox and PC. *Sonic Adventure* and its sequel landed on Nintendo's new machine, as did the once-exclusive *Resident Evil – Code: Veronica*. These and many more grew in appreciation after the Dreamcast's untimely demise, with former SEGA of America director of third-party development and publishing Kathy Astromoff telling gamedeveloper.com: 'If everyone who today tells me they loved the Dreamcast had actually bought it, and kept buying games for it, it would have been the most popular console of all time!'

That the Dreamcast sold so poorly – just 9.13 million worldwide, putting it *beneath* the Saturn's lowly performance – isn't reflective of all the things that it did right. GD-ROM might have been a misstep and ultimately did little to combat the impact of pirated games, but in so many ways the Dreamcast was a system ahead of its time, a brilliant piece of hardware that found itself caught between the disappointment of its makers' previous machine and the unprecedented commercial might of the PlayStation 2. Its first-party games might be the most varied that SEGA has ever produced for a single console, with the open-world life-sim (tinged with revenge) *Shenmue* and eye-popping skate 'em up *Jet Set Radio* two of the most striking experiences seen anywhere at that point. It was a home for wonderfully weird experiences like the bizarre *Seaman*, where you care for a human-faced aquatic creature who loves to insult the player, and *The Typing of the Dead*, which altered the on-rails arcade shooter to use swiftly typed words and phrases to mow down undead baddies.

The Dreamcast's online play was the best in the business for consoles, connecting players around the world; and it offered genuine arcade quality in the home thanks to its shared architecture with SEGA's NAOMI (New Arcade Operation Machine Idea) arcade system. Its Visual Memory Unit doubled as a mini-portable system all of its own and allowed for second-screen functionality on the controller – and inspired PlayStation's PocketStation – and its controller design still feels great in the hands, despite 20-plus years of design refinements and its lead being placed on the underside of the pad. How that passed QA, we'll never know (and no, the placement of the VMU slot is no excuse).

In a retrospective published in 2020, then-USGamer.net editor in chief Kat Bailey wrote that the Dreamcast was 'a bridge between gaming's classical period and the modern era that would follow', and that it was 'a platform for daring creators and even more daring ideas'. And as its enduring influence on today's games and hardware makers shows, while the console itself may have burned brightly but briefly, its legacy – its games are cited as influential and personally memorable by designers including Amy Hennig (Uncharted), Tim Schafer (Double Fine), Daisuke Sato (Yakuza) and Sam Barlow (*Immortality* and *Telling Lies*) – may well be more powerful than any other SEGA system … except, perhaps, for the eternally popular Mega Drive.

Dreamcast: Five Must Plays

Sonic Adventure (1998)
Translating the speed of a 2D Sonic game into the 3D realm was a huge challenge for its makers, SEGA's internal Sonic Team studio. But with original *Sonic the Hedgehog* lead programmer Yuji Naka producing and direction from *Nights into Dreams* lead game designer Takashi Iizuka, the 60-strong development team pulled it off to a chorus of critical acclaim. The Dreamcast's best-selling game with 2.5 million copies sold, *Sonic Adventure* was SEGA's biggest hope for course-correcting its commercial fortunes after the Saturn's slump, but it wasn't to be. Nevertheless, *Sonic Adventure* lived on after the discontinuation of the Dreamcast, with a version for PC and Dreamcast titled *Sonic Adventure DX* releasing in 2003, and a high-definition re-release coming out digitally for PlayStation 3, Xbox 360 and PC in 2010. The game also features on 2011's physical *Dreamcast Collection* for Xbox 360 beside *Crazy Taxi*, *Space Channel 5* and *Sega Bass Fishing*.

SoulCalibur (1999)
Namco's blades-swinging weapons-based fighter is, according to reviews aggregator Metacritic, the highest-rated game to ever release for the Dreamcast with a score of 98 (out of 100). This exceptional score also makes it the fourth greatest game of all time … according to the reviews that Metacritic has collected over the years, at least. Realistically, *SoulCalibur* is showing its age nowadays, and can't be compared directly, favourably, with many of its own sequels. But at the time its deep and rewarding mechanics, appealingly diverse roster of playable characters, and multiple modes of play made it a must-have for Dreamcast early adopters and latecomers alike. No collection is complete without it.

Shenmue (1999)
And that same sentiment is shared by this, Yu Suzuki's pioneering open-world adventure that moves at whatever pace the player decided to take (subject to a cut-off point, several months after starting the game). Protagonist Ryo Hazuki is on a quest for revenge after he witnesses a man called Lan Di murder his father. But to achieve that he'll first have to find out about a mysterious dragon mirror; poke around in the back streets of Yokosuka and take on a job at the local docks; and spend far too much money in (playable) arcade cabinets and on capsule toys. A major change of ambition and pace from the arcade racers and shooters that director Suzuki made his name with – including *After Burner*, *OutRun* and *Virtua Racing* – *Shenmue* sold 1.2 million copies but failed to turn a profit after SEGA spent around $47 million developing the game. Nevertheless, a Dreamcast sequel followed in 2001 and was later ported to Xbox, and *Shenmue III* came out for PlayStation 4 and

PC in 2019, having been partially funded by some 69,000 backers on Kickstarter. In May 2022, Suzuki stated he had no firm plans for a fourth Shenmue game but would like to see the series continue.

Jet Set Radio (2000)

Known as *Jet Grind Radio* in North America, this gorgeously stylised action game mixes in-line skating moves with hip-hop and funk grooves and graffiti tagging mission objectives. With its streets based on real-world neighbourhoods of Tokyo, and its cel-shaded visuals looking like nothing else in gaming at the time, *Jet Set Radio* really was a transportive experience of fast and free-flowing movement and middle-finger-to-the-cops satisfaction as you scooted away from chasing policemen. Developed by a team with an average age of under 25, the game's freshness is palpable – and what's most striking of all is that, somehow, it doesn't feel like it's aged a day. The game's sequel, *Jet Set Radio Future*, became a pack-in game for the Xbox in 2002, coming on a shared disc also featuring the racer *Sega GT 2002*.

Skies of Arcadia (2000)

Overworks' RPG of air pirates sailing between floating continents was a huge adventure that left an even bigger impression on those who played it – which, disappointingly for its makers, wasn't all that many at first, as the game struggled to sell well. They didn't know what they were missing as this epic tale of warring empires and massive mechanical weapons managed to distil its compelling drama down to the level of a few individuals caught up in the centre of this all-consuming conflict, as the player guides the cutlasses-wielding Vyse and his friends through memorable ups and downs. Known as *Eternal Arcadia* in Japan, *Skies of Arcadia* is another Dreamcast classic that was ported to another platform, coming out on the GameCube as *Skies of Arcadia Legends* in 2002. A sequel was planned in 2003 but never materialised, and an HD re-release of the original game, while widely requested, has yet to appear.

Dreamcast Collector Spot

Faith Johnson, aka Retro Faith on YouTube, is from London and has successfully collected every Dreamcast game released in the UK. She also has a huge collection of other SEGA and Sonic the Hedgehog items, from games and consoles to all manner of merchandise. She talks about what hooked her about SEGA's final console proper, and its lasting relevance in the independent development scene.

'What drew me to the Dreamcast? My top-level answer would be it was SEGA, and it had a proper 3D Sonic. *Sonic Adventure* was the first Dreamcast I played, and the first game I owned. I was lucky enough to import a Dreamcast from Japan early in 1999 and there were only a handful of games to choose from, including that. But if memory serves, I also bought *Virtua Fighter 3tb* at the same time, and a VMU. I was well into my arcade fighting games at this point. Capcom and SNK were both at the height of their powers and the Dreamcast was getting all of them thanks to the NAOMI hardware. The Dreamcast is a fighting fan's dream console.

'It was clear from the beginning that everything about the Dreamcast, from the VMU to its internet connectivity, made it feel futuristic. It was a true arcade machine at home – something we'd only seen before with the Neo Geo, but the Dreamcast was affordable. *The House of the Dead* and *Crazy Taxi* were games I was chucking 50p coins into – but now they were in my living room.

'The Dreamcast is, for me, the last console of the golden era of video gaming, when it was all about quick-fix, shorter games that had real arcade feel. The industry was evolving – people wanted longer, story-driven games. But SEGA stuck with what it knew, giving us high score-chasing, button-bashing wonderment. Most of the best Dreamcast games are straight from the arcade, and we've never had that since.

'But then, out of left field, *Phantasy Star Online* appeared. I'd played a few PC games online but had never experienced anything like this. This was the start of modern gaming, right there in those *Phantasy Star Online* lobbies. Every online console game owes a debt to it, and that juxtaposition of pure, arcade-style gaming coupled with opening the door to the future puts the Dreamcast in the realms of past and present, all mixed together.

'My Dreamcast collection just started naturally, from a combination of love for arcade gaming and a new-found ability to buy anything I wanted. It was about five or six years ago that I realised I had inadvertently collected about two-thirds of the UK releases. After a little research and list making it became clear that getting all of them would not be a hard task, so I started hunting for the rest. It took two more years, and I was lucky to already have a few of the more expensive ones. It was also around that point that I realised my collecting focus would just be Sonic and

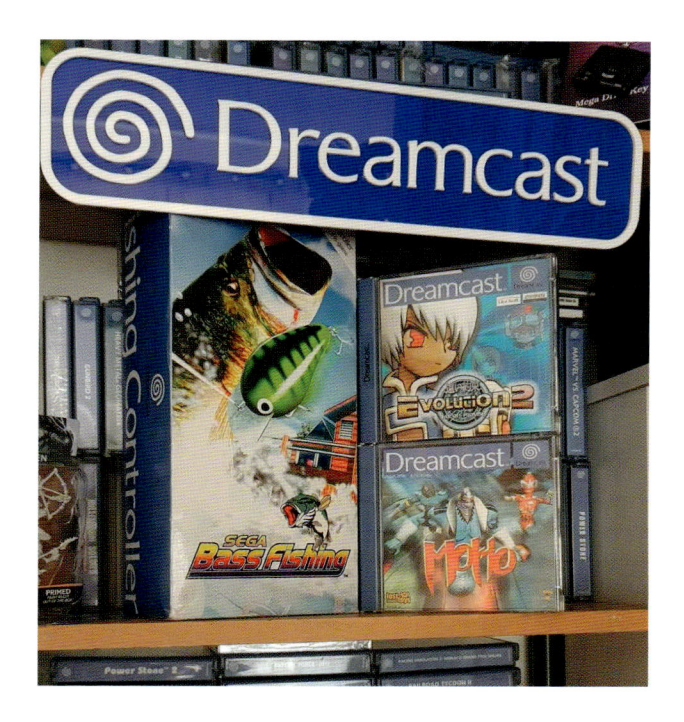

Dreamcast. There were piles of games for lots of consoles, and I cared little for most of them. I started becoming a player more than a collector and it felt like a relief to concentrate on something. I was so used to simply buying bundles of anything and everything that this new approach felt like I finally had an something to aim for. Seeing the shelves filled with games I had an affinity with was refreshing.

'The final purchase to finish my Dreamcast collection was a combination of the *Sega Bass Fishing* rod set, *Evolution 2* and *MoHo*, in September 2019. So, the whole collection started shortly after the Dreamcast was released in the UK and took 20 years to finish, with a massive gap in the middle. It is hard to say exactly how long because I have been constantly collecting games since the turn of the century. I have never had that "nostalgia" moment of, "I'm going to start buying games again." They have always been with me.

'My favourite five games would me *Ikaruga*, *Mr Driller*, *Capcom vs. SNK*, *Spawn: In The Demon's Hand*, and *Phantasy Star Online*. *PSO* is a game I still play on private servers to this day. It's the greatest game I have ever played – it's so simple, plays well, and is wonderful to play with your mates. I've moved onto the GameCube version now, purely because it has more levels, but I still love firing up the Dreamcast and its

broadband adapter for some *PSO*. I do play the games in my collection – not every single one, it'd be impossible to have the time. But I am working on playing every UK Dreamcast game I own – I'm about halfway through now, and my rule is that every game must be played for at least a couple of hours.

'My most prized possession isn't anything to do with the Dreamcast – it's my Sonic & Knuckles Mega Drive bundle from France. It took me 20 years to find one complete and it is the crowning glory of my Sonic collection. I also spent four figures on two Game Gear games to finish my Sonic collection, *Sonic Blast* and *Sonic 2 in 1*. The latter is exceptionally difficult to find in boxed and good condition. I only bought these to put on the shelf, to have a complete collection, and it felt strange to spend so much on cardboard and plastic. Beyond testing the carts on purchase, they'll probably never be played.

'I'm a huge advocate for the Dreamcast indie scene, for the games still being made for the console today. The architecture of the Dreamcast makes it very easy to port games to – being based on Windows, it's easy for developers to move their code over. Also, due to the lack of copy protection on most Dreamcast systems, you can professionally print games today that will automatically work on original machines without modifications. And the fan base also has a lot to do with why devs are attracted to it – Dreamcast nuts like me love having new games to play and collect. Each new release is celebrated like it's an AAA title, and you don't see this kind of renewed dedication with many other old consoles. Long may it continue – we dare to dream, and the dream is endless.'

THE 2000s
ONE CONSOLE TO RULE THEM ALL

While SEGA and Nintendo had both enjoyed triumphs in different territories through the late 1980s and early 1990s, neither company had dominated home console gaming across two consecutive generations on a global level. As the new millennium dawned however, PlayStation would aim for, and achieve, exactly that, taking the worldwide success of the PS1 into an even-bigger second system, the PlayStation 2. At the time of writing the PS2 remains the highest-selling console ever at over 155 million units – a figure that may never be beaten, although the sales trajectory of the Nintendo Switch gives it half a chance. While the PS2 was *the* console of the 2000s, the decade also witnessed the arrival of a new superpower in gaming, Xbox, and saw Nintendo embrace a diverse audience with the Wii's appealing library of motion-controlled 'casual' games.

PLAYSTATION 2

Manufacturer: Sony Electronics

Released: March 2000 (Japan), October 2000 (North America), November 2000 (Europe, Australia)

When Sony announced its original PlayStation in October 1993, the games industry was divided. Some felt that the electronics giant could ruffle feathers at Nintendo and SEGA, and that its 32-bit console would steal a healthy slice of the home gaming market. Others downplayed the PlayStation's appeal, confident that the established names would stay out in front. But by March 1999, when Sony officially revealed that its new, as-yet-unnamed console was coming soon, everything had changed. PlayStation owned around 60% of the lucrative North American market, and almost 50% of the global market. It was no longer chasing the pack but leading it, and every other major console brand braced itself to face a powerful new opponent. Nintendo and the newcomer of Xbox would survive going up against the PlayStation 2. SEGA, however, wouldn't.

Sony hadn't taken any chances when it came to making its second console a success. Development of the PS2 began as early as 1994, with the PlayStation itself yet to appear in Japanese stores. The driving force behind Sony's debut system, engineer and former chairman of Sony Interactive Entertainment Ken Kutaragi, also known as the father of the PlayStation, wasn't about to rest upon any laurels having shown that his company could go it alone in console gaming. The former chairman of Sony Computer Entertainment, Shigeo Maruyama, told Polygon.com in 2018: 'When the original PlayStation was being manufactured and getting ready to ship, he (Kutaragi) was already meeting with the staff about his vision for PlayStation 2.' He added: 'I thought he was going to take over all of Sony. I think that probably would have been for the best. He was the engine behind it all.'

Kutaragi's ambition was reflected by other prominent Sony employees, as the then-president of Sony Computer Entertainment Europe, Chris Deering, told eurogamer.net in 2010: 'From day one on PS1, I started thinking about what I would do to make sure PS2 could win round two. Nintendo and SEGA had never won two [console generations] in a row. We used to say it was like winning two gold medals in two back-to-back Olympics – it just never happened.' And while Kutaragi was acknowledged as a huge motivator for whatever Sony would do next, it was a different kind of engine that shipped with every PlayStation 2 console when it released in March 2000: the Emotion Engine.

The PlayStation 2's CPU, this Emotion Engine, was a collaborative project between Sony and Toshiba. Made up of eight different units handling memory, vector processing, image processing and more alongside the CPU core, Kutaragi spoke of this tech being able to simulate human-like emotion, hence its name. Twice as fast as leading PCs of its time and capable of incredible graphics, theoretically able to generate 66 million polygons per second, the Emotion Engine chips cost $1 billion to produce for the first couple of years that the PS2 was on sale, a huge sum of money. But Sony backed Kutaragi's concept, and it soon paid off as PS2 consoles sold at staggering speed around the world. 'Kutaragi was a visionary,' David Wilson, the former UK PR manager for Sony Computer Entertainment Europe told eurogamer.net in 2010. 'Taken on its own it might seem pretentious, but to call it the Emotion Engine was making a bold statement about what we were out to achieve.'

As great – iconic, even – as the Emotion Engine proved to be, generating headlines across the gaming media in the preamble to anyone being able to test a PS2 for themselves, Sony hadn't pursued just the one design for its new console. It also reached out to selected third parties, keen to see what other teams could come up with. British studio Argonaut Software had worked with Nintendo in the early 1990s to produce the Super FX chip, giving *Star Fox* and *Stunt Race FX* their polygons, and submitted a chip design for the PS2 based on the specs it was given – specs that, it turns out, were way below what Sony already had in the works. Argonaut founder Jez San later told pushsquare.com: 'They designed their own chip to be faster than the spec they told everyone else to design. If they'd said five million polygons per second or whatever, we'd have done that.' Rather like SEGA's development of the Dreamcast, it seems that Sony wanted to explore all the options it could while already having a favoured chipset in mind.

But it wasn't just what was inside the PlayStation 2 that mattered – its outer shell, designed by Teiyu Goto (who also designed the PS1 and its controller), was also striking, with a form factor that could be positioned vertically or horizontally. In contrast to its top-loading and rather toy-like predecessor, the PS2 had an aesthetic not too far removed from the CD-ROM multimedia machines of the 1990s that never really made it. It seemed designed to fit snugly beside hi-fi gear, or alongside a VHS beneath the television. This wasn't a games-only machine for the bedroom – it was the first console to properly understand how to infiltrate the living room and provide something for all the family (and this new place within the home is something Kutaragi would develop further with the PlayStation 3). Its shape wasn't plucked completely from Goto's imagination, though, and was based on the Falcon 030 Microbox, a home computer by Atari that was never produced but is referenced in the PS2's design patent documentation.

Knowing that the specs of the PlayStation 2 had been gradually leaking since 1997, Sony finally let the media get their hands on the console at the September 1999 Tokyo Game Show. Playable demos included *Tekken Tag Tournament*, *Dark Cloud*, and *Gran Turismo 3: A-Spec*. Now the complete picture of what Sony was offering could be seen, and many were in awe. It was, reported IGN, the 'master of ceremonies, the main feature, and the final act, all in one'. As well as games, the PS2's DVD functionality was shown off, and more details were firmed up: it would be backwards compatible with all PS1 discs and would use both the older console's memory cards and controllers for those games; its firmware was updatable (although this is something that never really happened, except for one disc); and its expansion bay would be used for an official Network Adapter, allowing online play through dial-up and broadband, and a Hard Disk Drive. The option to stream media, like music and movies, was hinted at, but running Netflix through your PS2 would only ever become a reality in Brazil.

Sony had learned from the mistakes of those who'd gone before them, and whatever additional uses the PS2 could have, akin to the likes of the Commodore

CDTV and Philips CD-i, first and foremost this was a video games console. Ten titles were ready for the system's Japanese launch on 4 March 2000, including *Ridge Racer V* and *Street Fighter EX3*, and many more had been previewed, whetting appetites for what was to come. Pricing was paramount, too. Retailing at ¥39,800 in Japan, and subsequently $299 in the US and £299 in the UK, the PS2 launched at the same price that the PS1 had several years earlier. And with dedicated DVD players often costing much more, the PS2 represented a great way to start watching movies and TV shows on this emerging format. 'The games were the real hook,' SCE UK and Ireland's Ray Maguire told gamesindustry.biz in 2020, but Deering remembers that things were different elsewhere in Europe, commenting in the same article: 'We really pushed the PS2 as a DVD player almost on an equal footing with it being a game machine in Southern Europe. Of course, once it got under the TV, then people started buying games.'

And it got under millions of TVs in no time at all. Pre-order demand in Japan was huge, and several thousand consumers queued to try to buy the PS2 when it went on sale at midnight. Every unit available was sold by 10am. According to a PS2 timeline published on gamespy.com in 2004, there were just under one million consoles available day one in Japan, but if Sony had produced three million, they'd have sold out too. 'We were underprepared,' commented the former president of SIE's Worldwide Studio, Shuhei Yoshida, at 2018's Develop Conference in Brighton, UK. 'Because of the fast transition between PS1 and PS2, we had no idea how the industry manages these things.'

By the end of March 2000 a very healthy 1.4 million PS2s had been sold in Japan, and when the console launched in North America on 26 October its 500,000 units instantly sold out too, Sony again met with greater demand than they were able to provide for. (For comparison, the Dreamcast had taken two weeks to reach the half-million milestone.) Second-hand units began selling on eBay for over $1,000 as stock remained limited for several weeks. With day-one titles including *Madden NFL 2001* and *NHL 2001* (EA having taken its huge sports games to PlayStation after falling

133

out with SEGA), *TimeSplitters*, *Tekken Tag Tournament* and *Unreal Tournament*, the stateside launch was an even bigger deal than the Japanese one had been, with sales earning over $250 million across hardware and software in 24 hours, an industry record. By the end of March 2001, a year after the console's Japanese debut and following successful launches in Europe and Australia, the PS2's worldwide sales stood at 9.2 million – and with the Dreamcast officially discontinued and Nintendo and Xbox not releasing their new consoles until much later in the year, Sony effectively had the home console market to itself.

Rather than be overly antagonistic marketing wise and setting their sights on the competition's shortcomings, for the PS2 Sony got weird, hiring feted avant-garde filmmaker David Lynch to oversee a TV ad promoting the console's ability to take the user to The Third Place, but showing nothing of the hardware or software at all. If the talking duck and a chap's head floating free of his shoulders didn't make much sense to the viewer, it didn't matter: as the letters P and S and the number 2 appeared at the end, it felt more like a statement of confidence, of comfort almost, than a campaign to persuade players over from SEGA or Nintendo. Sony already knew they had the best console, and the only other significant rival it had was on its knees. Further strange commercials gave us a fawn being struck by a truck, only for the vehicle to explode – 'Different Place, Different Rules', read the on-screen text – and a creepy animated number where a man wishes he was a werewolf, which is fine because with PS2, in The Third Place, you can 'be whatever you want to be'. David Wilson explained: 'These types of adverts were more about the experience than the product. It was about how you *felt* about PlayStation.'

One man in the UK felt a little too much for his console, however, as the BBC's Newsround website reported in 2002 that Dan Holmes, a 29-year-old man from Oxfordshire, had not only legally changed his name to PlayStation 2, but also joked about wanting to marry Sony's machine. 'I asked a few vicars if they would do the service,' he was quoted, 'but they didn't seem keen.' Wherever Dan is now, hopefully he's doing alright. And if that story seems wild it's got nothing on a brilliant rumour surrounding Japan's restrictions on exporting PS2s. What's true is that the Japanese Trade Ministry felt that the console was so powerful that it could be reappropriated for military use such as missile guidance, and therefore applied special export regulations. Anyone wanting to take more than $472 worth of products out of Japan would have to get a licence to do so. What *isn't* true is that the then president of Iraq, Saddam Hussein, managed to get around this restriction and stockpile 4,000 PS2s with the intention of constructing a military supercomputer. That's pure poppycock, but it's one of gaming's strangest urban myths and did pick up some coverage in late 2000.

If the Dreamcast represented the final games console that had ties to the high scores of the arcade, then the PS2 was absolutely the one that moved home gaming into wider, richer virtual spaces. Three of its top six best-selling games are from Rockstar's open-world crime series Grand Theft Auto, with the console's number one title with 17.33 million copies sold being 2004's *Grand Theft Auto: San Andreas*, which set its action across three whole cities (albeit small, fictionalised versions of Los Angeles, San Francisco and Las Vegas). The Final Fantasy series continued to sell in huge numbers too, and it was on the PS2 that the God of War franchise made its debut in 2005. Other names made the leap from PS1 with terrific new entries, including Gran Turismo, Metal Gear Solid and Resident Evil – but the PS2 was also home to a wide array of experiences that weren't aimed at a so-called hardcore audience. The motion-controlled mini-games of *EyeToy: Play* came out in 2003, using the camera peripheral, and *Guitar Hero* appeared two years later. The SingStar series had friends and families bellowing into a microphone attached to their console, and Buzz! brought TV quiz show formulas into play. All of these broadened the appeal of the PS2 substantially, attracting people who'd never played video games before.

While it predated consoles offering high-definition visuals as standard, four PS2 games could be played at 1080i – *Gran Turismo 4*, *NHL 2004*, *Valkyrie Profile 2* and *Tourist Trophy* – and many more supported 16:9 widescreen displays. In total, well over 4,000 games were released for the console, and at the time of writing the PS2 is the highest-selling games console of all time, with around 155 million units sold between 2000 and its worldwide discontinuation in January 2013

(to make way for that year's PlayStation 4). A smaller model, the PlayStation 2 Slimline (or simply Slim), was released in 2004 and swapped its motorised CD tray for a top-loading drive. Both the Slimline and original PS2 were available in a variety of colours other than the standard black, while a bright-white digital video recorder with PS2 compatibility, named the PSX, emerged for the Japanese market only in 2003. In 2010 Sony released a high-definition TV with an integrated PS2, the Bravia KDL-22PX300, which is something of a collector's item today.

Teiyu Goto's PS2 design didn't randomly select blue lettering on a black plastic case – his inspiration was the blue dot of our planet Earth against the vast blackness of space. And between that grand thinking and Kutaragi's ambitious Emotion Engine, the PS2 really was a console apart, something that brought new life and new lessons to the gaming world. Its runaway commercial success was never guaranteed, despite all the planning Sony had put into place. But there's a chance its 155 million units sold will never be surpassed, and that's all down to what it did – genuinely evolving the market with fresh features and stunning games – and when it did it, with a former champion announcing its retirement and other sometime powerhouses misfiring at the beginning of a new millennium. Back-to-back golds, achieved.

Playstation 2: Five Must Plays

Grand Theft Auto: San Andreas (2004)
While not an exclusive series to the platform in question, Grand Theft Auto is nonetheless tied in many players' minds to the PlayStation, with the original top-down cops-and-robbers experience coming out on the PS1 in late 1997 and receiving both a dedicated sequel and a standalone expansion on the console. The series' first 3D game, *Grand Theft Auto III*, released on the PS2 in October 2001 – two years before its arrival on Xbox – which further deepened this relationship between software and hardware. But it was 2004's *San Andreas*, the third full 3D game for PS2 and fifth main series entry, that stands out as the fan favourite of the GTAs of its generation. Set in three cities – fictional versions of Los Angeles, San Francisco and Las Vegas – it follows protagonist CJ after he's released from prison in 1992 and immediately finds himself embroiled in gang warfare and facing up to corrupt cops. An epic like few games to come before it, *San Andreas* set the standard for all GTA games to come after – not that there have been many, with the last main entry at the time of writing being 2013's widely ported and updated *Grand Theft Auto V* and the much-anticipated *VI* yet to receive an official announcement.

Metal Gear Solid 3: Snake Eater (2004)
A prequel to the Metal Gear games that came before it, *Snake Eater* is the fifth mainline game in its series and swaps hi-tech military facilities and gloomy internal environments for a lot of creeping through Soviet forests in the 1960s. More streamlined story wise than its numerical predecessor *Sons of Liberty* and featuring a more familiar-looking protagonist in Naked Snake – aka Big Boss, the father of *Metal Gear Solid*'s Solid Snake – this is still a tale of many twists and turns, of serious situations and dire straits, but it's also possessed by a wicked humour and appreciation for the flexibility of the fourth wall. The script is a mix of weighty drama and hammy nonsense that struggles to find a consistent tone, but so far as stealth-action gameplay goes, *Snake Eater* remains elite.

Resident Evil 4 (2005)
There's an argument that *Resident Evil 4* should appear on every Five Must Plays list in this book, providing it was released on the platform in question (and it's appeared on a lot of different consoles since its debut on GameCube a few months before this version), but the PS2 is as good a place as any for Capcom's masterpiece of over-the-shoulder third-person shooting with lots of horror high jinks stirred in. Indeed, the PS2 release expanded the GameCube original, adding a new part of the story called Separate Ways where the player takes on the role of Ada Wong instead of main protagonist Leon S. Kennedy (last seen in *Resident Evil 2*), and it also included other post-game unlockable extras. Both hugely influential on the action genre for its perspective and gameplay and a seemingly ageless appeal, *Resi 4* is an essential whatever your console of choice, and was remade for PlayStation 5, PC and Xbox Series consoles in 2023.

Shadow of the Colossus (2006)
This meditative, peculiarly empty-feeling open-world game from director Fumito Ueda is absolutely an acquired taste with its minimal guidance and slim narrative. But it's a game where just being in its world, the Forbidden Land, is what it's all about – not the end of

the journey you take through it. The pitch is fairly simple: you must fight and defeat 16 enormous creatures spread around these lands so that a mysterious and somewhat sinister force known as Dormin will restore life to a fallen friend. Every colossus is a puzzle as protagonist Wander must mount them to strike at select weak spots, while the gigantic beasts do their utmost to shake him free and crush him under foot, club, tail, whatever they can. It soon becomes evident why this place is known as the Forbidden Land – but there's no turning back, and *Shadow of the Colossus* will leave a powerful and lasting impression on any player willing to stick with its formula-eschewing design. The game was remade for PlayStation 4 in 2018 and received another round of universal critical acclaim.

Persona 4 (2008)

This murder-mystery role-player is a stylish and narratively satisfying epic that pits a group of teenagers in a rural Japanese town against a nefarious force that is orchestrating the killings of individuals, including a teacher at a local school and a TV presenter. The group discovers a parallel world, entered via a television set, where they gain powerful abilities channelled through fantastical entities called Personas. If that all sounds a little out there, well, *Persona 4* certainly does go places that other games don't – but it's grounded by realistic-feeling relationships between its core cast, and its sumptuous music is almost worth a playthrough in and of itself. The game earned an expanded re-release on the PlayStation Vita in 2011, as *Persona 4 Golden*, which subsequently came to PC in 2020 and has since released for Switch, Xbox One and Series consoles and PlayStation 4; and there are several *Persona 4*-specific spin-offs and adaptations, including a rhythm-action dancing game, an anime TV show, and even a theatre production.

GAMECUBE

Manufacturers: Nintendo, Foxconn

Released: September 2001 (Japan), November 2001 (North America), May 2002 (Europe, Australia)

PlayStation's approach of beginning work on its next console before its current machine had even released for consumers wasn't quite replicated by Nintendo, but the Mario makers wasted little time in commencing development on the system that'd ultimately succeed the N64. It was in 1997 that Chinese-American entrepreneur Dr Wei Yen founded ArtX with 20 former Silicon Graphics Inc employees, focused on the design and production of graphics chips. Yen had previously been senior vice president at SGI and had liaised extensively with Nintendo on the N64, so for its next console Nintendo already had a valuable ally in the GPU arena. In 1998 ArtX would receive the contract to produce the GameCube's GPU, code-named Flipper, and took the lead on the console's system logic. The reason for that name, Flipper, is connected to what the GameCube was called before its release. Having been the N2000 for a while both internally at Nintendo and in the games media, in May 1999 the console was officially announced as Project Dolphin – *Flipper* being the name of a TV show from the 1960s starring a dolphin interacting with human characters. Another name briefly used for the console was Star Cube, but it didn't stick despite trademark applications being submitted in 1999.

A year on from its reveal, however, Dolphin was clearly not the name the console would release with, as Shigeru Miyamoto told IGN in June 2000: 'I'm not in the position to tell you (its real name).' Miyamoto reportedly liked the Dolphin moniker and wanted to go with it, but not even the influence of the man who created Mario, Zelda and Donkey Kong was enough to persuade Nintendo to hold onto the cetacean-inspired handle. Select early GameCube titles played on the code name though, with the spacecraft in *Pikmin* called the SS Dolphin and the events of *Super Mario Sunshine* set on Isle Delfino, a dolphin-shaped tropical island ('delfino' being Italian for 'dolphin').

Like the Dreamcast, Nintendo wanted the GameCube to be friendly for third-party developers. The console's CPU, code-named Gekko, was made by IBM rather than being an internally designed proprietary chip, and its Mini DVD format for games was worked on in collaboration with Matsushita (now known as Panasonic). Each of these discs, 8cm in diameter compared to a regular DVD's 12, could hold 1.4GB of data as standard on a single layer (certain workarounds could push that capacity to 5.3GB), and the format was chosen to offer greater capacity than cartridges while guarding against game piracy. There was also the fact that Nintendo's research concluded that Japanese consumers liked smaller devices in their homes, which is why the GameCube is so little beside its generational peers like the PlayStation 2 and Xbox. Its carry handle was included as the same research showed that Japanese users moved their consoles between TVs in different rooms. Console sales would be a factor in turning ease of third-party development into regular third-party releases for the GameCube, however, and with the N64 selling fewer units than the SNES before it and the PlayStation – and later, the PlayStation 2 – enjoying such success, several studios were on the fence about lending their support to Nintendo's new machine.

Nintendo was also seemingly in no rush to get their new console to market. After announcing Project Dolphin in May 1999, it'd be over two years before the GameCube would come out in Japan on 14 September 2001, with the machine's final name confirmed in August 2000 and its launch line-up of titles only locked in at May 2001's E3 conference in Los Angeles. One anonymous developer told IGN in 1999: 'If titles like *Perfect Dark* and *Donkey Kong 64* do well, we're not going to see Nintendo's new hardware until 2001.' (Both titles would end up in the N64's top 20 best-selling games.) And Nintendo of America's then executive vice president of sales and marketing, Peter Main, also said at the time that he expected the company's new system to be out around the end of 2001. Nintendo felt that while the N64 wasn't as powerful as either the Dreamcast or PlayStation 2, the quality of its software would keep units ticking over. And with 1999 also seeing the release of *Super Smash Bros.*, *Pokémon Stadium* and *Pokémon Snap*, and 2000 *The Legend of Zelda: Majora's Mask* and *Banjo-Tooie*, all of which were multi-million sellers, they might have been onto something.

Both the GameCube name and its design – including the controller (also available in the wireless WaveBird model), which took three years to develop itself, moving through various iterations including a model that did away with Nintendo's traditional D-pad completely – were agreed by Nintendo's Japanese and American teams, ensuring there'd be no remodelling or renaming for Western markets. The console's Japanese launch was supported by just three games – *Luigi's Mansion*, Mario's brother taking a rare lead in his own game; *Wave Race Blue Storm*, a new entry in Nintendo's jet ski racing series; and the SEGA-published *Super Monkey Ball* (the Dreamcast having been discontinued several months earlier) – but for its North American debut two months later, on 18 November, several more were added including another SEGA game in the shape of *Crazy Taxi*, *Star Wars Rogue Squadron II: Rogue Leader*, EA's *Madden NFL 2002* (a must for the market in question), and *Tony Hawk's Pro Skater 3*. As day-one rosters in console history go, the GameCube's American selection was arguably one of the strongest ever. Even more games were added for the European launch on 3 May 2002, including a football game with *International Superstar Soccer 2* and yet another (expanded, in this case) SEGA port, *Sonic Adventure 2: Battle*.

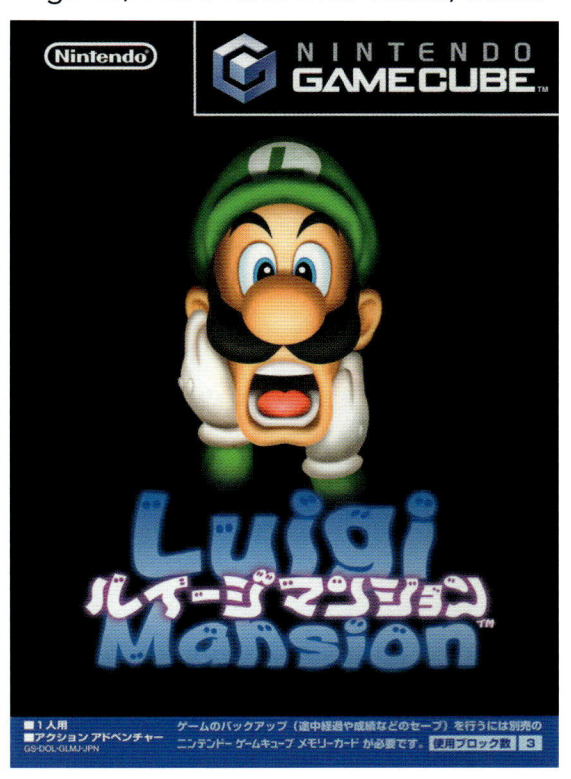

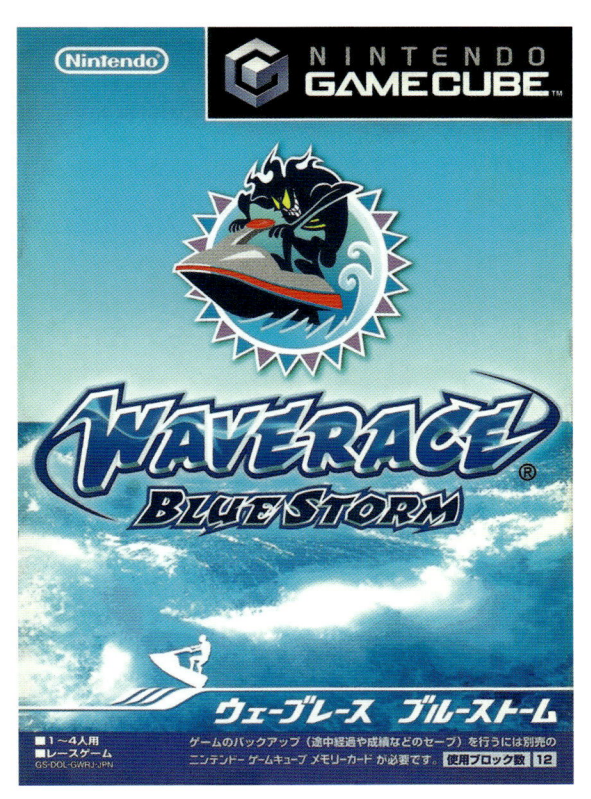

Initial sales in Japan weren't as strong as the N64's had been – up to 300,000 consoles were sold in the first three days, compared to half a million for Nintendo's previous system. Stores did sell out of their stock in the US, with launch weekend sales revenue stateside amounting to $100 million. But a shadow loomed large over the GameCube's chances in any territory: the PlayStation 2. Where Sony's machine offered DVD compatibility, allowing movies to be played, the GameCube was exclusively a gaming machine, much as the Dreamcast had been before it. Its online functionality was limited, with only five titles released in its lifespan supporting online play, and zero backwards compatibility with the N64 meant players effectively had to abandon their previous favourites when they switched to GameCube – not a problem for the PS2, which could play PS1 games and use the older console's controllers. The GameCube would let users run Game Boy Advance (and Color, and original 'DMG') cartridges on their TVs though, via the bottom-mounted Game Boy Player peripheral, but this didn't arrive until 2003. Despite costing $100 less at launch than the PS2 in the States, and only £129 at launch in the UK, the GameCube struggled to impose itself and ultimately achieved 21.74 million sales globally by the time of its 2007 discontinuation, under half of Nintendo's prediction of 50 million sales by 2005 and making it the company's lowest-selling home console at the time (discounting the Famicom Disk System, which required a Famicom to operate).

As sales were restricted by not only the PS2's market dominance but also the emergence of the Xbox in the West – Microsoft's console performed appallingly in Japan, where it sold fewer than half a million units – third-party developers eased their support for the GameCube, preferring to focus on the runaway leader of the time. SEGA, Nintendo's old enemy in the so-called 'console war' of the early 1990s, did stick by the GameCube though; as did EA, whose officially licensed sports titles released right up until the console's discontinuation. Strong sales of first-party games – the top ten best-selling GameCube releases were all published by Nintendo itself, and 18 of the top 20 (the exceptions being SEGA's *Sonic Adventure 2: Battle* and Capcom's *Resident Evil 4*) – prevented the console from being a total failure for its makers, but questions were asked in the media as to whether Nintendo could survive as a hardware manufacturer. Would it not be better, perhaps, to focus on making amazing games for other console platforms?

Nintendo was formally approached by a future competitor, Microsoft, about this very subject in 2001, just before the GameCube was released. Microsoft put forward an offer to buy Nintendo for $25 billion, and make its games – Mario, Metroid, Zelda et al – exclusives for its new Xbox console. The approach wasn't met favourably by senior Nintendo staffers. Years later, firm details emerged of the meeting that Microsoft had with Nintendo about this deal, with Kevin Bachus, then Microsoft's director of third-party relations, telling Bloomberg in 2021: 'Steve (Ballmer, then CEO of Microsoft) made us go to Nintendo to see if they would consider being acquired. They just laughed their assess off. Like, imagine an hour of somebody just laughing at you. That was kind of how that meeting went.' His colleague, head of business development Bob McBreen, added: '(Our) pitch was their hardware stunk compared to Sony PlayStation. So the idea was, "You're better at the games, with Mario and all that, why not let us take care of the hardware?" But it didn't work out.'

Nintendo's next console would improve its faltering commercial fortunes, and then some – but the seeds for the Wii, which would be backwards compatible with GameCube games and successfully achieve multi-generational appeal, were already being sown in the early 2000s. Nintendo patented a motion-control compatible control pad for the GameCube that didn't enter production but did get far enough for Factor 5, the developers of *Rogue Squadron II*, to use a prototype during the making of their Star Wars sequel. The GameCube didn't forget its past either, with its ambient menu music a slowed-down version of the start-up tune that played on the Famicom Disk System (perhaps a curse as it turned out, but it makes sense when you consider this was Nintendo's first standalone disc-based console). As well as a variety of differently coloured and patterned standard-model GameCubes coming out worldwide – everything from indigo and black, the most common versions, to a striped model themed around a Japanese baseball team and a Gundam-themed red release – Panasonic issued a machine of its own that played GameCube discs as well as DVDs and CDs (and more), the Panasonic Q, which even had its own dedicated Game Boy Player add-on.

Speaking in 2001, the late Satoru Iwata, Nintendo's president from 2002 to 2015, told IGN that the GameCube was, quite simply, 'an optimised machine for gaming'. That was all Nintendo wanted its sixth-generation system to be, and in hindsight it was a goal achieved. But the market around home games consoles was changing. The Dreamcast showed that just being a brilliant piece of gaming hardware wasn't enough when the PS2 could do so much more, and Nintendo was taught the same lesson with the GameCube's low sales. Unlike SEGA, Nintendo survived this shift in consumer wants and expectations, drawing upon its rich roster of intellectual properties to produce some stunning GameCube exclusives while being supported financially by its market-leading handheld consoles – the Game Boy Color had launched in 1998 and the Game Boy Advance in 2001, both of which sold multiple millions of units (all models combined, the Game Boy family sold around 200 million units). No need to sell to Microsoft or anyone else, then, otherwise home gaming in the 21st century might have evolved very differently indeed.

Gamecube: Five Must Plays

Luigi's Mansion (2001)
The GameCube launched with a very different kind of Mario-series game, as *Luigi's Mansion* made the green-clothed brother its star and put him in a haunted house that he's apparently won in a competition. Mario's rather flatter than he used to be, transformed into a painting, and it's up to Luigi to save him and defeat all manner of spooks along the way. But this is no game of dashing about and leaping on enemies' heads – Luigi is armed with specialist ghost-busting gear provided by one Professor E. Gadd, who helps him understand the true nature of this supernatural mansion. A refreshing twist on its series, *Luigi's Mansion* is a short but sweet adventure that received a 3DS sequel with 2013's *Dark Moon*, a remake for the same handheld in 2018, and a third game (*Luigi's Mansion 3*, predictably enough) was released on Switch in 2019.

Super Smash Bros. Melee (2001)
The second Smash Bros. game after the N64 original, this is where the series really found its footing and grew in both mainstream recognition and as a huge presence in the competitive fighting game scene. The GameCube's best-selling game with 7.41 million copies shifted, *Melee* is a multiplayer extravaganza of multiple game modes, many unlockable playable characters, and effortlessly accessible gameplay that clicks immediately but will take many months, or even years, to fully master. Its popularity led to GameCube-styled controllers releasing for the Wii U and Switch alongside those consoles' own iteration of Smash Bros. in 2014 and 2018 respectively.

The Legend of Zelda: The Wind Waker (2002)
With gorgeous cel-shaded visuals, *The Wind Waker* is a Zelda game that no passing of time will ever take the shine off. Looks aside, the gameplay loop of this title differed slightly from previous Zeldas by taking Link out onto the open sea with its dungeons set on islands, and many other patches of dry land available to optionally explore. However, its core is much the same as what came before it, as certain specialist items must be obtained before new areas can be accessed. With a plot that goes far deeper than first impressions suggest and a world that can't quite be fully appreciated from sea level, *The Wind Waker* is engrossing and affecting in a way that the very best entries in its series are. Re-released in HD on the Wii U in 2013, using the GamePad for Link's map and inventory screen, this is one of the most celebrated Zelda games of all time, right up there with *Ocarina of Time* and *Breath of the Wild* in many fan rankings.

Metroid Prime (2002)
The first 3D game in the Metroid series, *Prime* is set before the events of all the titles that came before it on NES, Game Boy and SNES, and finds protagonist Samus Aran exploring the history of the Chozo civilisation and encountering the Space Pirates for the first time. Played from a first-person perspective most of the time – it switches to third-person when Samus is in her Morph Ball form – *Prime* follows previous games' formula of poking around the environments for key, plot-progressing power-ups and other upgrades. It also features some minor Game Boy Advance compatibility as owners of *Metroid Fusion* can use Samus' suit in that game in *Prime* and unlock the original *Metroid* to play on their GameCube. With an average score according to review aggregator Metacritic of 97/100, *Metroid Prime* is one of the most critically acclaimed games of all time and spawned two direct sequels, *Metroid Prime 2: Echoes* on GameCube and *Metroid Prime 3: Corruption* on Wii. as of June 2023, *Metroid Prime 4* is in active development for the Switch and a Remastered version of the first game is available too.

F-Zero GX (2003)
At the time of writing the final F-Zero game to release for a home console (as Game Boy Advance titles came after it), *GX* is a super-speedy and super-punishing racer that enjoys compatibility with an arcade counterpart, the SEGA-published *F-Zero AX* – data from one can be shared with the other via a memory card. *GX* itself was developed not by Nintendo but by Amusement Vision, a division of SEGA that later became Ryu Ga Gotoku Studio and made a worldwide name for itself with the Yakuza series. With many game modes, difficulty options (although even 'novice' is a challenge) and even a story to progress through featuring Captain Falcon as its playable star, *GX* is considered by many to be the definitive F-Zero experience – which may be why Nintendo is yet to pursue a new entry in this futuristic series.

XBOX

Manufacturers: Microsoft, Flextronics

Released: November 2001 (North America), February 2002 (Japan), March 2002 (Europe, Australia)

In the mid-1990s, a trio of Microsoft engineers internally nicknamed the Beastie Boys developed a set of programming application interfaces (APIs) for PCs that enabled game developers to sort of bypass the constraints of the newly launched Windows 95 operating system. Instead, the collection of APIs worked simultaneously to enable different parts of a program to communicate with each other, meaning that developers didn't need to worry about incompatibility between MS-DOS games and Windows 95 as many of the latter's core routines could be worked around. The result: Windows could, and would, become a viable platform for video gaming. The trio – Alex St John, Craig Esler and Eric Engstrom – named their creation DirectX, and its first version was released in September 1995. Six years later, this same set of APIs would be the foundation for Microsoft's first-ever games console, which for a while had the work-in-progress name of DirectX Box, soon shortened to Xbox.

As reports of the PlayStation 2 started to circulate in 1997, Microsoft realised that Sony's new console represented a significant threat to PC gaming, the console's power comparable with many of the best home computers of the time. Microsoft CEO Bill Gates (pictured above) worried that the PS2 could shatter Windows' share of the PC gaming market and elected to pursue consoles as a new business direction. First Microsoft worked with SEGA, whose Dreamcast used a modified version of Windows CE as its operating system. Next, it reached out to Sony to see if the companies could work together, with Microsoft providing key software for the PS2. Sony declined.

Then, in 1998, four Microsoft employees – Seamus Blackley, Kevin Bachus, Otto Berkes and Ted Hase – began a project named Midway, the aim being the creation of a console that wouldn't just match the PS2 but surpass it and destroy Sony's market dominance. The name Midway was a reference to the Battle of Midway in World War II, where American naval forces crushed a Japanese fleet in the North Pacific, and was considered to be in poor taste by journalists – but it didn't carry through to the naming of the console itself, when a host of options were put forward for consideration.

As well as the DirectX Box came a slew of suggestions: the AIO, standing for All-In-One; the MOX, aka the Microsoft Optimal Experience; the MARC, meaning Microsoft Action Reality Center; and MIND, representing Microsoft Interactive Network Device (which at least highlighted the significance that Microsoft would place upon online functionality). There were many others, but focus testing produced one clear winner: Xbox. Nomenclature issues aside, various teams were busy within Microsoft on both the insides of the console to be and its exterior design. Gates demanded a kind of Trojan Horse machine, a device that would have the appearance of a video games console but ultimately put the Windows operating system at the heart of a household, right beneath the TV set.

And that was certainly the aim of its engineers to begin with. But after a short series of prototypes, it was clear that a Windows interface wouldn't work for the Xbox and that production costs were rising beyond expectation. Gates was frustrated at these developments but nevertheless gave the green light to go ahead, having been convinced that what was being built would outperform the PS2. And it would, with its Intel Pentium III CPU running at 733MHz to the Emotion Engine's 294.9MHz and its NVIDIA GeForce 3-based GPU essentially making it a state-of-the-art PC in console form. Compared to the PS2, the Dreamcast and the GameCube, on raw power alone the Xbox was leagues ahead of its competitors.

It was also substantially larger, a proper statement piece of hardware that would dominate any space, any room, it was placed in. Its look was created by industrial designer Horace Luke, who'd joined Microsoft after working at Nike, and who told IGN in 2000: 'When you purchase that console, and you put it on your living room floor, it should represent every brand value that Xbox brings to the picture, every strength that the platform brings.' Which is to say this was a bigger and better console than the competition on the inside, so it needed to look that way too. It was also Luke who gave the Xbox brand its green colour scheme, albeit more through limitation than deliberate design, as Blackley explained to IGN's Podcast Unlocked in 2015: 'Horace Luke, when we had to have a logo for a meeting or something, the only colour (marker) he had was green, so he made all this artist's stuff with green, and now it's still green. It's crazy.' And it was also Luke who finalised the form of the Xbox's hugely divisive original controller, called the Duke, which was bundled with the console in all markets except Japan and widely criticised for being overly large and uncomfortable. It was later replaced by Japan's smaller S controller as the standard pack-in pad worldwide.

The Xbox project was revealed to the media by Bill Gates late in 1999, with its official announcement coming in March 2000 during Gates' keynote presentation at the Game Developers Conference in San Jose. Here, two major features of the Xbox, billed in the on-show slides as 'the future of console gaming', were confirmed: its internal 8GB hard drive for saving data and downloads, and its built-in Ethernet port offering broadband connectivity, essential for what would roll out as Xbox Live in 2002. But the prototype on show was wildly different to the final console design, a giant X-shaped unit with a glowing green core. 'This is the box we take to trade shows and events like this,' commented Blackley, who'd joined Gates on stage, before confirming that this unit was only capable of around 10% of the final Xbox. Even so, the keynote left a huge impression, and while Microsoft's attempts to acquire outright companies like Square Enix, Midway and even Nintendo failed in the run up to the Xbox's release, it did secure console-exclusive titles from Tecmo and Bethesda. (Years later, in 2021, Microsoft would buy the latter's parent company, ZeniMax Media, bringing Bethesda into its Xbox Game Studios family.)

One acquisition that was completed at the time, however, was Bungie, a Washington State-based studio that was working on a new sci-fi shooter for Mac and Windows. Or rather, it *was* for those platforms, until Xbox intervened. That game, *Halo: Combat Evolved*, was reworked, shifting from a third-person perspective to first-person and prepared as a launch exclusive for the Xbox. And it hit its deadline, taking its place beside 19 other titles on 15 November 2001 when Microsoft's console finally released in North America. The promotional push for the system – the first American-made home console since the Atari Jaguar – had been substantial, with WWE superstar The Rock, aka Dwayne Johnson, brought out at CES 2001 to lend Gates some youth-market star

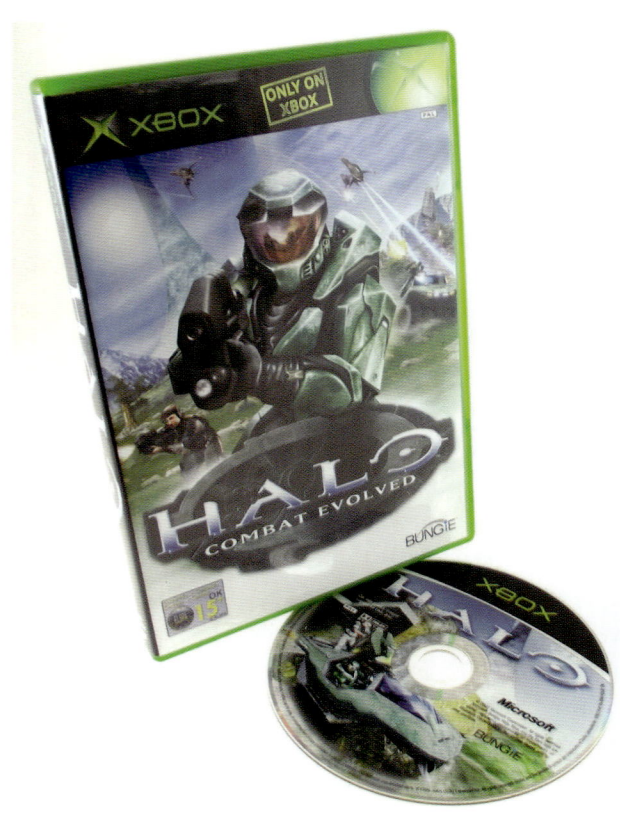

144

power. TV ads eschewed the PlayStation 2's cerebral style for a focus on the gameplay that only Xbox could provide, with their creative director at agency McCann-Erikson Worldwide Inc, Craig Markus, calling it 'an advertising campaign designed to speak directly to the gamers'. It worked, in the short term at least: by the end of 2001 1.5 million Xbox consoles had been sold in North America alone, outpacing the Nintendo GameCube, which had released in the region three days after the Xbox, and more importantly the PS2. Supply wasn't an issue as Microsoft worked with Flextronics to establish a factory in Mexico to ensure mass production and availability in North America.

Xbox's momentum wouldn't last though, and sales were somewhat hindered by a high hardware failure rate (up to 25% according to Flextronics CEO Michael Marks, who told Bloomberg in 2021: 'We had a lot of repair work that had to get done. Microsoft paid for everything, and we just kept iterating until we got it right.'). And as console sales slowed so did those of Microsoft-published software for the system, which were so essential for making back the losses involved with the machine's pricing: with an RRP of $299 at its US launch, the same as the PS2, Microsoft was losing an amazing $125 on every console it sold, and a price drop to $199 in 2002 only made things worse. Speaking to Bloomberg in 2021, Robbie Bach, the former president of Microsoft's Entertainment and Devices Division, said: 'Probably six months after we shipped, you could see the price curve and do the math and know that we were going to lose billions of dollars … The more volume we did, the worse it got.' Perhaps it was a good thing for Microsoft then that the Xbox didn't sell in the same numbers as the PS2, achieving total worldwide sales of 24 million by the time of its 2006 discontinuation – 16 million in North America, six million in Europe and two million in the rest of the world (including fewer than 500,000 sales in Japan, which to this day has never been a particularly successful territory for Xbox).

Xbox did a lot of things right. It was the first games console to offer a built-in hard drive, keeping memory cards optional (they were useful for taking your saved files to a friend's house), and its Xbox Live service was a genuine game-changer when it launched in 2002. Online play had simply never been so simple, assuming you had the broadband access to use it at the turn of the millennium, and it'd grow substantially in subscribers when new features were added, like achievements and Gamerscore, with the Xbox 360. But locking DVD functionality behind the purchase of a Movie Playback package lessened the Xbox's appeal beside Sony's machine, and its games library simply never rivalled the breadth and depth of the PS2's.

Poor sales outside of North America also dampened the original Xbox's legacy – but to those who owned an Xbox, in its standard black or widely sold transparent 'crystal' casing (other designs were available, including 'Halo green' and a Japan-only blue model), Microsoft's first console holds a special place in their hearts, and many of its games are playable today, with performance upgrades, on Xbox Series X and S. And even the Duke controller, aka the 'Fatty', so ridiculed at release in 2001, has been revived – peripherals manufacturer Hyperkin released an officially licensed version of it for the Xbox One and PC in 2018, and for Series X and S to mark Xbox's 20th anniversary in 2021.

Xbox: Play One Game

Halo: Combat Evolved (2001)
Halo is now a multi-platform, multimedia mega-brand with several games under its belt, a Paramount + TV show, feature-length live-action spin-offs, an anime series and many books and comics. But it all started with this game, originally in development at Bungie as a real-time strategy title prior to switching to third-person action and targeting a PC and Mac release, before Microsoft stepped in, put the player inside the helmet of its super-soldier protagonist, and the rest is history. Multiplayer modes represented a huge part of the game's appeal, with up to four Xbox consoles able to be connected for 16-player matches (the game releasing before Xbox Live was ready – its 2004 sequel, however, would be instrumental in popularising said service), and split-screen support for four players on one system. The game's campaign could also be played through in full in two-player co-op, its story of gigantic ringworlds and the Flood, of Master Chief and Cortana and all their allies, becoming legendary. A pivotal first-person shooter that helped the genre make sense on consoles, with a control pad in hand, the importance of *Halo: Combat Evolved* simply can't be overstated.

Child's Play: Questionable Consoles for the Younger Gamer

Consoles aimed at very young children didn't blink into existence in the 2000s, as the laptop-styled (but without a built-in screen, necessitating a TV) SEGA Pico had been released in 1993, targeting under-sevens and supported by over 200 pieces of educational-orientated software with themes ranging from SEGA's own Sonic the Hedgehog and Ecco the Dolphin to Sesame Street and Disney Princesses. But the first decade of the 21st century saw further toy-like devices emerge, albeit nothing that ever escaped the shadow of the main attractions from Sony, Microsoft and Nintendo.

VTech, the makers of 1982's CreatiVision console and 1988's Socrates educational system (as well as several home computer models), released the V.Smile in 2004. Using 'Smartridges' for its software, this was more of a product range for players aged between three and six than a single console, with a portable unit, the Pocket Generation, coming out the same year as the main system and motion-controlled variant, the V.Smile Motion, releasing in 2008. The V.Smile Baby, released in 2006, aimed its sights younger still, ostensibly designed for children aged between nine and 36 months. The V.Smile range was discontinued in 2010 with software support continuing until 2012, but a similarly positioned product, the LeapFrog Clickstart, remained on sale after Vtech's systems were retired and also targeted three- to six-year-olds.

Another name from home gaming's past resurfaced in the mid-00s, as Mattel – makers of the Intellivision – released the HyperScan in October 2006, exclusively in North America for $69.99. Its library of five released games (two more are known about but were cancelled) illustrates how its ambition was to target pre-teen players, with titles based on the cartoon *Ben 10* and a few Marvel franchises. Games came on CD-ROM but used radio frequency identification (RFID) cards to unlock otherwise inaccessible features, such as new moves for controllable characters. The pack-in *X-Men* game, for example, came with six of these cards – but Mattel also sold booster packs, six cards per set, to take the compatible total for this one game to 102. At ten dollars for six RFID cards, this was going to be a hugely expensive way to see everything one game had to offer. After a critical mauling and extremely poor HyperScan sales, however, only half of these cards were released. Eighty cards were available for *Ben 10*, taking a $20 game to a total cost of $150 to unlock it all, and 70 for *Marvel Heroes*, pushing its complete price to $130.

Even if the HyperScan had worked as a console, this predatory pricing structure would have doomed the machine – but the system was a mess anyway, with inconsistent performance, a horrible controller, painfully long loading times and a high hardware failure rate. Many consoles featured in these pages have been ranked as among the worst ever in lists across the gaming media, but perhaps none are as wretched as the HyperScan. Mattel cut its losses and discontinued the console in 2007, selling remaining systems for $9.99, games for $1.99 and booster packs for 99 cents. Fewer than 10,000 HyperScans were sold in total, and Mattel hasn't returned to console manufacturing since.

Oddities From Beyond the Mainstream

Despite PlayStation's untouchable market performance and Nintendo and Xbox fighting over whatever Sony didn't take for itself, there were other brand-new consoles released in the 2000s – not that any of them were more than the faintest blip on the radar for most players.

Following the 3DO model of establishing a games format that could be produced by several manufacturers, California-based company VM Labs released its NUON technology in July 2000. NUON units weren't strictly games consoles but DVD players with added gaming features, and these devices could also run (barely) enhanced movies. VM Labs didn't see why every maker of DVD players wouldn't want a NUON chip inside their goods, but many proved reluctant to incorporate the technology – Sony in particular saw little point in doing so when it had its PlayStation 2 in the works. Select manufacturers did take a punt though, including Samsung, RCA and Toshiba, selling their NUON-enhanced players at between $350 and $500. But VM Labs was out of money and declared bankruptcy in late 2001, selling NUON to Genesis Microchip, who subsequently dropped the entire thing in 2003. Only eight games, each with graphics more akin to a PS1 than the Dreamcast or PS2, were released for NUON machines, including *Tempest 3000* and *Space Invaders*

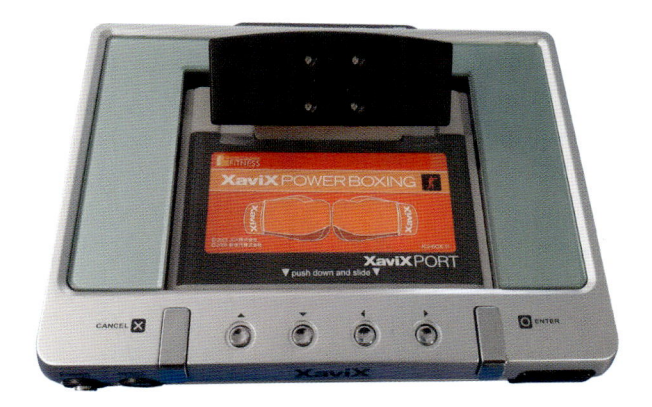

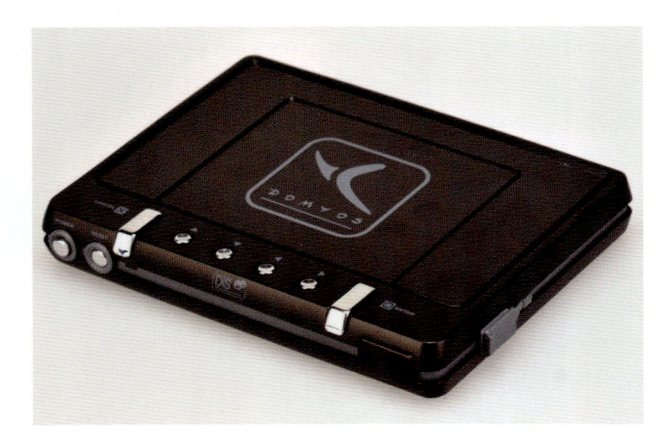

XL, and just four movies made use of the technology.

Released in 2004 for the North American market, the XaviXPORT was a sports-themed console developed by Japan's SSD Company Limited that used motion-controlled wireless peripherals shaped like tennis racquets and baseball bats to play games that left the user in no doubt as to what they were getting into, bearing as they did titles like *Baseball*, *Tennis*, *Golf* and *Bowling*. The system came to the UK as the Domyos Interactive System in 2007, sold exclusively through the Decathlon chain of stores, but represented a poor purchase when the Wii offered similar swing-the-thing experiences with its pack-in *Wii Sports* collection, but could also play *Super Mario Galaxy*. Nevertheless, old games continued to be sold online until 2017 when the official Xavixstore.com website shut down.

Sold as a 'Family Entertainment System' rather than a games console, ZAPiT Games' Game Wave launched in North America in October 2005 for an RRP of $99. Its makers secured a deal with the Christian media franchise VeggieTales, which increased its appeal to consumers who studied their Bibles more frequently than the gaming press, and its games were primarily trivia- and puzzle-based experiences – the TV remote-like controllers weren't well suited to traditional platformers and sports games. Thirteen titles are known to have released for the Game Wave prior to its discontinuation in 2009. Also debuting in the 00s was the Zeebo, which released mainly in Brazil and Mexico in 2009 and played digital games – 57 were released by the time of its discontinuation in September 2011, including versions of *Pac-Mania*, *FIFA 09*, *Resident Evil 4*, *Tekken 2* and *Ridge Racer*. Some of its titles were compatible with a special motion-control pad called the Boomerang, and planned releases for the console in China and Russia didn't come to pass.

Two notable pieces of hardware that were announced to the press but never came out were the ApeXtreme, shown at both CES and E3 in 2004 but cancelled by the end of the same year; and the Phantom, which appeared for pre-order in 2003 stating a release date of early 2004 but saw its launch delayed and delayed again until, in August 2006, the product was removed from its manufacturer's website. There are two known prototypes of the Phantom, but no further units have been found. Both the Phantom and ApeXtreme were designed as console devices that would play PC game discs, something that Alienware's Windows-based DHS Media Center product line would provide to limited success.

XBOX 360

Manufacturers: Celestrica, Flextronics, Foxconn, Wistron

Released: November 2005 (North America), December 2005 (Europe, Japan), March 2006 (Australia), September 2006 (South Africa), December 2006 (Brazil), February 2007 (Russia)

Sony knew that producing a successor to the PlayStation 2 was vital to maintaining its market position, and in 2001 it began work on a new multi-core microprocessor to power what would eventually become the PlayStation 3. Its partners on this project were Toshiba and IBM (together forming an alliance known as STI – catchy, no doubt). The resulting CPU, Cell, took four years to develop at a cost of US$400 million, with the PS3 debuting in Japan in November 2006. But Microsoft's second-generation console, a direct rival to the PS3, beat Sony's machine to market by a year, aided enormously in its production by none other than IBM, who in 2003 had graciously shared its designs for the PS3's CPU with Microsoft. Breaking no terms of its STI agreement, IBM subsequently produced a separate CPU code-named Waternoose, later Xenon, a modified version of the Cell microprocessor exclusively for Microsoft's new machine: the Xbox 360.

The *Wall Street Journal* would headline a 2008 article on this above-board betrayal 'Playing the Fool', highlighting Sony's failure to exclude Microsoft from the clients that its STI partners could sell their work to. Once Sony's bosses realised what had transpired, they acted with brutal efficiency, reportedly firing the very man who'd spearheaded the development of the first PlayStation, Ken Kutagari, from his position as president of Sony Computer Entertainment. Other accounts state he retired from his role in 2007, but whether pushed or not the so-called father of the PlayStation moved to an honorary position within the company shortly after the PS3's release and departed completely in 2011. In 2005, Kutaragi had called the Xbox 360 'more like an Xbox 1.5', a slight that would come back to haunt him as Microsoft's machine stole a sales lead on the PS3, a lead it would hold until the sunset of console gaming's seventh generation and the introduction of the PlayStation 4 and Xbox One.

The Xbox 360's relatively short development period began in February 2003 but didn't really hit its stride until August of that year, when ATI was signed up to produce its graphics processing unit, the Xenos (the planning of which goes back to 2002). Names for the new console came and went – for a while, as its CPU name suggests, the system was known as Xenon – but there was also Trinity (taken from *The Matrix*), and Xbox 2 and Xbox Next were tossed around. But the 360 stuck when the decision-making management at Microsoft realised it put the player at the heart of everything Xbox was now capable of offering. Like the Xbox before it, the 360 was produced with an internal hard drive, which scaled from 20GB to 500GB across the machine's impressive 11-year lifespan, and it was built to be a connected console like no other before it, putting Xbox Live at the core of the user experience. Speaking to United Press International in 2005, Aaron Greenberg, then Xbox's global marketing manager, said: 'We made a lot of big bets [with the Xbox], [on] online broadband gaming, voice [chat] in every game, and adding a hard drive to the console experience.' And the bets paid off: in January 2008 Microsoft revealed that it had passed ten million Xbox Live members; and in December 2020, a month after the Xbox Series X and S launches, its monthly users had passed 100 million.

Like the original Xbox, Microsoft looked outside of the games industry for inspiration regarding the 360's outward appearance. It commissioned Japan's Hers Experimental Design Laboratory and San Francisco-based Astro Studios to produce something striking, something different, something that'd make the 360 desirable as an object to have in your living room almost regardless of its function. (Swappable faceplates helped owners get the right look for their personal spaces, too.) They also worked on the packed-in wireless controller to avoid a repeat of the Duke situation, producing something far more ergonomic and comfortable that used its two AA batteries to its advantage, having a reassuring weight in the hands.

In 2005, Astro Studios' president Brett Lovelady told the website Gamasutra (now gamedeveloper.com) how the console design went through 'four or five refinement iterations', covering 'aspects from materials to control functionality'. He noted some realities of the process, such as how 'you can't put a heat-sensitive item near a super-hot chip' and the need for 'airflow around the product' – but the level of heat inside the console would prove to be a problem upon its release, as up to 54% of initial shipments suffered from General Hardware Failure, indicated by three red lights on the front of the system.

This problem, known as the Red Ring of Death (even though only three quarters of the ring around the power button are illuminated red at the time), was attributed by Microsoft to cracking solder joints connected to the GPU, the cause said to be thermal stress. Guarantees were extended and consoles replaced, with Xbox's then corporate vice president Peter Moore revealing to IGN in 2015 that the cost to Microsoft ran to $1.15 billion. Later production runs modified the 360's components to prevent the issue, and the 'slim' model Xbox 360 S of 2010 and Xbox 360 E released in 2013 were designed to automatically switch off if they were running too hot.

This failure risk wasn't known to consumers at the console's launch, however, and demand was substantial. Preceded by a few viral marketing campaigns and an official unveiling of the console on an MTV special hosted by Elijah Wood in May, the Xbox 360 was made available to the American public on 22 November 2005 for a price of $299 for its 'Core' model with a wired controller and no bundled hard drive (but one could be bought separately), or $399 for the 'Premium' model with an included and removable 20GB hard drive and wireless pad. Even $399 represented a loss per console of over $150, but Microsoft was confident that Xbox Live and its own published software would prevent its bottom line from being too badly beaten up. (And in late 2006, then-president of Microsoft's Entertainment and Devices Division Robbie Bach confirmed to the San Jose *Mercury News* that: 'Xbox is on the trajectory we thought it'd be on [and] we feel very good about that.') Eighteen games were available for the North American launch, including *Call of Duty 2*, *Quake 4* and *Project Gotham Racing 3*. But one name was conspicuous by its absence: Halo.

'We're not positioning a killer app for launch,' is what J Allard (pictured below), a co-founder of the Xbox project back in 1999 and both CXO and CTO of Microsoft's Entertainment and Devices Division, told eurogamer.net in in May 2005. When asked if there'd be a Halo substitute for launch, he answered: 'There will be. I think there will be. It's not up to us to call the winners, let the gamers decide.' Those same gamers had made *Halo 2* and *Halo: Combat Evolved* the number one and two best-selling games on the original Xbox, so clearly there was huge anticipation for the third game's appearance on Xbox 360, and disappointment that it wasn't right there day one. But Bungie was shattered from the development of *Halo 2*, and its staff were burned out – *Halo 3* therefore took time, eventually releasing in September 2007 backed by a $40 million marketing campaign but earning $170 million back in 24 hours. In IGN's review of the Xbox 360, it said that none of its launch titles was a 'knockout, AAA title like *Halo* was at the launch of the Xbox', but at least early adopters could use the new console's (selective) backwards compatibility to run both existing Halo games from the original discs.

As huge as *Halo 3* was for the Xbox 360 though, it was only the console's ninth biggest game with 12.13 million units sold. At number one: the 24 million sales of *Kinect Adventures!*, the pack-in software for Xbox's motion-sensing peripheral, Kinect. This add-on was developed under the code name of Project Natal and was aimed at making the Xbox 360 more attractive to people who weren't into shooters and action games, taking its family-friendly cues from Nintendo's Wii and the PS3's PlayStation Eye (the successor to the PS2's EyeToy). With sales of eight million in its first two months, Kinect earned a Guinness World Record as the fastest-selling consumer electronics device; but the peripheral's appeal would diminish in 2013 when it was initially announced as an essential component of the Xbox One. A less-popular Xbox 360 peripheral was its HD DVD Player, which failed to gain much attention as HD DVDs themselves were discontinued in 2008, Blu-ray discs proving the preferred DVD alternative (and the format that games for the PlayStation 3, 4 and 5, Xbox One and Series X would come on).

The Xbox 360 would reach sales of 84 million worldwide – over 47 million in North America and 25 million in Europe, but only 1.66 million in Japan, further highlighting what little market share Microsoft could achieve in the region. For much of its lifespan it kept the PS3 at bay, with Sony's machine's total sales only overtaking the 360 in 2013 (and even then, the two machines ended up close to being tied). Compared to the performance of the original Xbox, the 360's performance was a massive success for its makers – but it could have all been so different had the Red Ring of Death not been dealt with at such speed. 'If we hadn't made that decision, there and then, and tried to fudge over this problem, then the Xbox brand wouldn't exist today,' Peter Moore told IGN in 2015. 'I'll never forget that moment.' And for millions of players around the world, the Xbox 360 *was* gaming in the late-00s, an amazing, reputation-making piece of hardware that'll always be thought of favourably. And yet neither Sony nor Microsoft could match the commercial highs of the company that'd slumped so dangerously with its past two consoles, with Nintendo's Wii the only home system of its generation to break 100 million sales.

Xbox 360: Five Must Plays

BioShock (2007)
A console exclusive on Xbox 360 for more than a year, coming to PS3 in late 2008, *BioShock* combined thought-provoking narrative depth with intense first-person action in a setting that would soon become one of gaming's most-loved virtual worlds: the underwater city of Rapture. With inspiration drawn from the works of Aldous Huxley and George Orwell, and also Ayn Rand, it's provocative with its moral choices and dystopian politics, and was widely celebrated in the gaming press for its immersive qualities and consistently impressive sights and sounds. BioShock won several game of the year awards and spawned two sequels, 2010's *BioShock 2* and the Rapture-departing *BioShock Infinite* of 2013.

Gears of War 2 (2008)
The original *Gears of War* had gone some way to plugging the Halo gap in the 360's line-up in late 2006, becoming a huge hit with solo players and, perhaps more importantly, Xbox Live users. Taking perspective cues from *Resident Evil 4*, it was a third-person shooter of compelling cover-based skirmishes and cacophonous bombast. For its sequel, makers Epic Games maintained the furious action of the first game but took its campaign storyline in a deeper direction as these burly characters, all muscle and grit, took on both the Locust enemy and their own splintering emotions. Multiplayer was again the star though, with the co-operative Horde mode earning many plaudits.

Bayonetta (2009)
While many third-party games of the Xbox 360 and PS3 era came to both consoles, it wasn't unusual for the Microsoft version to be deemed superior in the press – and PlatinumGames' awesome all-action *Bayonetta* is a fine illustration of this. Put the two side by side and the Xbox 360 game looks crisper, it flows smoother, and its controls feel tighter. The recipient of an extremely rare 10/10 review from *EDGE*, *Bayonetta* was celebrated for being an easy game to leap into and have fun with but containing amazing combat depth that would take several hours to master if you were to attain perfect scores. An essential for fans of the Devil May Cry games, *Bayonetta* received a Wii U-exclusive (at the time) sequel in 2014 as publishing duties switched from SEGA to Nintendo, and the Switch-only *Bayonetta 3* released at the end of 2022.

Limbo (2010)
This skin-tinglingly creepy puzzle-platformer was one of the breakout titles from the Xbox Live Arcade (XBLA) service, which Microsoft ran in the 360 era to sell smaller, download-only games. Developed by the Danish indie studio Playdead, *Limbo* plays in a classic 2D left-to-right style – but this is no Sonic or Mario adventure. Almost every screen contains some kind of potential death for the game's child protagonist, and its mesmerising monochromatic art style earned comparisons to the work of Tim Burton and Lotte Reiniger. Challenging, horrifying and unquestionably unique, *Limbo* was

not only a massive game for XBLA but also indie games as a whole, earning a slew of award nominations beside titles from larger developers with far bigger budgets – and winning several of them. *Limbo* subsequently released for many other platforms including PS3, PC and Mac, iOS and Android, Xbox One, PS4 and Switch.

The Elder Scrolls V: Skyrim (2011)

Bethesda's massive fifth Elder Scrolls entry might be the source of untold memes and jokes about how it's coming to every platform under the sun, but at release *Skyrim* was a true epic, a role-playing experience not to be missed. And when it came to playing the game on console, like *Bayonetta*, Xbox 360 was the system to pick. Plagued by performance issues on PS3, the Xbox experience was far easier going, with only the occasional giant-flying-into-the-air bug to deal with. Refining the first-person swords-and-sorcery gameplay from the fourth Elder Scrolls title, *Oblivion*, *Skyrim* earned substantial praise for its Norse-inspired world, its player freedom, and its amazing number of side-quests to crack on with (and environments to explore, just because). Five years after its release, Bethesda revealed that *Skyrim* had sold over 30 million copies, making it one of the best-selling games of all time – and in 2021 new-gen console ports of the game released for Xbox Series X and S and PlayStation 5.

PLAYSTATION 3

Manufacturers: Sony Electronics, Foxconn, Asus

Released: November 2006 (Japan, North America), March 2007 (Rest of the World)

The PlayStation 3's development began in 2001 with Cell, the CPU co-developed by Sony, Toshiba and IBM. With the Cell project being overseen by Ken Kutaragi, it fell to Shuhei Yoshida, then vice president of Sony Computer Entertainment America, to work with a select group of programmers to understand the architecture of the new machine and help studios and their games developers make the most of its power. Mark Cerny, formerly of SEGA and Crystal Dynamics, was one of these programmers, and immediately saw problems. Speaking years later, at Barcelona's Gamelab Conference in 2013, he said: 'The SPEs (the Special Processing Element cores of the Cell structure) had huge potential, but huge effort was required to programme them.'

The extra lengths that developers had to go to in order to get the best out of the PS3 would see the console's games vary massively in presentation from the launch of the system to its final years – just look at (Sony first-party studio) Naughty Dog's *Uncharted: Drake's Fortune* from 2007 and then at the same company's 2013's *The Last of Us*, as the two games could almost be running on different generations of hardware. The more that teams worked with the PS3, going through cycles of trial and error, the more they could push what the player experienced – 'It really feels that sometimes it's this bottomless pit of processing power,' is what Naughty Dog co-president Evan Wells said of the machine in 2010 – but early on the reception to the console as a platform for game development wasn't entirely positive. In a 2007 interview with next-gen.biz, Valve founder and former Microsoft developer Gabe Newell called the PS3 'a waste of everybody's time', adding: 'Investing in the Cell, investing in the SPE, gives you no long-term benefits. You're not going to gain anything except a hatred of the architecture [Sony has] created.'

Newell was exaggerating somewhat, but his later comment in the same interview that 'it's harder to get [PS3 games] to the same standard as the Xbox 360 and PC versions' was borne out by several externally developed titles that came to both Microsoft's and Sony's seventh-generation systems during their lifetimes. Bethesda's *Fallout 3* and *The Elder Scrolls V: Skyrim* earned higher review scores on Xbox 360, so too *BioShock, Bayonetta, Saints Row IV, Lost Planet: Extreme Condition* and *Mass Effect*. Differences were usually minor – slightly muddier visuals or a mildly inconsistent frame rate, nothing especially game breaking – but there can be no doubt that the PlayStation 3 quickly earned a reputation for being a hard system to create games for. But Sony was confident in its longer-term strategy, as the company's Kaz Hirai told *Official PlayStation Magazine* in 2009: 'I'd like to think we'll continue official leadership in this industry. Unless things go really bad, there's no way that at the end of a lifecycle our competition is going to have a higher install base.' He also conceded, however, that the PS3 was 'hard to programme for, and a lot of people see the negatives of it, but if you flip that around, it means the hardware has a lot more to offer'.

Hirai was right on a couple of points: the PlayStation 3 would end up ahead of the Xbox 360 in sales, *just*, achieving 87.4 million units by the time of its 2017 discontinuation while Microsoft scored 84 million; and the hardware did begin to sing a few years into its life, as its top four best-selling titles were all released in 2010 or later. But at the PS3's launch it wasn't just the headaches of bringing games to the hardware that saw the gaming and tech press give the console mixed reviews and buyers not picking it immediately – the system's initial price and its early availability proved huge factors in consumers hesitating and perhaps leaning instead towards what the Xbox 360 and Wii were offering.

On 11 November 2006 the PS3 debuted in Japan at ¥49,980 (about $420) for a model with a 20GB hard drive, and ¥59,980 ($508) for the 60GB model – memory cards were a thing of the past, but due to backwards compatibility with PS1 and PS2 discs in these early PS3 units, a memory card adapter was made available. Just over 88,000 PS3 consoles were sold in Japan over its first weekend, a figure that would have been higher if not for manufacturing delays resulting in fewer-than-hoped shipments reaching retailers. Demand outstripped supply, and some early buyers cashed in by putting their new consoles straight onto eBay, where some over-eager users paid three times the RRP to get their hands on Sony's system. Six days later, the console's North American launch was marred by reports of violence as people actively fought over too-few units, with one patron of a Walmart in Connecticut shot while waiting to pick up their PS3. The US release of the console also saw its price go above the Japanese equivalents, with the 20GB model selling at $499.99 and the 60GB at $599.99. Compared to the $399 launch price for a hard drive-bundled Xbox 360, which was lowered to $329 in 2006, this was a bold strategy from Sony – and some of the company's comments didn't make it any easier for PlayStation fans to swallow.

Speaking with the Japanese economic website Toyo Keizai in 2005, just after the console's official announcement at E3 2005 (where it appeared with a different configuration of ports, including six USBs and two HDMIs), Kutaragi commented that Sony wanted 'consumers to think to themselves, "I will work more hours to buy [a PS3]"', adding: 'We want people to feel

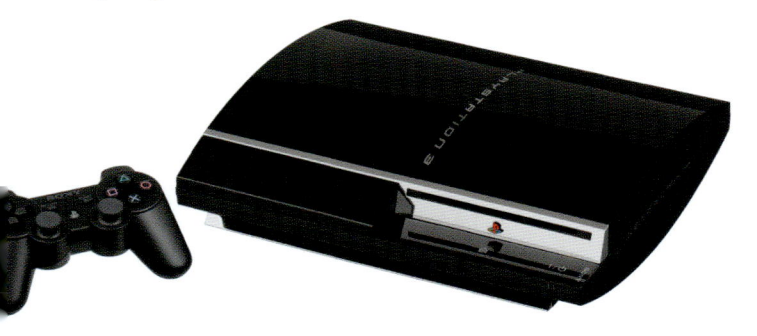

'Although the [PS3's] specification made it a £425 entry level machine, that was exactly the right thing to do because it gives us much more longevity in terms of lifecycle. The last thing I would want to be doing is replacing three cheaper machines over three years, rather than having something like PS3 that lasts for seven to 10 years.'

Perhaps expectedly though, the PlayStation 3 didn't perform at retail as well as Sony was hoping for. It saw an incredibly strong launch in Europe, with 165,000 units sold in the UK within two days and 600,000 across the continent, but sales fell by 82% the very next week. The company expected six million units to have been sold by the end of March 2007, with the console now available in all major territories; but the global number stood at 3.68 million. The Xbox 360, at the same time, had reached sales of 8.3 million worldwide, and the Nintendo Wii's sales were very nearly at six million, leaving Sony languishing in third place (how appropriate, given the PS2's advertising campaign). While the most powerful of this trio, games journalists commented that the PS3's lack of high-quality games was hindering its appeal in early 2007. But its fortunes would begin to change as the year ended, with the first Uncharted game releasing in November to significant acclaim, its production standards compared to Hollywood movies, and the racer *Gran Turismo 5 Prologue* arriving in December and offering then-unprecedented visuals that some reviewers considered almost photo real. The software worm was beginning to turn – and to support Maguire's comments, seven years after launch, in 2013, the PS3 would be home to critical and commercial heavyweights that were pushing the platform to its limits: *Gran Turismo 6*, *The Last of Us*, and *Grand Theft Auto V*.

that they want it, irrespective of anything else.' He'd also stress to *Impress PC Watch* that the PS3 was intended to be more than just a games console, and to be an 'entertainment supercomputer' for homes – hence the RRP. 'We never once called it a games machine,' he added. 'Maybe he was using video games as a stepping-stone to realise his vision,' is how Yoshida remembered Kutaragi's ambitions, speaking at Develop Conference in 2018. 'He wanted to become the next Intel or something.' Hirai also made it clear that this was a big leap from the PS2, not just in hardware terms but also impact on consumer's bank balances, as he said onstage at E3 2006 during the reveal of the PS3's final, retail-ready design, in front of a slide showing the US launch prices: 'It requires huge financial investment.' Yoshida would later remark, again at Develop 2018, that the console's price confirmation in 2006 was a 'horrifying moment'.

But the decision to go with a high-spec machine with a large price tag was, according to former Sony UK managing director Ray Maguire, a good one. He told *CVG* in 2010, referencing the console's equally substantial launch RRP in the UK:

The pad that Sony shipped with the PS3 was incredibly familiar to players who'd used the PS1 and PS2. While the console's main controller was initially showcased at E3 2005 as a sort of boomerang- or banana-shaped device (never intended to be the final product, according to Sony, which begs the question: why show it off?), the wireless controller that did come out, the Sixaxis, was modelled exactly after the PS2's DualShock 2 (itself based on the PS1's DualShock), only with slightly different insides. It dropped the previous controller's rumble functionality but did feature motion-control compatibility, Sony's line on the vibration-free approach being that including such components would interfere with the motion sensitivity, with the then-president of Sony Worldwide Studios Phil Harrison later adding that rumble was a 'last-generation feature'. This was nonsense, however, the truth being that Sony had been sued for patent infringement by Immersion Corporation, who specialised in vibration haptics. The matter was settled in March 2007 – and just months later, in November that same year, the Sixaxis was replaced by the DualShock 3, which combined the motion functionality of the previous pad with haptic rumble feedback.

A great many other official peripherals released for the PlayStation 3. The Move controller, a wand-like device a little like a Wii remote, was used in conjunction with the PlayStation Eye camera for a selection of motion-controlled games and would really come into its own as a primary control option for the PlayStation 4's VR headset. As the PS3's games came on Blu-ray discs, the console could also run Blu-ray (and DVD) movies – a huge plus for consumers, as dedicated Blu-ray players at the time of the PS3's release could cost up to $1,000 – and Sony released traditional-looking remote controls for easier use of this feature. A keypad was released that could attach to the DualShock 3 pad, making inputting information (such as searching for games on PlayStation Network) that little bit faster; and the PlayTV tuner allowed users to record television shows to the PS3 hard drive.

Movie streaming via Netflix and other services was now possible as Sony embraced online interactivity with its PlayStation Network, which also enabled online multiplayer access and supported a store full of downloadable games. A paid subscription service, PlayStation Plus, launched in 2010 allowing PS3 owners to get discounts on purchased games, access to exclusive demos and a handful of free games each month. In an industry first, the PS3 could also be controlled by both of Sony's handheld consoles, the PlayStation Portable and PlayStation Vita.

In 2009 the original PS3 design – featuring lettering straight from the 2002 *Spider-Man* movie (distributed by Sony Pictures) – was updated as Sony's manufacturing costs fell by around 70% and the so-called 'Slim' model (pictured above), otherwise called the CECH-2000, was released. This was, as its immediately adopted nickname suggests, a smaller, thinner console than the launch system, and its on-unit labelling was shortened to simply 'PS3'. However, the 'slim' abandoned backwards compatibility for PS2 games, so its quieter performance and cheaper RRP of $299 came at a price. A further revision, the 'super slim' (CECH-4000, pictured below), released in 2012 with its 250GB model retailing at $270 with *Uncharted 3: Drake's Deception* included. In CNET's review, the super slim's slot-loading disc drive was deemed to 'feel cheap' and a 'step back' for the console. VentureBeat's coverage called it 'ugly and clunky', and 'not worth upgrading to'. Something of a disappointing end for the PS3, then, but Sony itself wasn't all that impressed with how the console had fared commercially either.

Over 87 million sales places the PS3 at number six on the list of the world's best-selling home consoles. But many players saw the Xbox 360 as the better of the two machines, an impression built around its year head start and several games' improved performance on Microsoft's machine, and the PS3 was the first of Sony's home consoles to not break 100 million sales. So while the PS3 has its fans, its collectors and plenty of outstanding games, plus it introduced PlayStation Network and PlayStation Plus, it's a relative misstep for its makers in the grand scheme of gaming history. In 2011, when asked about the next major console from Sony, Shuhei Yoshida told eurogamer.net: 'As far as we're concerned, we have no desire now to do that … I see no need to transition into a newer generation.' But behind the scenes the wheels of progress were already turning: development of the PlayStation 4 had started in 2008, and Sony was adamant that it would avoid the mistakes made with the PS3.

PlayStation 3: Five Must Plays

Uncharted 2: Among Thieves (2009)
Probably the best of the original PS3 trilogy of Uncharted titles, *Among Thieves* sets protagonist Nathan Drake off on an adventure to find the real location of the mythical kingdom of Shambala. It's all very Indiana Jones-style stuff, as Uncharted always is (and likely always will be), but there are sequences in this second title that set it apart, like its opening climb up a shattered train that's slowly slipping off the edge of a snowy cliff, and keep the player's blood pumping. A blockbuster experience that built on the foundations of its predecessor excellently, showcasing its makers Naughty Dog's growing confidence with the PS3's Cell CPU, *Uncharted 2* sold over six million copies and was included (remastered) in the PS4's *The Nathan Drake Collection* compilation of 2015.

Dark Souls (2011)
Though it was preceded by the PS3-exclusive *Demon's Souls*, developer FromSoftware's so-called Souls series of punishingly difficult action-RPGs really broke through to a global audience with *Dark Souls*. With its complex level designs, demanding (but never unfair) combat and environments full of lethal traps and irresistible secrets, *Dark Souls* was and remains an enigmatic experience that managed to enrapture as many players as it confused others. Director Hidetaka Miyazaki drew influence from real-world locations and several dark fantasy works, and the result was a wickedly magical adventure that made trial and error a kind of artform. *Dark Souls* was simultaneously released on Xbox 360 (albeit notably not in Japan), and later came to PC, Xbox One and PS4, and in late 2018 it finally received a Nintendo port on Switch.

Journey (2012)
Made by indie studio thatgamecompany with support from Sony's Santa Monica Studio, *Journey* is a short game with a minimalist narrative but an atmosphere and aesthetic that made it instantly captivating. Its effortless gameplay, all sliding down sand dunes and gliding over collapsed ruins, and serene soundtrack from composer Austin Wintory (which earned a Grammy nomination in 2013, the first gaming soundtrack to do so) combined to incredible effect. Exceptional review scores were accompanied by remarks about its 'startling power' (*EDGE*) and how it was 'the most beautiful game of its time' (IGN), and the game won several industry awards. *Journey* was released for the PS4

in 2015 to comparable acclaim and is also playable today on iOS and PC.

The Last of Us (2013)
With a list of award wins as long as your arm, *The Last of Us* was the final PS3 game from Naughty Dog, makers of Uncharted and Jak and Daxter, and showed users exactly what the console was capable of. Its incredible visuals, high-quality voice and motion performances, and a story that critics considered one of the interactive medium's best made it an immediate essential for PS3 owners. The game raced to sales of over seven million, making it the third-highest seller on its system – and this figure had increased to 17 million by 2018, including copies of its PS4 remaster. Downloadable content titled *The Last of Us: Left Behind* served as a prequel to events of the game, and a complete ground-up remake of the original game came out for PS5 in September 2022. A film adaptation was planned but cancelled, but an HBO TV series was filmed during 2021 and 2022, and at the time of writing is set to debut in early 2023.

Grand Theft Auto V (2013)
The biggest selling game on PS3 with almost 30 million copies sold, around seven million more than the Xbox 360 version, Rockstar's *Grand Theft Auto V* is a phenomenon that continues to attract players, with the game reappearing on PS4 (and Xbox One) in 2014 and then on PS5 (and Xbox Series X and S) in 2023. Its total copies shipped now stands at over 180 million, making it the world's second highest-selling game ever after *Minecraft*. As well as its captivating solo campaign of big-money heists and triple-protagonist tomfoolery, the game's multiplayer mode, *Grand Theft Auto Online* – allowing for both co-operative and competitive play in the game's massive open world – has grown into a huge part of the title's appeal.

NINTENDO WII

Manufacturer: Foxconn

Released: November 2006 (North America), December 2006 (Japan, Australia, Europe)

Nintendo knew that it had to change its approach to home consoles with the successor to the GameCube. With its hardware sales falling since the Super Famicom/SNES era, the feeling inside the Japanese giant was that directly competing with Sony's PlayStation 2 and 3 and Microsoft's Xbox and 360 wasn't the way forward. The core gaming audience was growing up and moving on, attracted to the mature thrills provided by Grand Theft Auto and Halo. Instead, diversification was necessary, and a wider audience needed. Nintendo would have to reach people who'd never really played video games before and make them want to buy its hardware.

Perhaps the required direction had been in front of them for a few years already. In a 1999 interview with *Gamers' Republic*, legendary Nintendo designer Shigeru Miyamoto had said: 'Although it's a part of Nintendo's responsibility to provide new games to hardcore gamers, we should instead always think about new entertainment possibilities for everybody.' And this 'for everybody' attitude was taken into the company's development for its next console, which began around the time of the GameCube's launch in 2001. In May 2002 Satoru Iwata (pictured above) took over as president of Nintendo and he had concerns over how complex video games were becoming, how off-putting they could seem to non-players. In his 2006 GDC keynote speech, Iwata reflected on how this inspired what they made next: 'We started with a very simple question: why is it that anyone feels comfortable picking up a remote control for a TV, but many people are afraid to even touch the controller for a video game system? This was our starting point.'

Genyo Takeda, the general manager for Nintendo's Integrated Research and Development Division, and who'd been at the company since 1972, met with both Miyamoto and Iwata in 2003 and was told to design a console that would achieve this incredibly broad appeal. Speaking in one of Nintendo's regular Ask Iwata features, in conversation with Iwata himself, Takeda would later say: 'Ordinary engineers and developers use a roadmap as a reference when creating machines that will be released in the future … I have the impression that this has become a machine that is completely different from the machine of the roadmap.' And that 'this', that machine, was the Nintendo Wii – a system created to quite deliberately be out of step with its competition, so much so that neither the same-generation Sony or Microsoft console was really a competitor at all.

In 2006, Miyamoto would talk to *Business Week* about this early period of the Wii's development, saying: 'Our goal was to come up with a machine that mothers would want – easy to use, quick to start up, not a huge energy drain, and quiet while it was running. Rather than just picking new technology, we thought seriously about what a game console should be.' And that thinking meant not aiming for cutting-edge tech, instead installing lower-spec components inside the Wii to keep costs down – the console's IBM Broadway CPU is only around a third of the power of the chips inside the Xbox 360 and PlayStation 3, and its ATI Hollywood graphics processor was based on the GameCube's Flipper. Miyamoto had wanted to Wii to retail for $100 or less, but the console debuted in North America (launching there before Japan) on 19 November 2006 at $249.99 – higher than hoped for but lower than the other options on the market.

'My idea was to spend nothing on the console technology,' Miyamoto would tell *Business Week*, 'so that all the money could be spent on improving the interface and software.' And Iwata also emphasised the Wii's prioritising on the player experience over raw hardware power in his 2006 GDC keynote: 'Some people put their money on the screen, but we decided to spend ours on the game experience. It is an investment in actual market disruption. Not simply to improve the market, but disrupt it.' And disrupt the market the Wii most certainly did: Nintendo sold 600,000 consoles in eight days in North America, despite the console lacking HD output, having no DVD functionality (although the first model did feature backwards compatibility for the GameCube), no internal hard drive (flash memory and SD card support aside), and no robust online multiplayer service. Of its 21 launch titles *The Legend of Zelda: Twilight Princess* racked up over 450,000 sales in the period. But the real killer app of the Wii was its pack-in title, *Wii Sports*.

To understand the appeal of Wii Sports – and several other games that came after it – one first has to understand the brilliance of the Wii Remote. A motion-sensitive controller that resembled a TV clicker more than a traditional game pad, the key inspiration for the Remote was Nintendo's own dual-screen handheld, the Game Boy line-succeeding DS. The DS had succeeded in reaching an audience of people who weren't considered core gamers, and a lot more female players than was typical of gaming hardware. Its touchscreen interface took away the need to know what all these buttons did, and Takeda adapted that thinking into a point-and-click controller for the Wii. 'Being able to directly touch the screen was intuitive and easy to understand,' he said in another Ask Iwata feature. 'When making the [Wii] controller, I had in mind how to maintain that DS line.' His colleague at Nintendo IR&D, Kenichiro Ashida, added that he felt the GameCube pad was 'the culmination of conventional controllers', that he 'had a strong feeling [the Wii] would be a game machine that I and my family could use', and that 'the concept of resetting [that controller design] is very futuristic'.

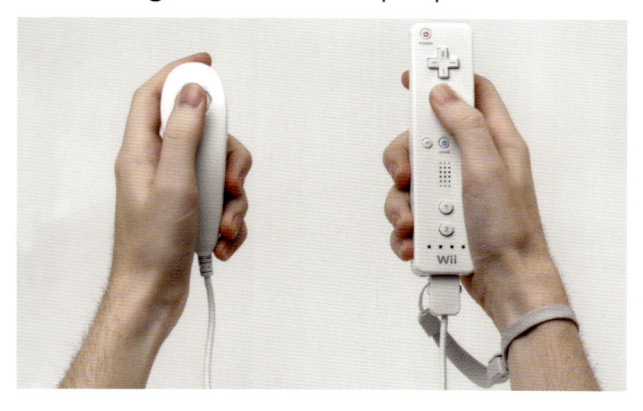

The Wii Remote was entirely designed around pick-up-and-play immediacy, fuss-free and intuitive functionality – you point it at the screen, you select what you need to, and you press a button. It did much more than that, naturally, and could be flipped sideways to be played as a more conventional pad (and the Wii also launched with the Classic Controller, offering a very familiar form factor), but at a basic level the Remote was all about connecting non-gamers with Nintendo's software. And the connection of *Wii Sports*, with a Wii Remote in hand, was instant. 'As a bundled game, Nintendo could not have chosen a better title to relay, in a simple way, the true strength and appeal of the console and its unique control system,' wrote

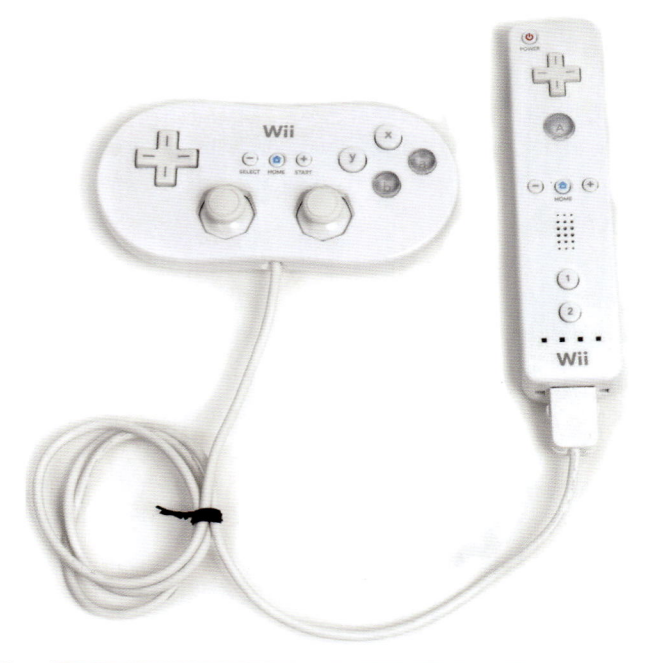

Trusted Reviews of the Wii's box-in collection of motion-controlled sporting attractions. And yet, *Wii Sports* came close to not being included with every console.

When former president of Nintendo of America, Reggie Fils-Aimé (pictured below), released his book *Disrupting the Game: From the Bronx to the Top of Nintendo* in 2022, it contained a recollection of conversations he had with Miyamoto and Iwata about *Wii Sports*. Fils-Aimé had to really fight to convince his Japanese colleagues of the benefit bundling the game would bring to the Wii, but Iwata told him: 'Nintendo doesn't give out precious content for free.' Miyamoto suggested that the party game *Wii Play*, or at least some mini-games from it, be included instead, but Fils-Aimé stuck to his guns (or, perhaps, his Wii Zappers). An agreement was reached: Wii Sports would be included with Wii consoles sold in North America and Europe, but not in Japan, where it was sold separately. It's naïve to say that the Wii would have stumbled in the States without *Wii Sports*, but few bundled games were ever so great at showcasing what the new hardware in question was all about.

That name, though: it certainly caused some titters and spawned some jokes in certain parts of the games press when it was officially announced in April 2006. Nintendo's new console had gone under the code name of Revolution prior to that point, and for a brief period it'd been referred to as the GameCube Next – and Revolution was a title that some developers involved with the system preferred, aware of the childish responses that would greet Wii. But Nintendo hadn't picked the name at random: it was meant to represent two players and the Wii Remote with its attached Nunchuk (which featured an analogue stick and two trigger buttons, increasing the inputs available for games that required them). And with the moniker pronounced 'we', it was felt that all players in all territories, of all cultures, would be able to say the system's name easily. The Wii Shop Channel, an online service for the downloading of new digital games (WiiWare) and older Nintendo titles (via the Virtual Console), launched at the same time as the Wii itself, and its catchy menu music became the soundtrack to a widely shared internet meme (have a search for 'Wii Shop Wednesday', and enjoy). The offline Wii Menu also featured a selection of channels, covering the weather, news, Mii avatar creation (Nintendo's popular Mii versions of their players debuting on the Wii, as the name implies), and more.

By February 2007, the Wii had shipped close to two million units in Japan, and even more in North America, but Iwata was stressing caution, not allowing himself to be too optimistic about the console righting the commercial wrongs of the GameCube. 'There will come a time when it stops selling,' he told IGN, and then painted Nintendo as the underdog, as its new system wasn't aimed at the same core gamers as the PS3 and Xbox 360: 'So long as we continue the fight against the lack of interest in games from the general consumer, Nintendo will always be the challenger.' But by the end of the fiscal year in April 2008, worldwide Wii sales stood at nearly 25 million. A year later, that figure had doubled; and the next year saw

Nintendo sell a further 20 million units. By the time of the Wii's official discontinuation in 2013, it'd passed 100 million sales – and as remaining stock was sold off that number went higher still, the total reaching 101.6 million. The Wii had become Nintendo's best-selling home console of all time – until the Switch flew past it in early 2022.

Though it was underpowered beside the PS3 and Xbox 360, both Sony and Microsoft took inspiration from the Wii in the creation of the PlayStation Eye camera and Move controllers and Kinect motion-sensing peripheral respectively. Both appreciated that the 'hardcore' audience they'd targeted wasn't entirely where the money was and aimed to take a slice of the casual crowd away from Nintendo (something Microsoft would achieve fairly successfully, selling 24 million Kinect sensors between 2010 and 2013, and PlayStation less so). The Wii would be re-released as a costs-reduced model in 2011, which removed the GameCube compatibility and was also released in black as well as the Wii's traditional white; while a wi-fi-free model with no internet connectivity, the Wii Mini, came out as a bare-bones basic option in late 2012, sporting an entirely new (slightly smaller) look and coloured red and black. And while the Wii's discontinuation coincided roughly with the release of the Wii U, boxed software for the older console surprisingly outlasted its successor's library, with the final physical Wii U game releasing in 2018, namely Ubisoft's *Just Dance 2019*, but the Wii receiving a version of *Just Dance 2020* the following year.

By going against the gaming industry grain with the Wii, Nintendo set itself up as the company creating games for everyone who wasn't into what Xbox and PlayStation was putting out. Its focus on other audiences was a winning 'blue ocean' strategy, doing what its competitors weren't, and while the Wii's legacy perhaps isn't as respected today as either the PS3's or Xbox 360's, Nintendo's efficient production of the console, using lower-spec tech, ensured that it turned a profit on every unit sold. Its games library might lack quite as many all-timers as the SNES, N64 and GameCube catalogues, but all the best Wii titles felt uniquely created for the platform in question, and not simply ported over as another revenue stream. Fils-Aimé would call the Wii a 'gutsy call that paid off' in a 2019 lecture at New York's Cornell University, but Iwata – who died in July 2015 – would speak of it being the only decision Nintendo could have made. 'For me, I found that it would have been more frightening to take the conventional path,' he said in an Ask Iwata piece of 2006. 'When we decided to change the direction of the ship, so to speak, we didn't know how long it would take people to understand the path we were trying to achieve, [but] we knew there was no future on the conventional path.' The Wii gave Nintendo new life, an injection of followers and massive profits at the end of the 00s, and fresh hope for its future – but its next home console would be a reminder that success is never to be taken for granted.

Nintendo Wii: Play One Game

Super Mario Galaxy (2007)

After a mixed reception to the GameCube's *Super Mario Sunshine*, Nintendo's mascot needed a terrific debut on the Wii – and *Galaxy* absolutely delivered. Visually beautiful, blessed by a magical orchestral soundtrack and with gameplay that just clicked from the first time you moved Mario around with the Nunchuk and fired off Star Bits with the Remote, *Super Mario Galaxy* is a dream of a game, a near-unmatched masterpiece of a 3D platformer, and an experience that'll always be special however many years pass between playthroughs. Speaking to *Official Nintendo Magazine* in 2007, its co-producer Shigeru Miyamoto commented that he hoped *Galaxy* would help the Wii's audience of new players 'discover the joy of video games', and you have to say that mission was successful. If you've no Wii (or Wii U) to hand, *Super Mario Galaxy* was released with updated control options on the Switch in 2020 as part of the *Super Mario 3D Allstars* collection, alongside *Sunshine* and *Super Mario 64*.

THE 2010s
THE COLLAPSE AND COMEBACK OF AN ICON

As the first decade of the 21st century faded into the rear view, Nintendo had comprehensively proven itself to be the dominant force in console gaming once again, as the Wii achieved a market share healthily ahead of its rival systems from Sony and Microsoft. But the company's next system would confuse consumers and critics alike, becoming a cult favourite amid afficionados but selling a minuscule number of units compared not only to its immediate predecessor but every other Nintendo home console before it. The end of the 2010s would see the longest-serving name in gaming, which celebrated its 125th anniversary in 2014, storming back, however, with hugely successful hybrid hardware that changed how users interacted with consoles. Elsewhere, Sony and Microsoft released a new PlayStation and Xbox respectively, and all other contenders had to be content with whatever market scraps they could get.

Micro Consoles Come, Micro Consoles Go

As internet connectivity in homes became abundant and touchscreen smartphones ubiquitous, a selection of companies felt the time was right to enter the home console market with digital-only devices – none as powerful as the PlayStation 3 or Xbox One but intended as a middle ground between those machines and the iPhones et al that were bouncing around in consumers' pockets. Some streamed games, others stored them on hard drives. None were especially successful.

OnLive was a streaming service that aimed to bring console-quality games to users via PCs, Macs, smartphones, tablets, Android televisions and other internet-connected TVs. It did this through cloud gaming, the titles running on remote servers and streamed to the user's device of choice, and it was launched in the United States in June 2010. OnLive also had a dedicated console, named the MicroConsole TV Adapter, which came with an OnLive wireless controller that split the difference between Xbox's and Sony's pads deign wise, with dual analogue sticks and all the buttons needed for the big-budget games of the time.

The OnLive model made sense on paper: pay a monthly subscription and get access to a wealth of games without having to invest in an Xbox 360 or PS3, or high-spec gaming PC. Positive previews at gaming industry conferences drummed up interest in the service and its console, but subscribers didn't materialise in the numbers that were needed, developers cooled their support, and OnLive was sold in 2012 for $4.8 million – far lower than its approximated value in 2010 of $1.8 billion. OnLive was shut for good in April 2015 with most of its assets sold to Sony, whose own PlayStation Now subscription service had launched in 2014 and was merged with PlayStation Plus in 2022.

In 2013 there was a flurry of micro-console systems (not to be confused with the 'minis' we see from SEGA, Sony and Nintendo, based around older systems), with BlueStacks Gamepop – a diminutive cuboid-styled device – announced for pre-order in May. It offered users over 500 Android games, playable on their TVs rather than phones or tablets. CEO Rosen Sharma said the company wanted to be a 'Netflix for gaming', and potential customers had two options: the cube console, which was over $100 upfront, or a smaller rectangular plug-in that was delivered for free, but subscribers then paid $6.99 each month. The consoles didn't attract much interest, and after Samsung investment in 2014 BlueStacks reworked its business model to provide Android cloud gaming for PC and Mac rather than dedicated devices.

A very similar device to the Gamepop, PlayJam's GameStick was a USB drive-sized plug-in that released in November 2013 and ran Android as its operating system (but was also iOS compatible). It shipped with a chunky controller – which the console itself could be stored inside of for portability – and could also connect with third-party peripherals like Bluetooth keyboards and even dance mats. A poor selection of games let this modestly powered device down, and the GameStick store closed in early 2017. Arriving a month after the GameStick, initially in the UK and US only, was Mad Catz's M.O.J.O., also running Android and connected to the Google Play Store for game downloads to its 16GB of flash memory. A high launch RRP of $249.99 led to minuscule sales, however, and a price drop to $199 stateside and £179 in the UK in March 2014 did nothing to improve its commercial performance. The M.O.J.O. added both OnLive streaming support and the ability to play OUYA games in June 2014, but it was already effectively a dead platform by its 2015 launch in continental Europe and its dedicated game store was closed in 2019.

Amid these relative makeweights were a couple of names that did break through to countless games and tech media articles and mainstream awareness: the OUYA and Sony's PlayStation TV. The Android-based OUYA was a huge crowdfunding success, making $8.5 million on Kickstarter, and launched in June 2013 for $99 in the US and £99 in the UK, supported by a dedicated store and powered by a NVIDIA Tegra 3 quad-core CPU. Despite strong pre-release enthusiasm however, the OUYA stalled as a commercially viable complement to players' existing consoles and computers, with criticism aimed at its laggy and uncomfortable wireless controller and sub-par performance for games that would otherwise run perfectly on a smartphone. The OUYA's total sales peaked at around 200,000 units before its July 2015 discontinuation, with its top-selling game *TowerFall* having only been downloaded 7,000 times.

The PlayStation TV (PSTV), meanwhile, was a compact console roughly the size of a pack of playing cards that enabled users to both download games onto its 1GB hard drive (expandable with proprietary memory cards), stream titles via PlayStation Now, and use physical Vita cards. It was compatible with both PS3 and PS4 controllers, making it an attractive way for owners of those consoles to get Vita (and PSP) games onto their TVs. The PSTV could also stream PS4 titles from one TV in the house to another – handy for taking your games from the lounge to the bedroom in the pre-Switch era. Launching first in Japan in November 2013, the PSTV came to North America, Europe and Australia around a year later and was initially recommended, with IGN calling it 'one of Sony's most exciting new products', and it won a Good Design Award in 2014 from the Japan Institute of Design Promotion. But with Vita-specific features not universally replicated on the PSTV, meaning some games were compromised (including big-name releases like *Uncharted: Golden Abyss*), lessening the machine's appeal massively, and with the Vita itself only selling in relatively low quantities (top estimate, about 16 million globally before its 2019 discontinuation) the PSTV sold poorly – making it an increasingly desirable item on the second-hand collector's market today.

Further big names involved in micro-consoles during the 2010s include Amazon, which released the fireTV in April 2014 – its makers not aiming to rival the high-end consoles of the time, but instead appeal to people who wanted to take smartphone games onto their televisions – and NVIDIA, whose Android-based Shield (pictured below) was marketed as a games-playing device in 2015, but its full title of Shield TV is illustrative of its more common use as a way to stream content from providers like Netflix and YouTube. Shield devices remain in use today and support GeForce NOW cloud gaming, allowing users to run their PC games on their living room TV. In late 2019 the Capcom Home Arcade, made by Koch Media, offered users 16 (mostly brilliant) Capcom arcade games, including 1994's hard-to-find *Alien vs Predator*, wrapped up in a chunky tabletop device that was basically two full-size arcade sticks stuck together on top of an enormous Capcom logo. Subtle. Expensive at a launch RRP of around £200, the Home Arcade was a niche product aimed at coin-op superfans, but it earned praise for its high-quality controller components and excellent game emulation.

WII U

Manufacturer: Nintendo, Foxconn, Mitsumi

Released: November 2012 (North America, Europe), December 2012 (Japan)

Nintendo's decision to focus on a 'casual' audience with the Wii was paying off financially, with worldwide sales sitting at around 45 million by the end of 2008. But that same year minds began to turn to the company's next home console, and to the players they weren't speaking to anymore. Whatever came next had to be closer to the Xbox 360 and PlayStation 3, with high-definition visuals and online functionality allowing for multiplayer gaming. In a 2011 edition of Nintendo's Iwata Asks features, the then-president of the company, Satoru Iwata, said: 'Shortly after the Wii was released, people in the gaming media and game enthusiasts recognised it as a casual machine aimed toward families, and placed consoles by Microsoft and Sony in a similar light with each other, saying these are aimed towards those who passionately play games.' Nintendo wanted those passionate players, who'd been with them with the N64 and GameCube, back.

Wii sales were slowing by 2010, and after that year's E3 conference, where Nintendo showcased *The Legend of Zelda: Skyward Sword* on Wii but the demo was beset by connectivity issues and the 3DS handheld was revealed, Iwata remarked to BBC reporter Daniel Emery that new hardware wasn't immediately on the horizon: 'Do we need to launch a successor to Wii right now? I don't think so.' He added, however, that it was normal for Nintendo to start work on its next generation of home console hardware almost as soon as the current system is launched, 'and the Wii is no exception'. In May 2011 the games media reported on the first notable leak of this hardware, which was being developed under the code name Project Café, immediately replacing talk of a Wii 2, Wii HD, or Nintendo Feel or Stream (all of which had been used in the press). Project Café's most notable advance over the Wii was its controller, featuring as it did a screen in its centre. 'Is this Nintendo's move to have the console with the most ground-breaking controller again?' asked stuff.tv's Dan Grabham – and just a few weeks later, at E3 2011, that controller would be available for the press to get their hands on.

E3 2011 was also the start of a headache for what'd eventually release not as Project Café but as the Wii U, as Nintendo placed its focus almost entirely on the controller – which was indeed a large peripheral with a screen at its centre (*not* the retail model, with 3DS-like flush circle pads instead of proper analogue sticks and no ergonomic rear curves) – rather than the Wii U as an all-new console. 'Switch from the TV to the New Controller', said its promotional video for the event, showing how the Wii U GamePad – as it'd be called at release – could run games solely on its screen, leaving the television free for other uses. The console wasn't shown in detail, and when seen sitting beside the TV in the video could easily be mistaken for a regular Wii – an impression reinforced by showcased compatibility with the Wii Remote and Balance Board. Viewers could be mistaken for thinking the Wii U was the controller itself, a new add-on for the existing Wii. And when the console's final specifications were shown at E3 2012, again the emphasis was on the GamePad and its games, not the all-important box that'd sit beside or beneath your television.

But the GamePad *was* a revelatory piece of hardware for home gaming. Twice prototyped by sticking two Wii Remotes to the side of a small monitor and a display atop a Wii Zapper, it brought across the 3DS's gyroscopic control options, and its built-in screen allowed for menus and maps to be displayed at the same time as the on-TV action (and many games could be easily played off the TV, as advertised in 2011). With nine-axis motion detection, near-field communication (leading to the use of Amiibo figures to unlock game features), a 1.3-megapixel front-mounted camera and a touchscreen suited to fingertip poking and swiping (although a stylus was included to avoid greasy smears), this was cutting-edge stuff. And while the system it supported, *not* the Wii, wasn't as powerful as its peers, its custom multi-chip module containing a 1.24GHz tri-core CPU and 550MHz GPU did make it capable of standing side by side with a lot of Xbox 360 and PlayStation 3 games when it came to looks, at least in static screenshots, and its crisp HD output and online functionality brought it up to feature-set pace with its competitors.

And several of those rival consoles' games were available at the Wii U's launch in North America on 18 November 2012. In an attempt to get some of those passionate players engaged with Nintendo's new hardware, the console's day-one line-up in the States featured a new 'Armored Edition' of Warner Bros.'s *Batman: Arkham City*, which had previously come to PS3 and Xbox 360 in 2011; a 'Special Edition' of EA's *Mass Effect 3*, which had come out on other platforms that March; and its own second screen-enabled (showing the map and supporting off-TV play) version of Ubisoft's *Assassin's Creed III*, which had debuted on PS3 and Xbox 360 a few weeks earlier. Other third-party produced games at launch included Ubisoft's (then) Wii U-exclusive *ZombiU*, a rare adults-only Nintendo release, as well as Activision's *Call of Duty: Black Ops II* and THQ's *Darksiders II* – clearly, Nintendo was committing to courting the so-called 'hardcore' audience with the Wii U. Not that the system didn't emerge without some first-party games more familiar to Nintendo fans, and some casual party-style experiences. One of the best was *Nintendo Land*, a collection of multiplayer mini-games based on Nintendo IP that used the on- and off-screen capabilities of its platform to amazingly entertaining effect.

Wii U support from non-Nintendo developers did slow, however, from over 40 by major studios in its first year to substantially fewer. In 2014, a 'Secret Developers' story on eurogamer.net quoted an anonymous dev who told of how making games for the console was 'harder than it should have been', and that when it came to online functionality for games it was useless referencing what was on Xbox and PlayStation as 'nobody in [Nintendo's] development teams used those systems'. In March 2014 a blog entry on Gamasutra (now gamedeveloper.com) observed that just 28% of Wii U games were from third-party studios, and that 'without strong unit sales for the Wii U console itself, third-party support is unlikely to catch up to what was seen on Wii' (third-party software sales on the Wii exceeded those on PS3 and Xbox 360). Iwata himself seemed to acknowledge and accept this, posting on Nintendo's official site in early 2014: 'Software publishers are not necessarily keen on making games in genres that have weaker affinities with audiences that Nintendo has not been as strong with, where making a huge investment does not guarantee a sufficient return.'

The 'passionate players' pitch had failed, and as Wii U hardware sales slumped – the ten million mark was finally passed in mid-2015, over three years on from the console's launch, whereas the Wii had achieved that in just over six months – so too did support from developers who could be confident of profits on other platforms. Also damaging the Wii U's commercial fortunes was the release, in November 2013, of both Microsoft's Xbox One and Sony's PlayStation 4, consoles that massively outperformed Nintendo's hardware. On the plus side for Nintendo, its first-party developed and exclusively published Wii U games were some of the greatest of the first half of the 2010s – *Super Mario 3D World*, *Donkey Kong Country: Tropical Freeze*, *Mario Kart 8*, *Bayonetta 2*, *Pikmin 3* and *Captain Toad Treasure Tracker* all earned later Switch ports or updates due to their high quality, while the acclaimed *Super Mario Maker*, *Splatoon* and *Super Smash Bros. for Wii U* received sequels on Nintendo's next console.

There were enough missteps with the Wii U that its failure to emulate the Wii's success was probably never in doubt. It launched with two models, the white $299 Basic and the black $349 Deluxe/Premium with 8GB and 32GB of storage each – but neither was substantial enough given the growing size of big-budget games, and users quickly had to invest in an extra hard drive. Just like the Wii, the Wii U did not support DVD or Blu-ray movie playback – something that came as standard with the PS4 and Xbox One. A TV service – note the TV button on the GamePad – only rolled out in Japan and North America, leaving European users with a useless feature built into their new console. It might have fared better had Sony and Microsoft not released their new machines when they did, but its confusing early marketing emphasis on the GamePad and shift of focus from families and newcomers to gaming left it distanced from what'd made the Wii so compelling, so perhaps the Wii U would have been doomed whatever its competition did.

Nowadays the Wii U is a great way to play the Wii library through an HDMI input, as it's fully backwards compatible and can use all the previous console's main peripherals, and there are a handful of brilliant games that remain locked to the system, often because of its unique twin-screen interface – *Nintendo Land*, *Xenoblade Chronicles X* and *Affordable Space Adventures* among them. With many of its best games already on Switch though, it's hardly a must-have system for anyone picking their way through Nintendo history. The Wii U's last hurrah was *The Legend of Zelda: Breath of the Wild*, a genuine greatest-game-ever contender, which released on 3 March 2017 after six years of development – and simultaneously came out for the Switch, which launched worldwide on the very same day. The Wii U had been officially discontinued a few weeks earlier, on 31 January, and by the end of 2019, allowing for the clearance of existing stock at retailers, it made its way to 13.59 million sales, making it Nintendo's lowest-selling home console. But those declining revenues would turn around before the decade was done.

Wii U: Play One Game

Nintendo Land (2012)

A lot of the Wii U's best games can be played on Switch – but not this one, which features gameplay that's entirely reliant on using the GamePad alongside TV play controlled using Wii Remotes or other compatible controllers. Featuring a selection of minigames presented as if they're attractions in a Nintendo theme park, *Nintendo Land* uses familiar franchises in a variety of fun ways, including asymmetrical co-op and competitive play on the likes of 'Mario Chase', 'Animal Crossing: Sweet Day' and 'Metroid Blast'. It's not much fun on your lonesome, but if you have a Wii U and three or four friends available to invite over, *Nintendo Land* is both an excellent showcase for its platform's features and, more importantly, a brilliant time with pals.

PLAYSTATION 4

Manufacturer: Sony Electronics, Foxconn

Released: November 2013 (North America, Europe), February 2014 (Japan), May 2014 (China)

From the very start of the PlayStation 3's lifespan, Sony was hurting. It'd seen its expensive research and development for the system's Cell multi-core processor essentially hijacked by Microsoft for its Xbox 360, which got to market a year ahead of the PS3. The console had been tricky to develop for, and few studios managed to really get the most from the hardware – those who did generally being first-party teams, their best games coming out years after its 2006 launch. A combination of these and other factors led to Ken Kutaragi's departure from Sony's gaming business, and a change at the top was the catalyst for changes in development: the Cell structure would no longer be the way forward, and designer and programmer Mark Cerny, who'd been critical of the PS3's architecture, was brought in by SCEA's then-vice president of product development, Shuhei Yoshida, to lead the development of the PlayStation 4. According to comments made by Cerny to Gamasutra in 2013, his research into the CPU for the PS4 began in 2007, and in 2008 he asked developers what they'd like to see: 'We wanted our tools to be much richer and much more accessible to our developers.'

The result was a semi-custom eight-core CPU using an x86 instruction set and running at 1.6GHz (boosted to 2.13GHz in the PS4's Pro model of 2016), integrated into an Accelerated Processing Unit that its manufacturers AMD called 'by far the most powerful APC we've made to date'. This suited game developers perfectly, as the PS4-specific x86-64 was comparable to what was being used in high-end PCs. Speaking after the PS4's formal reveal at Sony's 'See the Future' event of February 2013 (which didn't actually feature a console to see on stage, at all), the head of British studio Just Add Water, Stewart Gilray, told eurogamer.net: 'It's closer to PC architecture, so it's easy to develop for and easier to get something up and running relatively quickly, maybe in half the time it would take to get a PS3 [game] off the ground.' Cerny himself had referred to the PS4 as being based on 'supercharged PC architecture' aimed at supporting 'a breadth of experiences'.

Also detailed (but again, not shown in person) in February 2013 was the PS4's box-in controller, the DualShock 4 – an evolution of the DualShock pads before it with a very familiar form factor but now with a click-enabled central touchpad and a share button, used for recording gameplay sequences and taking screenshots. There was talk of using the PlayStation Vita as a second screen, in a manner comparable to the Wii U and its GamePad, and while this didn't happen the Vita could be used to play PS4 games, streamed to the handheld from your console under the TV (although it wasn't always easy, with the portable system's fiddly rear touchpad making up for its shortage of shoulder buttons).

Far more would be shown at June's E3 2013 in Los Angeles: the final console design, its pricing of $399 in the US and £349 in the UK – a fantastic call-back to 1995, as Sony undercut the launch RRP of Microsoft's Xbox One by 100 dollars – and a feast of visually stunning games coming to the new system including *The Order: 1886*, *Killzone: Shadow Fall*, *Watch Dogs* and *Destiny*. One of the biggest cheers of the presentation wasn't for a new game or hardware feature, however, but for the confirmation that the PS4 would support used games and allow games to be leant between friends. Hours earlier, during Microsoft's conference for the Xbox One, they'd announced that the console would cost $499 and that it would use always-online digital rights management software to prevent game sharing and the distribution of used copies. Days later Microsoft would walk their DRM policy back, but the damage was already done – while neither console would be out for several months, PlayStation had already scored a comprehensive victory over the company that had it on the backfoot for much of the previous generation.

The PS4 launched first in North America on 15 November 2013, and in Europe exactly two weeks later, and the impact was immediate: over a million consoles were sold in just 24 hours in North America, making it Sony's fastest-selling console at the time, and in the UK 530,000 units were shifted in five weeks to make it the territory's highest-selling console of the year. By the end of 2013 the PS4's global sales had reached 4.2 million, closing rapidly on the November 2012-launched Wii U's then-total of 5.86 million, and comfortably ahead of the Xbox One's three million. When it launched in Japan on 22 February

2014, sales of the PS4 raced to 322,000 in two days, and at the beginning of 2015 the system's worldwide total was 18.5 million – a figure the Xbox One wouldn't hit for another year. While the Xbox 360 and PS3 had as good as tied when it came to who finished second in the previous console generation, behind the Wii, in just over one year the PS4 had established an unassailable lead – and it was yet to receive what many consider to be its greatest first-party games.

The PS4 has been home to a procession of massively acclaimed exclusives, albeit some timed and subsequently ported to PC after their console releases to open a new revenue stream for Sony. In 2015 came *Bloodborne*, FromSoftware taking its demanding Souls-series action-RPG gameplay into a new Gothic setting, and Supermassive's exemplary jump-scares 'em up *Until Dawn*. In 2016, Fumito Ueda's long-awaited follow-up to *Shadow of the Colossus*, *The Last Guardian*, came out, having originally been shown as a PS3 game in 2009; and *Uncharted 4: A Thief's End* brought the curtain down on Nathan Drake's adventures in true Hollywood style. 2017 brought *Horizon Zero Dawn* and *Nioh*; 2018 *God of War*, *Marvel's Spider-Man* and the remake of *Shadow of the Colossus*; 2019 Hideo Kojima's first game since departing Konami, *Death Stranding*; and 2020 *The Last of Us Part II*, *Ghost of Tsushima*, the fascinating game-creation tool *Dreams* and Square Enix's revival of a PS1 classic *Final Fantasy VII Remake*. While these big-ticket experiences came along only rarely, they earned accolades that made Xbox's own exclusives appear meek by comparison; and with the Switch lacking the processing power of either the PS4 or Xbox One, Nintendo was once again (successfully) focusing on fantastic gameplay over striking production values and targeting the audiences that Sony and Microsoft weren't naturally engaged with.

The PS4's online features received what might have been a shot in the arm if handled differently when the PlayStation Now subscription service launched in early 2014, offering users cloud gaming access to titles from the PS1 through to the PS4 itself, some of which could be streamed to a PC, and ultimately console downloads for everything but PS3 software. This helped offset the lack of backwards compatibility somewhat, but although PlayStation Now's available titles had reached 800 by 2020, the service never caught on with Sony users as Game Pass had with Xbox and PC owners, with PS Now having 3.2 million subscribers in March 2021 compared to over 18 million using Game Pass. PlayStation Now was merged with PlayStation Plus in mid-2022. Another key product launched during the PS4's lifetime was the PlayStation VR headset, developed under the code name Project Morpheus and released in October 2016. By December 2019 PSVR had sold five million units, compatible with over 600 games and experiences (some made specifically for VR, others with optional VR features or modes), and a follow-up peripheral for the PS5, the aptly titled PSVR2, was released in early 2023.

The PlayStation 4 console itself splintered into two distinct models in 2016, both simultaneously revealed at an event in New York in September of that year. The so-called PS4 Slim (not its *official* name) reduced the size of the original system by 40% and acted as its replacement, with the chunkier 2013 design phased out accordingly. Of more note was the PlayStation 4 Pro (pictured on previous page), developed under the code name Neo, which featured an upgraded GPU and was capable of 4K visuals. The Slim came out on 15 September and the Pro launched worldwide on 10 November. Then in 2019 came the inevitable: Sony was preparing a fifth PlayStation, which would release globally in late 2020. As of June 2023 though, the PS4 remains supported, up to over 117 million sales and with new games scheduled for release thanks to Sony having committed to keeping the platform active into 2024. In 2022 PlayStation-exclusive sequels to previously successful titles, *Horizon Forbidden West* and *God of War Ragnarök*, came to PS4 and PS5, and many third-party studios continue to release games for both systems.

PlayStation 4: Five Must Plays

Bloodborne (2015)

Set in the Victorian-inspired and maze-like Gothic city of Yharnam, *Bloodborne* was FromSoftware's highest-rated game on reviews aggregator Metacritic until the 2022 release of *Elden Ring*, and a port to PC or PS5 remains much requested. While generally presented in a similar style to the preceding *Dark* and *Demon's Souls*, *Bloodborne* places a greater emphasis on risk-and-reward combat, encouraging players to be daring and not chip away at an enemy's health from behind a gigantic shield. The story is, as Souls games so often are, a tangled web of disparate plot points that the game's makers leave the player to piece together, so *Bloodborne* won't be for everyone narratively, just as its demanding action can also see people bounce off it. But if you've patience to unlock its secrets, this is one of those all-timers that you'll never forget.

The Witcher 3: Wild Hunt (2015)

This isn't a PS4 exclusive, also releasing for Xbox One and PC (and later Switch, and later still Xbox Series X and S and PS5), but *The Witcher 3: Wild Hunt* sold twice as many copies on Sony's machine than it did Microsoft's, hence its inclusion here. With one of the richest open-world environments ever created for a video game, and intervened plot threads that culminate in one of the role-playing genre's most riveting and rewarding endings, CD Projekt Red's third game based on the dark-fantasy Witcher series (which also covers novels, comics, and a Netflix TV show) is an engrossing and moving adventure that is regularly cited as one of the very best games of all time. Once you've walked in the boots of the White Wolf, Geralt of Rivia, it's unlikely you'll look at games of this ilk the same way again.

Titanfall 2 (2016)

First-person shooters like those of the Battlefield and Call of Duty series are abundant on PS4, but Respawn Entertainment's *Titanfall 2* (also on PC and Xbox One) is the go-to for any genre fans wanting a compelling story that matches the intensity of the action. While its Xbox-and-PC-only predecessor was a multiplayer-only affair, for this release the studio looked to buddy cop movies for inspiration and emerged with a narrative where protagonist Jack Cooper forms a strong bond with an almost-sentient Titan-class exoskeleton, BT. The relationship between the two underpins the epic encounters (including a couple of truly inspired levels) they go through on the way to the campaign's climax, which will undoubtedly see many players shed a tear or two. An FPS experience with a lot of heart, *Titanfall 2* also shipped with several multiplayer modes, and Respawn would take some of the game's characters into its next multiplayer-only release, *Apex Legends*.

What Remains of Edith Finch (2017)

Developed by Giant Sparrow and published by Annapurna Interactive, and available for other platforms, *What Remains of Edith Finch* was the unlikely winner of the best game category at the British Academy Game Awards in 2018, beating the fancied *Horizon Zero Dawn* and *The Legend of Zelda: Breath of the Wild*. But play the game and its triumph begins to make sense: this is a expertly paced narrative adventure that taps into themes of loss and love in a very affecting fashion, unpicking a family's history of misfortune and playing out across what are essentially a series of mini-game vignettes. Beautiful of visuals and music, it's a highly immersive meditation on what it means to let go, and numerous other award nominations and wins for its story are illustrative of its strengths in that area.

God of War (2018)

Sony Santa Monica's reboot of a PlayStation-exclusive series known for its over-the-top and exceptionally gory Greek mythology action took its traditional protagonist Kratos to the magical lands of Norse legend, gave him a kid and set the two off on a journey to scatter his late wife's ashes atop the highest peak of the nine realms. Simple enough, but annoyingly for father and son a seemingly invincible stranger shows up at their door before they depart, eager to pound Kratos into pieces. Who he is becomes just one of this tale's many mysteries to unravel; and what follows his introduction is an experience of tightly orchestrated action, cleverly designed puzzles, narrative intrigue and visual majesty. *God of War* picked up several game of the year awards and its popularity resulted in incredible anticipation for its 2022 sequel, *Ragnarök*, the coming of which is teased at the end of the 2018 release.

XBOX ONE

Manufacturers: Flextronics, Foxconn

Released: November 2013 (North America, Europe, Australia), September 2014 (Japan, China)

By 2011 the Xbox 360 had proven itself a more-than-capable console, selling at a competitive pace against its peers and providing a home to a host of enthralling games. It was the perfect sequel to the system that had come before it, the original Xbox of 2001: faster, sleeker, more adventurous and forward-thinking, and the massively improved sales were there to prove it. But change was coming. In June of that year Xbox's EMEA vice president Chris Lewis remarked that the 2005-launched 360 was halfway into its lifecycle, telling MCV that the console was 'defying the normal curve' of machines of its ilk, which traditionally were phased out by now – the Xbox itself was discontinued after five years. And behind the scenes, development was under way.

Following rumours of PC-shelled next-generation Xbox hardware being used at EA in 2011, by mid-2012 official development kits for Microsoft's new console were confirmed to be with game studios, under the code name Durango. Until this information was revealed in the media the assumption had been that the third main Xbox console would carry the name 720. As it turned out, Xbox One would be chosen as it represented what this machine was supposed to be all about: an all-in-one device covering gaming, media content, television and movies. That approach would lead to some problems when the console was properly revealed in May 2013, but before then further rumours circulated about the Xbox One being an always-on device, requiring a constant internet connection to function properly; and that its games would be subject to digital rights management (DRM) restrictions, meaning that a disc-based game would be registered with an individual console, bringing an end to second-hand sales.

On 21 May 2013, inside a gigantic tent at Microsoft's Redmond headquarters, a selection of the world's gaming media gathered to watch the company's president of its Interactive Entertainment Business, Don Mattrick, officially unveil the Xbox One. He told attendees that with this machine, Microsoft was focused not just on games but entertainment – 'It is time for technology to step behind the curtain and you and your entertainment to take the stage' – and for the first 30 minutes of the presentation no video games were shown. Instead, there was talk of Skype use, interactive TV, and further analysis of the hardware – including the new controller, which improves upon the 360 pad with better ergonomics, a new D-pad and featuring haptic feedback in its triggers. Only then came the games, and not many of them. EA Sports showed its new FIFA and Madden, and *Call of Duty: Ghosts* was premiered at the event's climax, but the small number of games featured increased the pressure on the next month's E3 delivering what the Xbox 360 was known for. Which is to say: games.

Fast-forward to 10 June 2013, at 9.30am local time, and Microsoft's E3 press conference began in Los Angeles with an in-depth look at *Metal Gear Solid V: The Phantom Pain*. Mattrick returned, but this time he came with a different message: 'It's all about the games.' And many are showcased, including *Ryse: Son of Rome*, *Killer Instinct*, *Quantum Break* and *The Witcher 3: Wild Hunt*. But the always-on element of the console wasn't fully addressed and Mattrick ended up in hot water with his bosses when it was revealed that he told gametrailers.com, prior to the conference: 'Fortunately, we have a product for people who aren't able to get some kind of connectivity. It's called Xbox 360. If you have zero access to the internet, that is an offline device.' Nine days after the Microsoft E3 show, Mattrick wrote on the Xbox Wire blog that an internet connection would *not* be required to play offline Xbox One games. Pre-owned games were also back on the menu, and whether related to his comments or not, Mattrick left Microsoft on 1 July 2013.

Another area that Microsoft backtracked on was the necessity of its remodelled Kinect 2.0 peripheral for voice control, originally bundled with new Xbox One consoles and part of the reason why the system launched at $499, 100 dollars more than the PS4. The Kinect about-turn and the DRM reversal led some in the press to jokingly call the new Xbox the 180 – but later in its lifespan the Xbox One would make some moves that were widely celebrated. Backwards compatibility with a large selection of Xbox 360 games was introduced in 2015, and the range soon expanded to include further previous-gen games as well as original Xbox titles. In June 2017 Xbox Game Pass launched, a subscription service that gave console users access to a wide array of downloadable Xbox One and older games for a monthly fee, and which later came to Windows PCs and introduced cloud streaming options. By January 2022 Game Pass had 25 million subscribers, and it's become one of the Xbox ecosystem's greatest assets with new first-party games arriving on the service on day one since early 2018.

Inside the Xbox One – which launched in several territories simultaneously on 22 November 2013, but didn't release in Japan and China until September 2014 – was an AMD APU formed of eight x86-64 cores, making it similar to the CPU structure of the PS4 and PCs of the time. Powerful on paper, but not every critic of the time was impressed by the on-screen performance, with arstechnica.com's review of the console commenting that its initial games 'don't pack the visual oomph you might expect'. IGN's generally positive coverage concluded that the Xbox One 'offers a broader set of home entertainment features than its closest rival, the PS4', and that was how Microsoft's machine was widely perceived in its release window: a multimedia device first and a games-playing superpower second, even though it could more than match the grunt of the latest PlayStation.

By the end of 2013 Microsoft had sold three million Xbox One consoles, including a million in North America in its first 24 hours. Sony, however, had sold over a million more and would accelerate away from its most significant market rival over the next few years. A price reduction to $349 in June 2015, helped by taking the Kinect sensor out of the package, made the console more attractive to latecomers, however, and the system's steadily improved software and services saw it grow in critical appreciation; and by June 2016 a 500B Xbox One was down to $279, although by this point Microsoft had stopped publicly sharing sales figures for its console, switching instead to engagement numbers on Xbox Live. The original Xbox One was replaced by a new model in August 2016, the One S, which would later receive an all-digital variant in 2019; and in 2017 the Xbox One X was released offering a 31% performance boost compared to the original Xbox One. Code-named Project Scorpio when it was initially revealed at E3 2016, the One X was, at the time, the most-powerful games console on the market, fully compatible with all previous Xbox One software and relevant backwards-compatible titles but supporting 4K resolution and running on a six-teraflop GPU compared to the PS4 Pro's 4.2.

All Xbox One models were discontinued at the start of 2021, with the Xbox Series X and S consoles launched at the end of the previous year. While exact sales figures for the Xbox One range aren't available from Microsoft, estimates put it at between 50 and 51 million units, less than half the total of the PS4 and over 30 million behind the Xbox 360's total. With fewer big-name exclusive games than PlayStation – the once-hyped likes of *Scalebound* and *Fable Legends* were cancelled, and certain games that did release, like *Sunset Overdrive* and *Quantum Break*, are more commonly appreciated today as underrated gems rather than the system-sellers Xbox had hoped for – the Xbox One struggled to not only keep up with the PS4 but also the Switch once it'd released in 2017, with Nintendo's hybrid machine representing a more attractive second console for those already possessing a PlayStation. When Game Pass was added to PC in 2019, Microsoft's most appealing Xbox service was no longer bound only to its console, effectively retiring it from relevance a year before its successor was released.

Xbox One: Five Must Plays

Halo: The Master Chief Collection (2014)
Is this cheating? Perhaps, but no Xbox One collection is complete without this compilation of Halo titles, featuring graphically upgraded versions of the original Xbox's first and second entries (as Anniversary Editions), *Halo 3*, *Halo 3: ODST*, *Halo: Reach* and *Halo 4*. That's a whole lot of exceptional sci-fi FPS action for the cost of a single game – and *The Master Chief Collection* also supports several multiplayer modes for when its campaigns have been completed. Later released (in individual game instalments) on PC from 2019 and with an enhanced version coming to Series X and S in 2020 with previous-gen crossplay, this is not just a Halo fan's dream come true but the perfect jumping on point for players yet to take a tour or two through the eyes of Master Chief.

Cuphead (2017)
This 2D run-and-gunner drew gameplay influence from the likes of retro favourites *Contra* and *Gunstar Heroes*, but its looks could only have been achieved with 21st-century processing power. Its surrealist and vibrant visuals take cues from American animation of the 1920s to the 1940s, from studios like Fleischer and Walter Lantz Productions, and combined with a boisterous jazz soundtrack summoned from the 1930s, *Cuphead* is a game like no other. The game sold two million copies within two weeks of release as a timed console exclusive on Xbox One, alongside a PC version, and later came to Mac, PS4 and Switch. An expansion to the original game, *Cuphead: The Delicious Last Course*, was released in June 2022, and a Netflix series based on the game, *The Cuphead Show!*, debuted in February of the same year.

Forza Horizon 4 (2018)
Set in a condensed open world based on the British regions of Edinburgh and the Scottish Highlands, the Lake District and the Cotswolds, *Forza Horizon 4* is a racing game for everyone who isn't especially into racing games. Its map is full of events to participate in, from dragstrip blasts to cross-country rallies and stunts that see your car of choice fly off a hillside – but there's so much joy in just enjoying the scenery, the sounds of the countryside and its amazing views, changed as they so often are by the game's dynamic weather system. It's a lovely game to spend a Sunday morning with (and if the UK's a little too dull for your tastes, 2016's *Forza Horizon 3* is set in Australia and 2021's fifth series entry transports the same kind of gameplay to Mexico). *Forza Horizon 4*'s multiplayer component supports 72 simultaneous players per server, and with 750 licensed vehicles to add to your garage it's something you'll always find something to do in, however long you've been playing for. And when you're done with its real-world thrills, one of the game's DLC packs, 'Lego Speed Champions', takes players away to a map constructed from Lego bricks. An enhanced version of *Forza Horizon 4* released for Xbox Series X and S in 2020, and the game is also available on PC.

Control (2019)
Finland's Remedy Entertainment had already made a name for itself as masters of third-

person action games, with *Max Payne* and *Alan Wake* under their belts, but *Control* felt like the ultimate culmination of years of refinement. It mixes breathless cat-and-mouse encounters between the player and deadly foes with electrifying gunplay and gives its protagonist, Jesse Faden, supernatural-like powers courtesy of her interaction with the game's paranormal setting, the headquarters of the (fictional) Federal Bureau of Control. Within its walls are stored all manner of objects that are possessed by powers from another dimension, and somehow a malevolent force known as The Hiss has broken through the barrier dividing its world and ours. With loads of areas to explore, powers to wield and plot points to pursue, *Control* is a deep and complex title of *X-Files*-like spookiness and best-in-class gameplay. The game is also widely available on other platforms.

Outer Wilds (2019)

Using a time-loop mechanic like that seen in *The Legend of Zelda: Majora's Mask*, Mobius Digital's *Outer Wilds* is a small game of massive scale, in which the player must uncover secrets of an extinct race, explore a multitude of planets and environments to solve puzzles and progress the story, and keep their energy levels and their ship's fuel topped up so they can function correctly. Every loop lasts 22 minutes, and you take everything you learned in one into the next, until eventually – hopefully – you can work out how to prevent the actual destruction of the solar system you're in when its central star goes supernova. It's a tricky game with a level of fussiness that won't be for everyone, but *Outer Wilds* is incredibly unique too, and it won in the best game and game design categories at the 2020 British Academy Game Awards. A timed Xbox One exclusive that released for PC on the same day, *Outer Wilds* later came to PS4, PS5 and Xbox Series X and S, with a Switch port having been due in mid-2021 but still unreleased at the time of writing.

Valve's Machines Run out of Steam

Launched in November 2015, Valve's Steam Machines series was intended to take the PC gaming experience from desktops to living rooms, using the Linux-based Steam operating system. While the console units were to be manufactured by other companies in agreement with Valve, the all-important pad for Steam Machine use would be exclusively made by the Gabe Newell-fronted Bellevue, Washington state-based developer and was designed in such a way that mouse-like control was possible using twin touchpads.

But by June 2016 only around a combined 500,000 Steam Controllers and Machines had been sold, including devices made by Alienware and Zotac. Another manufacturer was Digital Storm, whose marketing manager Rajeev Kuruppu told PC Gamer in 2017: 'Nobody was buying [our hardware] with SteamOS.' Instead, consumers were picking up the company's Eclipse gaming PC with a Windows operating system. In the same 2017 feature, Alienware co-founder Frank Azer is quoted as saying that SteamOS and the Machines were 'not a major initiative for us … because it's not necessary right now'. Like Digital Storm, Alienware was seeing far better results with Windows systems.

Valve itself undermined the appeal of the Steam Machines at the very time they were being made available by simultaneously releasing the Steam Link, which could stream user's PC games directly to their TV, no dedicated console-like hardware required. The Steam Link cost $50, when Steam Machines could cost over $400, making the decision an easy one for PC gamers wanting a longue-session solution. The Steam Link was discontinued in 2018, and at the time of writing an Amazon search for 'Steam Machine' is as likely to bring up a washer-dryer or pressure cleaner than it is a device for playing video games.

Not that the Steam Machines' failure put Valve off from future hardware, as in February 2022 its handheld Steam Deck was released offering access to the user's Steam library and allowing for the play of Windows games through a compatibility layer. Its reception was a lot more positive than that of Steam Machines with upbeat comparisons drawn to the appeal of the Switch, although critics still complained of its noisy fans and limited battery life.

NINTENDO SWITCH

Manufacturer: Foxconn, Hosdien
Released: March 2017 (worldwide)

The Wii U's slow start had Nintendo immediately planning its next console move. By shifting the Wii's M.O. of appealing to people who weren't core gamers and promoting the machine with some confusing messaging around its GamePad and the integration of older peripherals, the 2012-launched system left the mainstream cold and the company's profits were falling. Something new was needed – but like the Wii and the Wii U before it, whatever it was should also represent a new way to play, a new way to fit games into users' lives. Nintendo would again have to take a blue ocean view on development, working towards whatever its competitors weren't. And this is how the Switch blinked into existence.

Inspiration came from Nintendo's own past: from the Remotes of the Wii, revisited and reformatted with updated functions, including HD rumble feedback and an infrared depth-tracking sensor, into the Switch's detachable Joy-Con controllers (a pair per unit, allowing for immediate two-player interaction); and from the Wii U's GamePad when it came to the layout of the new system's handheld mode. The Switch's development began under the code name NX, and Nintendo even looked back to the philosophy of its late employee Gunpei Yokoi, credited with the creation of the D-pad and the lead designer on the Game & Watch line and Game Boy console.

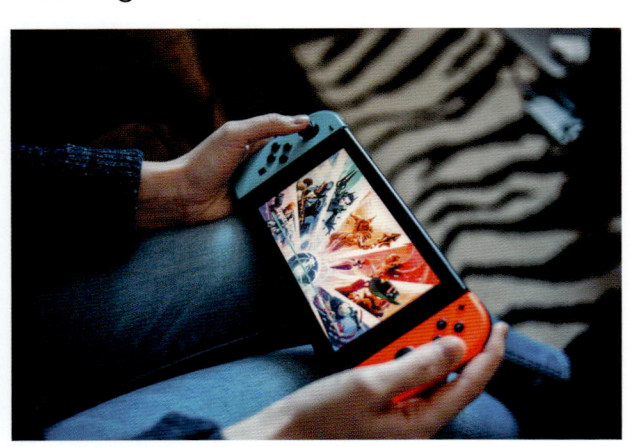

Yokoi, who died in a road accident in 1997, worked following an attitude of 'lateral thinking with withered technology' – using existing, mass-produced and inexpensive technology to create fun and engaging experiences. That's why the Game Boy came out as it did: not the technical equal of the Atari Lynx or Game Gear with its shades-of-green screen, but much cheaper, with better battery life, and arguably a far better software library. The Switch's choice of CPU was four ARM Cortex-A57s, available since 2012; and it also used an NVIDIA-made system on a chip, the Tegra X1, aimed at high performance but low

178

power usage. Off-the-shelf components selected for their affordability, helping Nintendo to make an immediate profit on every console sale (which wasn't the case with the Wii U or 3DS handheld) and making development of games at third-party studios easier. No more second screen to occupy was a blessing, too.

This spec made the console substantially underpowered beside the PlayStation 4 and Xbox One, but Nintendo wasn't interested in delivering the greatest graphics or fastest frame rates. The company's aim really was to revolutionise how people interacted with video games, and the name Switch reflected that: it not only referred to the system's docked-for-the-TV play or handheld use, but how its makers aimed to genuinely switch how its audience used its products, for both deep sessions sat on the sofa and leisurely play on the move (or in bed, or simply while someone else in the house was using the TV).

Although an early 2017 release date had been confirmed, Nintendo showed nothing of its new console, still NX at that point, during E3 in June 2016. Shigeru Miyamoto said at a shareholder meeting at the time: 'Normally we would have shown the NX at E3, but we didn't. We're worried about imitators if we release too early.' He also spoke to Associated Press the same month, stating: '[The NX's unique design is] why we can't share anything at this point. If it was just a matter of following advancements in technology, things would be coming out quicker.' The secrecy was of paramount importance as so much was at stake. Former president of Nintendo of America, Reggie Fils-Aimé, would later comment in early 2021 during the New York Gaming Awards: 'Wii U underperformed pretty radically in the marketplace, and when your only business is video games, that next [console] had to be successful. The Switch really was a make-or-break product for the company, and luckily it was a hit.'

'A hit' might be an understatement. Although the Switch absolutely isn't without flaws – a not-unsubstantial number of its Joy-Con controllers have malfunctioned over time, with their analogue sticks drifting, and the out-the-box storage of 32GB (under 26GB of which is actually useable due to the space taken up by the console's custom operating system, Horizon) wasn't nearly enough given the size of modern software (the memory is expandable with microSD cards up to 2TB in size) – the console has become a major success for Nintendo. By the end of March 2023, the Switch – across its three models – had sold in excess of 125 million units since its worldwide launch on 3 March 2017, making it Nintendo's highest-selling home console ever. It outsold the Wii U inside 12 months and passed the Wii in February 2022. And it has plenty of road ahead of it, with Nintendo president Shuntaro Furukawa telling investors in February 2022 that the Switch range was only now reaching 'the midpoint of its lifecycle'.

The original Switch – capable of being played on the TV through its dock, in 'tabletop' mode with its kickstand flipped out and Joy-Cons removed, and in handheld mode like a conventional portable console – received some minor updates in 2018 and a new version rolled out in mid-2019, its Tegra X1 replaced by the X1+. This took the Switch's battery life from between three and six hours to between four and a half to nine, depending on the software used. A dedicated handheld-only model, the Switch Lite, released in September 2019 offering a cheaper alternative to the hybrid unit, selling at $199.99 rather than the original Switch's $299.99. The Lite also added a conventional D-pad, as the standard Joy-Cons feature four individual face buttons instead due to their multi-functional design (each can be used sideways for two-player games). In October 2021 the Switch OLED Model came out, replacing the console's LCD screen with a crisper OLED alternative but still running at 720p in handheld and outputting at 1080p while docked, and by May 2022 had raced to almost six million units sold.

What hasn't been confirmed at the time of writing is a so-called 'Pro' model Switch, which would boost performance significantly with an improved CPU and potentially feature 4K output. In June 2021 Nintendo of America president Doug Bowser, who replaced Fils-Aimé in 2019 (and yes, his surname is Bowser – perfect, really), addressed the rumours of a more powerful Switch, telling *The Washington Post*: 'We are always looking at technology and how it can enhance gameplay experiences. It's not technology for technology's sake. How can technology enhance a gameplay experience? And where do you apply that technology – on current hardware, or do you wait for the next platform? There's a host of factors that go into it, and it's something we're always looking at.' Which could mean a fourth Switch model, a 'Pro', does release in this console line's later years, or that Nintendo implements this technology on whatever hardware follows it. With sales as healthy as they are, an all-new Switch to succeed the OLED probably isn't what many among its main audience are looking for – although if Nintendo did want to see the Switch overtake the PlayStation 2's record sales of just over 155 million, a high-end version could represent an entry point for players yet to pick up a Switch, those who previously felt its lack of horsepower was too much of a disadvantage.

While designed as a flexible piece of hardware, Nintendo has stated that the Switch – the Lite excepted – is a home console, shying away from the word hybrid in official messaging. That may have been because for a few years it shared support with the 3DS but speaking to Polygon in 2016 the company said: 'Switch is a home gaming system first and foremost.' It added that the 3DS had 'many more games in the pipeline', which was true at the time – but that dual-screen, stereoscopic portable was discontinued in 2020, leaving the Switch as the only console Nintendo has on sale, a situation it's not been in since the pre-Game Boy Famicom and NES era. Throughout the N64, Game Cube and Wii U lifecycles, the handheld side of Nintendo's business, with the Game Boy and (3)DS families, was crucial in keeping the bottom line relatively agreeable. With Switch, however, there's evidently no need to maintain a dedicated handheld range.

Reflecting on the Switch in early 2017, just ahead of the console's release, Miyamoto told *Time* magazine: 'All we had to think about was, really, providing fun. There's also the idea of having this original, unique thought, which means not doing the same as other people. This is something obvious in the world: if you're trying to do the same thing as everyone else, you get further and further from the top. But if you're doing something unique, when the spotlight hits, you're already at the top before you know it.' The make-or-break in Fils-Aimé's words was a 'make' like Nintendo had never seen before, and the company's return to having a market-leading machine – in the first quarter of 2021, the Switch sold more than double what the PlayStation 5 achieved and over four times Xbox's total for Series X and S – has put it in a fantastic position to pioneer further in future hardware generations. Just so long as it doesn't pull another Wii U out of its R&D department.

Nintendo Switch: Five Must Plays

The Legend of Zelda: Breath of the Wild (2017)
Nintendo's final significant game for the Wii U was also the first major reason to own a Switch – and arguably *Breath of the Wild* remains, years later, *the* game for Switch newcomers. With beautiful visuals that land halfway between the cel-shaded triumph of *The Wind Waker* and the grittier aesthetic of *Twilight Princess*, and a go-where-you-like Hyrule full of secrets (some key to the plot, some just there for fun) and memories to recall, *BOTW* is perhaps the zenith of open-world gaming, a playground for rewarding exploration and cause-and-effect experimentation. There's a quest to complete, of course, but there's also recipes to invent, a village to build, swords to smash over enemy heads (*literally*, as weapon degradation is a key aspect of the gameplay loop), challenge shrines to conquer, mazes to solve, dragons to shoot scales from, and even a golf course to thump a gigantic ball down. (Really.) *BOTW* is as close to any game that has end credits has ever come to being endless, and even when you're done kicking Calamity Ganon's fiery behind, you'll want to spend more time journeying to all the locations you've yet to see with Link's eyes. *BOTW*'s 2023 sequel, *Tears of the Kingdom*, is equally recommended.

Mario Kart 8 Deluxe (2017)
The expanded version of the Wii U's *Mario Kart 8* is the greatest Mario Kart entry to date – and it quite possibly will remain so, as rather than make any noise about a ninth entry in the racing series Nintendo instead introduced a Booster Pack for *MK8 Deluxe*, which adds more tracks and cups via downloadable content. With a huge cast of characters available and countless combinations of vehicles, wheels and gliders, and some of the best circuits (and music) in the series – including remade versions of old-school classics – this is Mario Kart at its smile-guaranteeing best.

Super Mario Odyssey (2017)
Nintendo's reliable mascot's big 3D adventure on Switch is one of his best, the newly introduced cap-throwing gameplay not only allowing the famous plumber to take control of various baddies to use their abilities, but also letting a second player join the Luigi-less fun. *Odyssey* isn't quite as revered as either *Super Mario 64* or *Super Mario Galaxy*, but it was somewhat overshadowed in its year of release by the startling originality of *BOTW*. With almost 24 million copies sold though, *Odyssey* has been no underdog at retail, and it brings plenty enough creativity to the table to make it the number one platformer on Switch.

Into the Breach (2018)
Subset Games' *Into the Breach* is a beautiful and devastating strategy game about the end of the world – or at least, it'll be the end of the world unless you manage to push back an army of giant monsters that's invading Earth and demolishing every city and power station it comes across. Using turn-based moves set on a board of squares, with clear sightlines for gunshots and pre-event warnings of imminent disasters, *Into the Breach* is all about thinking ahead and strategizing in a way that lets you lose a unit or two for the greater good. Think chess, just with colossal mechs and aliens. Oh, and with time travel, as if you're facing defeat one of your pilots can teleport back to the start of the game, where you can carry all your experience forward in a new campaign against the Vek. A winner at The Game Awards and the British Academy Game Awards, *Into the Breach* is a special strategy experience that remains a console exclusive on Switch.

Hades (2020)
A Switch console exclusive until its release for Xbox and PlayStation systems in mid-2021, *Hades* is a loop-based roguelite action game where every defeat builds your confidence, your strength, and your abilities. The aim, playing as Zagreus, is to escape the underworld ruled by the protagonist's father, Hades – and the player must do this from start to finish in one run, each death taking our protagonist back to the House of Hades where dad can chide him for his insolence. Near incessant of action and with its level layout shifting with each run, *Hades* isn't one for the easily overwhelmed; but its vivid art and propulsive music keep the attention locked, and the enjoyably pithy dialogue is the icing on a most delicious and multi-layered cake.

Streaming Services Come of Age, But do Players Care?
At the end of the 2010s high-speed broadband had reached enough homes that dedicated cloud gaming services were back on the menu – this time with the knowledge that millions of players could easily use them, if they wanted to. Google launched its Stadia service (controller, below) in November 2019, streaming games at 4K resolution and at up to 60 frames per second to TVs, computers and compatible smart devices. As well as free-to-play titles, Stadia also

sells games – games that the user can never actually *own*, downloaded to local storage, but merely rents in perpetuity through the service. Stadia received a mixed early reception, with the tech largely working as advertised but reviewers noting inconsistent streaming performance and criticising its paltry exclusives (just one at launch), while its familiarly designed controller, wrote *The Guardian* in its coverage, 'looks a bit like a fake prop knocked up for a BBC TV show that was a bit too strict about the rules for product placement'.

By the end of 2020 around 130 games were available for Stadia but despite expensive marketing campaigns from Google it never established itself as a genuine, hardware-free alternative to PlayStation or Xbox consoles (as both also feature their own streaming options and subscription services). Google's Stadia Games and Entertainment division, established to develop exclusive titles for the platform, was closed in February 2021 before successfully shipping a single game; and as of mid-2022 Stadia is the preserve of a relatively small but refreshingly dedicated audience while its makers reportedly look to license its streaming tech rather than support a service of its own – a Plan B that was perhaps always a likelihood given how dominant Sony and Microsoft are when it comes to TV-play blockbusters.

Amazon launched its own cloud gaming service, Luna (controller, below), in October 2020 as a limited-user beta, before releasing in the United States in March 2022. (The service later came online in Canada, the UK and Germany in March 2023.) Useable on PC, Mac, Android, iOS and Amazon Fire TV devices, Luna can be controlled with keyboard and mouse or the standard Xbox One/Series X and S and PlayStation 4/5 pads, while its own wireless controller, which looks a lot like a Switch Pro Controller, retails for $59.99. The service's various channels differ in price depending on what sorts of experiences are available, with a family-friendly channel of games featuring SpongeBob SquarePants and Adventure Time titles priced at $5.99 per month and one dedicated to Ubisoft games costing $17.99 for the same period – on top of a necessary $9.99 each month to access Luna in the first place. Reviews for Luna's rollout were about as mixed as Stadia's, with IGN commenting that it has its 'own set of hiccups' including a 'meek catalogue' of available games, but that its controller was 'the star of the show'; while PCMag.com concluded that most channels were reasonably priced (except Ubisoft's).

THE 2020s
BRAND NEW, YOU'RE RETRO

With the Switch going strong, it's been left to Microsoft and Sony to release new hardware in the early 2020s, albeit with systems that are effectively enhanced versions of their previous consoles. Which isn't to say that the PlayStation 5 and Xbox Series X (and all-digital S) aren't excellent machines, but they're more refinements than the reinventions seen in past generations. However, the decade is seeing a pronounced comeback of older titles through dedicated devices based on classic arcade hardware and a new console line in the shape of Blaze Entertainment's Evercade. Also, one of the very first big names in home gaming, Atari, is back with a fresh take on the VCS – assuming you can find it.

XBOX SERIES X AND SERIES S

Manufacturer: Foxconn, Flextronics

Released: November 2020 (most major territories), June 2021 (China)

Code-named Anaconda and Lockhart respectively, the Xbox Series X and Series S released simultaneously on 10 November 2020, offering players the choice between a $499/£449 model with a superior CPU and GPU and Ultra HD Blu-ray disc drive and a $299/£249 all-digital option with slower-running internal components. Both feature Microsoft's Velocity Architecture storage, reducing download sizes and improving load speeds; and both are backwards compatible with Xbox One and select 360 and (2001) Xbox games, with the Series X able to run them from the original discs.

Media reports of the new systems had started gathering steam in early 2018, and Microsoft's CEO of gaming and head of the Xbox brand, Phil Spencer, confirmed in June of that year that the company was 'deep into architecting the next Xbox consoles'. The plural in Spencer's statement made it clear that Microsoft was (perhaps confusingly, naming wise) following the model of the Xbox One X and One S, with one console aimed at more casual users and the other at those wanting the very best performance. A detailed breakdown of the Series X hardware was released in March 2020 with the Xbox Wire blog writing: 'The next generation of Xbox is defined by three primary characteristics: power, speed and compatibility.' And anyone who's used either the Series X or S will probably feel that Xbox achieved its ambitions.

The Series X's CPU is a custom AMD Zen 2 running at between 3.6 and 3.8GHz, with the Series S features the same Zen 2 running at slightly slower speed. The Series X's integrated graphics processor is capable of 12 teraflops of power, whereas the Series S tops out at four teraflops.

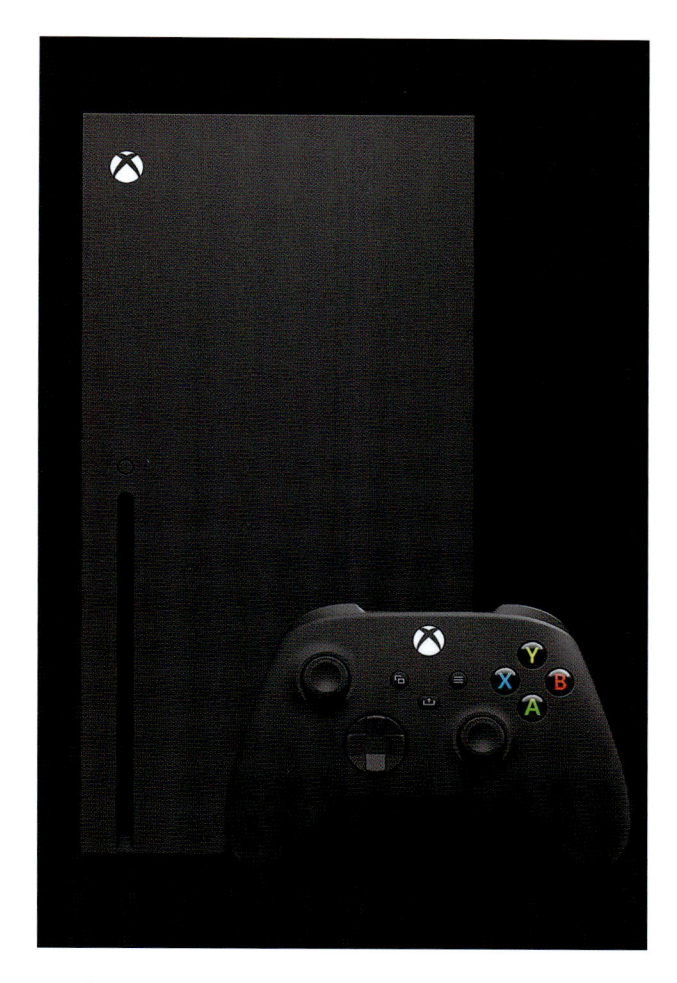

Both consoles use the same controller – a slightly upgraded version of the Xbox One pad, with an additional share button and sculpted grips – support ray tracing, Dolby Vision and Atmos features, and can be expanded with proprietary SSD storage. Ergo, the two machines are very comparable, with the Series X appealing to players with a collection of previous-gen Xbox game discs and the Series S to newcomers to these consoles who aren't fussed about second-hand games (as all software must be downloaded and is subject to Microsoft Store pricing).

The Series X's design was compared to a fridge – and to lean into this, Microsoft has manufactured a short run of Series X-themed mini-fridges, showing that it has a sense of humour. Like the PS5, however, both the Series X and S launched without much in the way of essential software to make the systems immediately attractive to those already owning a form of Xbox One, and as of January 2022 sales of the newer consoles had reached an estimated 12 million. In mid-2022 something exceptionally rare happened, however, with both the Series X and S outselling the PS5 in Japan for a few weeks – although that might have had more to do with PlayStation supply issues than the unique appeal of Microsoft's systems.

Xbox Series X/S: Play One Game

Microsoft Flight Simulator (2020)
Although many newer games released for Xbox One have Series X optimisation providing increased performance, *Microsoft Flight Simulator* can't run at all on previous-gen hardware. Using Bing Maps to recreate *the entire Earth*, this simulator also features real-time weather effects and became a terrific means with which to escape living rooms when the COVID-19 pandemic had so many people in lockdown. *The Guardian* wrote that the game 'captures the wonder of flight, and the spiritual and emotional rush of seeing the world in a different way', and it's safe to say that no other video game can show players their own planet in such beauty and at such scale.

PLAYSTATION 5

Manufacturer: Sony, Foxconn
Released: November 2020 (most major territories), May 2021 (China)

Having been formally revealed by lead architect Mark Cerny in an interview with *Wired* in April 2019, the PlayStation 5's full specifications were outlined in a somewhat dry online presentation given by the very same developer in March 2020. The specs were as expected, in as much as they improved on what had been in the PS4 but didn't represent a gigantic leap into the unknown. More power, yes, but this was Sony playing safe to an extent, sticking to its strengths and not risking anything while enjoying such a healthy slice of the home console market.

Inside the PS5 – which released on 12 November 2020 in two models, a $399/£359 digital-only version and a $499/£449 'base' unit with an Ultra ND Blu-ray drive for physical games and other media – is a custom eight-core Zen 2 processor by AMD running at 3.5GHz, packing in a lot more horsepower than the PS4's CPU set-up, and its AMD RDNA 2 GPU is around eight times more powerful than Sony's previous console, delivering 4K resolution and 120 frames-per-second gameplay. Both CPU and GPU are supported by a boost system that optimises their performance and manages power usage. The PS5's custom Tempest engine sound chip allows for many more simultaneous audio channels than the PS4 could handle, and its solid-state drive storage (of which 667GB is useable out of the box) reduced loading times for installed titles dramatically.

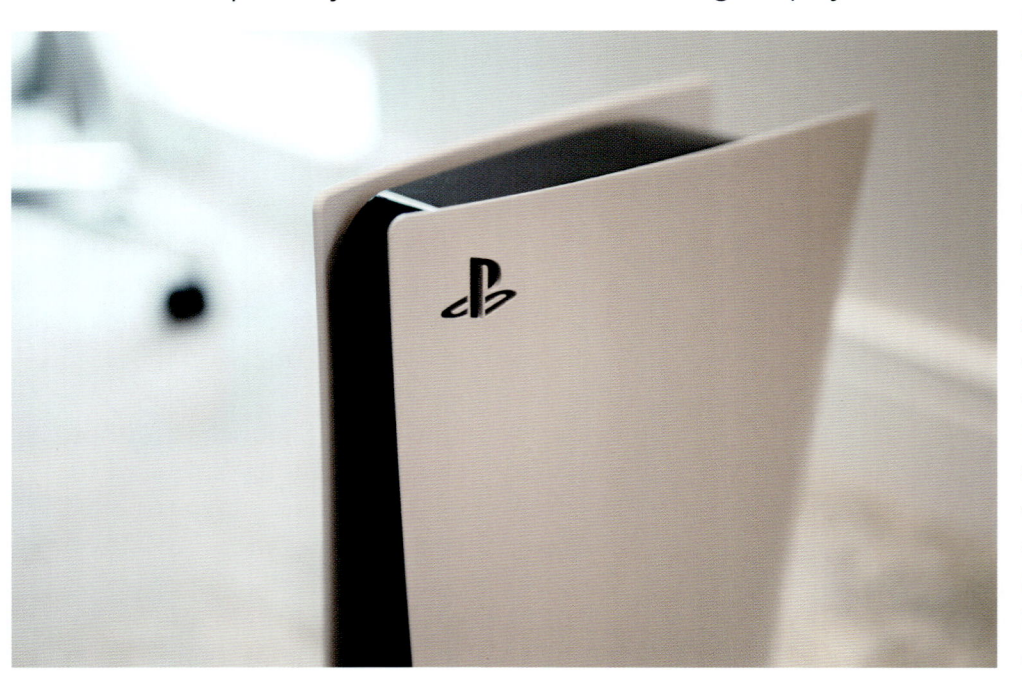

Aesthetically eschewing the PS4's blocky design for something far curvier and adopting a white finish as standard instead of the traditional black, the PS5 certainly looks different to what came before it – but experiences wise, it's so far offered much the same as the PS4. Sony's first-party games are mostly launching (at the time of writing) for both the PS4 and PS5, foremost among them *God of War Ragnarök* and *Horizon Forbidden West*, and there haven't been many genuine new-generation exclusives of note to tempt more casual players away from their outdated but still-supported hardware. The PS5 supports the same online features as the PS4, giving users access to the multi-tiered PlayStation Plus service, the PlayStation Store for downloading content, and multiplayer functions through PlayStation Network, and is also backwards compatible with most PS4 discs – a big plus for Sony after the PS4's lack of such a feature.

Where the PS5 did take a major step forward though was with its standard, boxed-in controller, the DualSense. This pad, designed in the same white and black as the console, is bigger and curvier than the PS4's DualShock 4, and its haptic capabilities are vastly improved, not only providing different levels of rumble depending on the action the player's controlling but also force feedback on its triggers to feel the tension on a string or the resistance of a trigger. While many titles on the PS5 don't feel so different to what came before them, loading times and a little visual crispness aside, having this pad in hand is a game-changer all of itself; and its showcase software, the pre-installed *Astro's Playroom*, is one of the system's best exclusives as a result of its pronounced use of the DualSense's various features.

Supply problems slowed sales of the PlayStation 5, the cause being a shortage of semiconductors necessary to the console's manufacture. This saw secondhand-market prices skyrocket. But by July 2022 total global units shipped was standing at over 21 million, and Sony issued a press release in late 2021 saying that the system had been the largest launch in PlayStation history, outperforming the PS4's 2.1 million machines sold in two weeks (albeit without specifying the PS5's total). Demand, Sony said, was unprecedented. It's remained exceptionally high since, but stock issues were a thing of the past by early 2023, ensuring that anyone wanting a PS5 could finally find one easily at retail.

PlayStation 5: Play One Game

Returnal (2021)
An incredibly unsettling and unapologetically challenging roguelike shooter, Housemarque's *Returnal* is a time loop-based sci-fi nightmare brought to skin-creeping life by the PS5's powerful insides. It casts the player as Selene Vassos, an astronaut trapped on an alien planet and who simply cannot die, respawning where she started whenever she's slain. Unfortunately, not being slain is quite the task in *Returnal*, and its environments change with each fresh run. Earning many high-scoring reviews and the winner of best game at the 2022 British Academy Game Awards, *Returnal* is a rare PS5-only release that's almost worth buying the console for.

ATARI VCS

Manufacturer: Flex, PowerA

Released: 2020 (crowdfunding backers), June 2021 (North America, Australia and New Zealand)

Yet to receive a global release, the Atari VCS is a micro-console running a Linux-based operating system and – despite its retro-influenced faux woodgrain and shared name with Atari's 1977 home console – is largely focused on the playing of relatively modern games, its AMD-made R1606G Zen CPU capable of handling PC games from the late 2010s. (It was showcased handling 2017's *Fortnite* without any trouble.) This VCS uses neither cartridges nor discs, being an all-digital device supported by a custom store, and its built-in Atari Vault includes over 80 2600 titles and a handful of Atari arcade games for that out-of-the-box retro kick.

As well as operating as a console, the Atari VCS can be set up to basically be a mini-PC, which makes its $299 asking price (for its base system) slightly more palatable. The system's small size and cute design were deemed as positives in preview coverage, but critics noted that its streamlined features and reduced power put it at a substantial disadvantage when it came to competing with Sony and Microsoft consoles – although, that isn't really the market this thing is going after, appealing more to retro enthusiasts attracted to new Atari hardware. What was better received, ahead of release and after the VCS's launch, was its Classic Joystick, a modernised take on the iconic CX10/40 joystick; and for anyone who prefers a standard-shaped pad, the VCS is also available with a Modern Controller. That's its name, the Modern Controller. Does what it says on the tin.

Reception so far to the VCS, which was originally announced under the name Ataribox, has been decidedly mixed, with tomshardware.com concluding that it didn't offer enough content for the asking price, techradar.com commenting that its UI was cumbersome and it was for 'retro fanatics only', and IGN writing: 'If you want a $300 machine to emulate old games, buy an Xbox Series S.' As of mid-2023, the only 'new' VCS you can buy from UK stores is a Lego model of the original Atari console (albeit the 1980 four-switch version), with this piece of actual gaming hardware nowhere to be seen.

Arcade-Perfect Desktop Play

Following the rise of SEGA, Sony and Nintendo mini-consoles in the 2010s, and the similarly presented Neo Geo Mini of 2018 with its built-in screen, a handful of shrunken-down arcade cabinets featuring pre-installed games have released in the 2020s. The first of note, the SEGA Astro City Mini, launched in late 2020 and perfectly recreated, at desktop scale, the full-sized arcade cab that was so ubiquitous in Japan in the 1990s. Its 37 included games ranged from mid-1980s coin-ops like *My Hero* and *Wonder Boy* to the 3D polygons of 1993's *Virtua Fighter*, with rare titles like *Dark Edge* and *Arabian Fight* rubbing shoulders with familiar names *Altered Beast* and *Golden Axe*. The Astro City Mini can be connected to a TV for bigger-screen play, controlled with either a dedicated six-button control pad or a chunky arcade stick, and it was generally well reviewed in the games media, with The Verge writing that 'it should be considered essential for SEGA fans'.

A second small-scale SEGA arcade machine, the Astro City Mini V, released in 2022 and featured a vertical 'TATE'-style screen (the 'V' standing for 'vertical') best suited to shoot 'em ups, which it's suitably loaded with. Its total of 22 games, many of which aren't SEGA-developed titles, include *Action Fighter*, *Batsugun* and *Gunbird*, and the V is more of a niche product than its Astro City predecessor. In early 2022 the Taito EGRET Mini II offered users the option to play with its screen set horizontally or vertically thanks to a very satisfying rotation function – the clunk-click when it snaps into place feels so good – and like SEGA's machines it can be played on the TV using either a control pad or arcade stick (and even a trackball peripheral for a few games). Out of the box the EGRET Mini II contains 40 pre-installed games, including the brilliant platformer *Bubble Bobble* and exceptional shooter *Darius Gaiden*, and its great build quality and diverse array of games earned the machine several positive reviews.

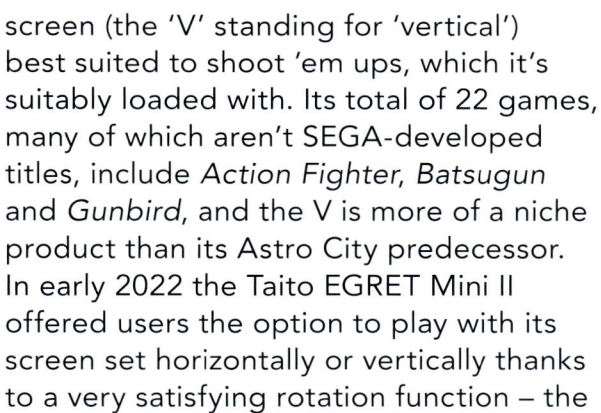

EVERCADE VS

Manufacturer: Blaze Entertainment

Released: December 2021 (Europe), February 2022 (North America)

Plug-and-play retro consoles weren't uncommon before the emergence of the Evercade brand – Retro-Bit's Super Retro-Cade of 2017 being a surprisingly excellent mini-system loaded with an array of fully licensed console and arcade games from developers like Capcom, Data East and Irem. But what Blaze Entertainment brought back with its console line, which started with a well-received handheld in May 2020 and progressed to the VS home console the next year, was something many retro-gaming enthusiasts had missed for years: swappable and collectible cartridges.

Compatible with all but two of the cartridges for the handheld console (two Namco collections that were only licensed for portable play), the VS is a machine with multiplayer fun firmly in mind, with four controller ports on the front just like the GameCube and Dreamcast before it. Its NES-style front-positioned flap lifts to reveal two cartridge slots, allowing the user to run a pair of its multi-game carts through its Linux-based operating system at once (the combination of certain carts can also unlock otherwise inaccessible games). Shipping with its own wired pads, the VS can also support third-party wireless peripherals and the original Evercade handheld can be plugged in to use as a controller, too.

With a quad-core CPU capable of supporting games from the 8-bit era through to the original PlayStation and a host of arcade titles, all of which come on compilations housed on Game Gear-like carts (with numbered boxes and manuals for each), the VS is unashamedly aimed at players who want a dose of nostalgia without messing around with (legally questionable) emulation on other devices. And with licensed collections in its library from the likes of Atari, Codemasters, Jaleco and Interplay, there's a huge number of old-school favourites available to jump right into.

Some critics weren't won over by the VS hardware, feeling that the pads were light and hollow and that it was too niche a product to find a mainstream audience. But by mid-2022 Evercade had established a healthy community of both dedicated enthusiasts and fair-weather followers, and in late 2022 its handheld was succeeded by a new portable machine, the 'TATE' mode-compatible and higher-resolution EXP. With retro collecting more popular than ever, and some games featured on Evercade collections selling individually for three figures, picking up a VS for less than £100 and its cartridges for under £20 a time represents a more-affordable way to either check out some of gaming's history for the first time or explore its weirder and wilder past without an eye-watering asking price.